Praise for *Loving through Enmity*

The deepest flaw in our antiracist efforts is our constant failure to understand what a racial enemy is. In this groundbreaking and beautifully written book, Wickware offers a sophisticated account of racial enmity and how to address it. There is nothing like this book, and there will be nothing to surpass it for generations to come.

—Willie James Jennings, Andrew W. Mellon Professor
of Systematic Theology and Africana Studies,
Yale University Divinity School

Wickware's *Loving through Enmity* is a brilliant, subversive tome that tests the perimeters of Christian antiracist engagement by exploring how genuine love for our "enemies" can drive meaningful societal transformation. Wickware's intuitive grappling with structural enmity calls readers to confront accountable benevolence and forge deeper connections even with those whose interests oppose their own. This consequential read offers a solid approach for anyone dedicated to breaking down white supremacy and fostering change with love at its core.

—Linda E. Thomas, professor of theology and anthropology,
Lutheran School of Theology at Chicago

Dr. Wickware is brilliant. This is a much-needed contribution to the work of antiracism at a critical time in our nation's history. What makes this project so powerful is that it is derived from lived experience, by a scholar who is able to do the sort of deep analysis that makes it all legible. This is a must-read for everyone.

—Reggie L. Williams, associate professor of
Black Theology, Saint Louis University

Loving through Enmity

Healing the Broken Heart of Christian Antiracist Work

loving THROUGH enmity

Marvin E. Wickware, Jr.

FORTRESS PRESS
MINNEAPOLIS

LOVING THROUGH ENMITY
Healing the Broken Heart of Christian Antiracist Work

30 29 28 27 26 25 1 2 3 4 5 6 7 8 9

Library of Congress Control Number: 2024947032 (print)

Cover image: Abstract pattern by CSA Printstock/Getty Images with Vibrant Abstract Chaos: Dynamic and Textured Background by mammuth/Getty Images
Cover design: Kristin Miller

Print ISBN: 978-1-5064-9716-7
eBook ISBN: 978-1-5064-9717-4

For Beth, who is always on my side

Contents

Acknowledgments

Writing this book was exhausting. This work demanded more than I had to give, and I could not have completed it without years of day-to-day support from my family. More than anyone, I am grateful to my wife, Beth. I can't account for decades of love and care here, so I will simply say that each time I have come to Beth to let her know I felt I needed to choose between career security and faithful integrity, she has encouraged me to do what God is calling me to do and has assured me that we will make things work. My kids, Nathaniel and Gabriel, have simultaneously saved me from burnout, demanded that I never stop growing as a person, helped me reconnect with things I had forgotten I love to do, and required me to strive to live up to what I teach. My in-laws John, Suzanne, and Paul Kilner have provided support and loving presence throughout the highs and lows of the past few years. And I couldn't make sense of myself without the influence of my parents, Jenifer and Marvin, and my sibling, Carmen. My mom died while I was writing this book, but I will always remember her as the person who first taught me that no one is better than anyone else, then challenged me to follow through on what that means in our complex, overwhelming world.

Three people have shaped my thinking so thoroughly that I couldn't have written this book without them. James Cone was my first theological mentor. He set me on this path. He made it his mission to foster future generations of Black theologians, and I hope my efforts in this book honor his work. Amy R. Barbour was my closest conversation partner throughout seminary and grad school. If I have anything meaningful to say about emotions or anything insightful to share about Cone, it is because I was blessed to benefit from our many conversations. Willie James Jennings has pushed me to write theology that is creative, faithful, and accountable to both the people who've shaped me and those with whom I am surprised to find myself in community. I don't write a word without thinking about how these three would respond, and when I write something I know they'd disagree with, I only do so after thinking it through three or four extra times.

At the Lutheran School of Theology at Chicago, I have found support among my colleagues. Brooke Petersen, Karri Alldredge, Erik Christensen, Kimberly Wagner, and Eunyung Lim have all been close confidants during this early stage of my career. I am grateful as well for the encouragement I've received from my senior colleagues, including Kadi Billman, James Nieman, Richard Perry, José David Rodríguez, Barbara Rossing, Mark Swanson, and Peter Vethanayagamony. I am particularly thankful for the womanist mentorship of Linda Thomas, a fellow student of James Cone who has consistently worked to help me find breathing room at LSTC. I have also been blessed by amazing students who have challenged, encouraged, and stood by me. I certainly can't name all of them, but some who have made a particular impact on this book are Emerson Remmers, Immanuel Karunakaran, Eddie Rosa Fuentes, and Vinod Wesley. Alexandra Clare has worked as my research assistant during the final stages of publication, making the work of constructing an index for this book much easier and much less lonely.

Beyond those already named, I have benefited from the mentorship of a community of Black scholars, including Eboni Marshall Turman, J. Kameron Carter, Joseph Winters, Reggie Williams, Joanne Marie Terrell, Brian Bantum, Terrence Johnson, Adam Clark, Steed Davidson, Anthony Reddie, and Beverly Wallace. Friends from my years at Duke University and Union Theological Seminary have been faithful conversation partners over the years. Among these, Matthew Elia, Matt Jantzen, Angela Parker, and George Schmidt stand out. M. Wolff has been a particular source of persistent encouragement and constructive feedback, without whom I would have taken even longer to get this book together. The Forum for Theological Exploration and the Wabash Center for Teaching and Learning in Theology and Religion have each provided community and financial support at key points in my writing. I learned much from my experience co-teaching a course on enmity with Klaus-Peter Adam. Durham Church has been a source of encouragement over the years, and I am particularly grateful to its pastor, Franklin Golden, who has been a faithful friend. The People's Lobby Faith Liberation Movement has been a vital group through which I can ensure that my work is always challenged to connect to the hard work of societal transformation. I have benefited from the efforts of a group of editors at Fortress Press. Daniel José Camacho helped me navigate the proposal process, while Laura Gifford has provided insightful feedback and grace-filled encouragement, showing me why so many scholars offer their editors such glowing praise. Marissa Wold Uhrina led the production process, helping to clarify my writing and ensure that this book says what I mean it to say. Last, I am grateful to my body. Through its aches, limits, needs, and joys, it has made the day-to-day work of writing possible.

Many of these relationships are complicated. Some of the folks I have named might not ever come back into my life, while others might not realize their impact on me. At the end of this work, though, I can genuinely express my gratitude to each of them. I hope that this book properly honors the time and beauty they have shared with me.

Introduction

I sometimes wonder if I will make it through life without having my heart broken by white supremacy. As the son of a Black man and a white woman, the husband of a white woman, and the father of two young children with quite different skin tones, white supremacy has insinuated itself into each of the relationships that most definitively makes me who I am. As with many children of interracial couples, well-meaning family questioned the possibility that I might have a good life before I was even born. Now that I have children of my own, I have to try to help them make sense of the fact that one of them basically looks white while the other looks more like me, that one of them will face more scrutiny from teachers and the police, that one of them can choose to be white while the other is consigned to racial ambiguity. Each of these interactions wears on me, and this kind of heartbreaking labor is precisely the kind of worldly trouble I would love to bring to church.

Now, I didn't grow up in church. My parents had been hurt badly by church people by the time I came along. Setting their childhood experiences aside, churches in 1980s Terre Haute, Indiana, didn't have much kindness to offer an interracial couple who were skeptical about Christian faith. Though I had a positive experience attending a Roman Catholic elementary and middle school, I grew up hating churches and struggling to trust in community of any kind. Still, as so many people have, I found my way to Christianity through InterVarsity Christian Fellowship during college. In time, I even found my way to seminary, then to doctoral studies in Christian theology.

During my PhD program at Duke University, I found myself in two communities that echoed my desire for the church to be a community where the heartbreaking impact of white supremacy could be met with healing and perhaps even liberation. By that point, I had worked to set aside my original suspicion of churches in favor of openness to the possibility that church could offer a powerful response to the lifelong struggle into which I had been born. In the context of these two communities, I found myself asking the questions that would lead me to write this book. A pair of stories will provide some context for why I ask these questions.

The first story takes place in the church in which my family were members during our time in Durham, North Carolina, and which we still love and visit as often as we can. This Presbyterian Church (U.S.A.) congregation was formed in 2012 out of the remnants of a pair of congregations that hadn't quite survived their attempts at becoming multiracial churches. When we arrived in 2013, it was a predominantly white church, but its members expressed a deep commitment to racial reconciliation. I accepted this commitment as stated, partly because folks I trusted vouched for its leaders and partly because it just felt like the kind of church that I wish could have been there for my parents in their earlier days.

In the spring of 2015, our church began a sermon series on race and the church. A few weeks in, a former pastoral intern gave a sermon in this series. He's a Black man who is soothing smooth jazz personified (he even played the saxophone during worship from time to time). Well, one Sunday he stood up in the pulpit and condemned white supremacy. He called the congregation—himself included—to repent for what he named our deadly addiction to whiteness. He bared his pain before the congregation and before God. And when he preached the word of God to the people of God, the people of God got angry. Not at the white supremacist violence that had wounded their brother's heart, though. They got angry at *him*. "This isn't church," one white elder said in this church that claimed racial reconciliation as central to its mission. "I come to church to get away from all of this hate," said another white elder. As for me? I did not know what to say. The first church that truly felt like church to me had just shown a very ugly side of itself.

Around the same time, I was working as a teaching assistant for a course on womanist theology and ethics at Duke Divinity School. At the time, several prominent Black faculty members were having a substantial impact on their students, many of whom in turn expressed a desire for their school to be a Christian community marked by its commitment to racial reconciliation. The professor of this course on womanist theology and ethics—herself a Black woman and a womanist theologian and ethicist—was hardly one to let people walk all over her, but with this class, she was beyond patient and gentle. As Duke Divinity School required students preparing for ministry[1] to take a class in Black Church studies, I suspect the professor was trying to make sure that even those students who were skeptical about a course on womanism would feel welcome and encouraged to learn. The readings were chosen with care, and class discussions left plenty of room for students to express their concerns. Still, each week in my section, a group of white women would express some variation of the same frustrated sentiment: "It feels like the professor and the authors hate white women. We care about racial reconciliation, but all we get in return is anger." I assured them that this was far from the case, but as was the case in my church, I did not know how to respond effectively.

These two incidents—and my lack of clarity in responding to them— left me with the questions that would lead me to writing this book: What is wrong with these white people? Why do they see hate when Black people try to help them understand how they are involved in the problem *they* say their faith leads them to fight?

These questions might not have gone further than frustrated venting if it weren't for one more story and one more insistent question. This story centers on Pappaw—my maternal grandfather—and begins before my birth, in the early days of my parents' relationship. While my mom was in college, she started dating my dad and quickly received an ultimatum from her parents: she had to stop dating that Black man, or they would stop paying for college. Luckily for my future existence, my mom dropped out of college and moved in with my dad. They made it work with help from my dad's family and got married after a while. My mom's mother came to the wedding, but her father refused. When I was born a few years later, my maternal grandparents came around to try to patch things up.

I don't believe my mother ever forgave them or that their relationship was ever really fixed, but I did get to have a wonderful relationship with her parents, especially Pappaw. He was a beautiful person. He died over a decade before I wrote this book, but if I'm still alive while you're reading this, I guarantee that I still miss Pappaw and fondly remember how proud he was of me for whatever I happened to be doing. That's how he was the entire time I knew him. He loved everyone for who they were, and when he died, an entire community mourned. In the end, he had even loved my dad well enough that when Pappaw died, my dad tearfully said he had lost one of the best friends he'd ever had.

More than anyone, he's who I learned to think of when I think of what it means to love unconditionally. See, it wasn't until I was in college—not too many years before Pappaw's death—that I learned the story of how he had broken my mother's heart. And that left me with a question that it took me years to even articulate: How could someone whose love was so powerful—and who it turns out was capable of significant change—do something so cruel to his daughter?

This lingering question about my Pappaw helped me to take that other question seriously: What *is* wrong with these white people? I found myself considering the possibility that those white Christians I had encountered in grad school really were trying to love the Black folks with whom they were in community, but somehow their love was distorted. I rejected the idea that they were acting in bad faith, that they did not really believe they were committed to reconciliation. I accepted that they truly felt attacked, that they truly were frustrated and burnt out. Ultimately, I came to the conclusion that they perceived themselves to be loving friends who were being treated as if they were enemies. They couldn't realize the truth that they *were* their Black friends' enemies and that they *were* being loved . . . *as enemies.*

WHY FOCUS ON ENMITY?

Contemporary antiracist[2] work in US churches has its roots in the response to Jesus's command to love our enemies, exemplified by Martin Luther King Jr.'s public leadership during the civil rights movement. Contemporary antiracist work in US churches falters and fails because US Christians generally have little to no understanding of what it truly means to be enemies across lines of race. Failing to understand enmity, US Christians fail to properly love their enemies, instead embracing a distorted understanding of love that has been clouded and consistently co-opted by white supremacy and anti-Blackness.

To put it bluntly, US Christians do not understand that to be caught within the reality that is race is to necessarily be the enemy of anyone of a race other than your own. Even the most intimate interracial relationships cannot escape this fundamental enmity. If you are white and you are reading this sentence, you are my enemy, and I am yours. If we can accept what that means—and understand what it does not mean—we might be able to love one another *as enemies* in new, more powerful ways.

I should be clear that in naming "US Christians," I am particularly interested in folks whose faith in Jesus is intimately connected to a stated commitment to antiracism. When I critique US Christianity in the coming pages, I am not striving to convince millions of US Christian nationalists that their faith is deeply corrupted. When I lay out an imagination of divine love and power that rejects the desire for mastery and control in favor of an embrace of need, desire, and mutuality, I dare not hope that this imagination will be compelling to those whose desire for mastery and control compels them to work toward a transphobic and misogynistic Christian theocracy. The critiques and imagination I offer in these chapters are offered in hopes of equipping those whose faith calls them to seek justice. I hope to help them deepen their commitment to antiracism, productively question their faith, and believe that their faith can thrive when it is called to account for the demands of justice. This book was written for Christians who desire beloved community and yet find their pursuit of that community too exhausting and demoralizing to maintain for the years and decades required.

These are the Christians with whom I feel the deepest bonds of community and care. I have encountered them among my students and in the churches to which my family has belonged. These are the people who give me the most hope that faith in Jesus might actually strengthen the faithful in their pursuit of justice. And yet, among these very Christians—the folks who register to take an elective course on antiracism or join their church's antiracism team—I have consistently encountered a fatal flaw in their work of loving their enemies: the rejection of the notion that there truly are *enemies* to be loved.

I have encountered this rejection of the concept of enmity by Christians of all races, and it is most commonly expressed in two forms. On the one hand, there are those who claim, "I have no enemies" or "Christians can't have enemies." This is a popular set of claims among white and BIPOC Christians alike. On the other hand, there are those who argue, "*Enemy* is a scary, unhelpful word to use if we want people to love each other."

This resistance to naming another person—especially another Christian—"enemy" is understandable. *Enemy* is a horrible, deadly word. It implies that you have a relationship with someone that tends toward hatred and exclusion, not love and embrace. Enmity leads those caught in it toward the death we claim Jesus overcame, without the promise of new life we are offered through baptism. To name someone "enemy" is to state, unequivocally, that your existence and theirs are opposed to such an extent that one or both of you must fundamentally change for true peace to exist between you. Acknowledging enmity across lines of race can feel like a denial of the possibility of any kind of interracial collaboration. For Christians who are actively committed to dismantling white supremacy, then, the idea of naming someone of another race their "enemy" can feel like it is both unchristian and counterproductive to the work of antiracism.

If you are reading this book, chances are you are a Christian who is deeply uncomfortable—if not wholly resistant—to the idea that someone might be your enemy simply because they are of a different race. So why do I lead with this potentially alienating insistence on the importance of enmity?

Jesus calls us to love our *enemies*, not posture as if we are so pure and loving that we have somehow transcended the concept of enmity. To be so convinced of our own righteousness that we believe we could not have an enemy is to believe we have no need of the healing grace offered by the one who calls us to love our enemies. To assume that our desire for beloved community somehow makes irrelevant our positions in a political and economic landscape structured by white supremacy and anti-Blackness is to believe that the call to love our enemies is, in fact, irrelevant to our world. To deny the reality of enmity between people of different races is to ignore the truth that sin and death are deeply woven into the lives of our churches and the communities of which they are a part.

Enmity structures the reality in which we live. The structural nature of enmity is why I favor the term *enmity* in this book over the more familiar *enemies*. Enmity is the state of being within which people exist as enemies, and when it comes down to it, that state of enmity is what we need to understand if we're going to engage in effective antiracist work for the long haul. We are called to love our enemies, but to do so, we need to understand how it is possible to love *through* enmity rather than trying to love by denying the reality of enmity.

Antiracism work collapses when Christians who have not been prepared for the intractable nature of enmity across lines of racial difference discover that such enmity is not eliminated by friendship. They find themselves coming together in the wake of tragedy or conflict—yet another police shooting, deportation, or hate-fueled election—only to realize that they are distressingly alienated from one another, distraught that so many white folks are still surprised about the depth and breadth of suffering caused by white supremacy or wounded by the fact that so many BIPOC folks are reaching the limits of their patience. They come together in church only to find that their faith cannot sustain them. Further, they discover that their faith actually undermines the antiracist work to which it led them in the first place.

I begin this book with the horror of enmity rather than the beauty of love because I long for us to break this cycle of kindhearted commitment to antiracism followed by brokenhearted retreat from our awareness of enmity. When it comes down to it, if we are called to love our enemies, we had better understand who our enemies are and what it means to say that they are our enemies. From this starting point, *Loving through Enmity* is intended to steer US Christians from the misguided grind of frustration in which so much antiracist work is caught, offering instead the no less difficult—but far more productive—challenge of faithful, loving action. To be clear, this book does not offer a comprehensive guide to antiracist work. Rather, it reimagines core concepts in US Christian antiracist work—enmity and love—in hopes of inspiring US Christians to commit to making their antiracist work more sustainable and rigorous.

Before more fully diving into this work of reimagining enmity and love, I'll take the rest of this introduction to briefly answer three questions and flesh out the context of US Christian antiracist work in which I hope this book will be helpful:

1) What's going on when it comes to race in the United States?
2) What has gone wrong with US Christian antiracist work?
3) What more needs to be said about US Christian antiracist work?

WHAT'S GOING ON WHEN IT COMES TO RACE IN THE UNITED STATES?

There are, of course, entire books covering mere aspects of the reality of race in this country. I will settle for briefly sketching out the situation of interracial enmity that continues to demand a response from US Christians, with particular attention to the twin problems confronting most US Christians who are committed to antiracism: white supremacy and anti-Blackness as they operate in the United States.

There are many ways to talk about white supremacy and anti-Blackness as they shape life in the United States. When I discuss these intertwined evils, I focus on how they create a racialized arrangement of *exploitation* and *violence* in this country that promotes the superiority of whiteness, enforces the inferiority of Blackness, and demands that all people orient their lives in relation to this white/Black binary. Theological and emotional elements of white supremacy and anti-Blackness will be central to this book's treatment of enemy love, but when it comes down to what destroys some and enriches others, white supremacy and anti-Blackness are about how folks are made subject to—or exempted from—structures of exploitation and violence, based on how they are perceived in relation to the influential social construction that is race.

In order to illuminate what's going on with race in the United States, I will focus on Chicago as an example.[3] In part, I choose Chicago as an example because it is where I live and work and should be understood to provide a certain basic context within which my thinking about race is being formed—and by which it may be limited. Just as important, however, Chicago is the focus of a set of clear, well-researched reports on racial justice produced in 2017 by the University of Illinois Chicago (UIC) Institute for Research on Race and Public Policy. Though these "State of Racial Justice" reports have their limitations, as all research does,[4] they highlight both the structural nature of race as it functions in the United States and the particular kinds of social and economic systems impacted by it. When I refer to *interracial enmity*, these systems and the resources they regulate are that in relation to which we find ourselves positioned as enemies.

Five primary categories of social and economic structures are addressed in the reports—housing, economics, education, justice, and health—in relation to five racial groups: white, Black, Latine, Asian, and Indigenous American. In all categories, disparities favor white Chicago residents, with other racial groups suffering from differing levels of inequity. Often Black and Indigenous American Chicagoans fare worst, with some Asian nationalities (Cambodian, Bangladeshi, Thai, Pakistani) faring similarly. These reports are extensive, but for the purposes of briefly illustrating the reality of white supremacy and anti-Blackness in the United States, I will simply list the range of metrics along which racial injustice in Chicago was discovered to be significant in these reports.

Housing: segregation,[5] homeownership, appreciation of home value, loan approval rate, housing availability, foreclosure rates, and percentage of renters being cost-burdened by rent (spending 30 percent or more of their annual income on rent)[6]

Economics: unemployment (including among folks with advanced degrees), poverty rates, income, percentage of workers earning a living wage, wealth, and commute length[7]

Education: segregation, funding, school closures, challenges finding teachers who look like students, disparities in preparedness for college, school punishment (including police intervention), and overrepresentation of white students in advanced courses, gifted programs, and top-ranked high schools[8]

Justice: incarceration rates,[9] impact of prison populations on political redistricting that leads to overrepresentation of white voters, police surveillance and intervention, use of force by Chicago police (including among youth), and effectiveness of complaints against police officers[10]

Health: access to health-care providers and pharmacies mirrors patterns of housing segregation, such that they're concentrated in white neighborhoods (with health-care provider availability ratios of up to 10:1), rates of heart disease and obesity, and rates of infant mortality and low birth weight[11]

Even presented in this truncated form, the findings of the UIC Institute for Research on Race and Public Policy gesture toward the reality of white supremacy in the United States. In short, exploitation and violence are consistently organized by race across a wide range of activities and institutions in ways that favor white people and disadvantage BIPOC people to varying degrees. Schools, prisons, real estate patterns, lending practices, health-care systems, urban planning principles, and any number of factors are woven together into a disturbingly coherent and terribly complex racialized societal arrangement. These myriad manifestations of racial injustice are complicated by their entanglement in further systemic evils—such as environmental degradation,[12] violence against LGBTQIA+ folks, immigration policy, and inequity experienced by women—all of which compound one another in an intersectional nightmare.

While the shape white supremacy and anti-Blackness take in even this single US American city is the subject of numerous books, I hope I have adequately highlighted the *kinds* of systemic racism that exist in this country. In some areas of the country, segregation is primarily town by town rather than neighborhood by neighborhood. In some areas, Latine folks experience disparities in income and housing value as severe as those experienced by Black folks and suffer as high a degree of police surveillance and use of force. In some areas, education helps Black folks to have greater access to privilege than in other areas. Poor white folks are more intensely marginalized in some areas than others. Still, despite these variations, white supremacy and anti-Blackness consistently coordinate exploitation and violence in ways that favor white people, harm Black people, and force other BIPOC folks to navigate this racialized dynamic.[13]

Going a step further, I could discuss the broader entanglement of white supremacy, anti-Blackness, and Empire. The exploitation and violence of white supremacy and anti-Blackness in the United States are intimately intertwined with both the historical, global realities of colonialism and the contemporary realities of global Empire.[14] Historically, colonialist white supremacist exploitation in the United States included the dispossession of Indigenous Americans' land through practices as complex as colonists' claiming of lands in North America through specious interpretation and imposition of European common land laws and as openly unjust as broken treaties. The enslavement of African laborers evolved into the exploitation of Black agricultural labor through sharecropping and Black industrial labor through the exclusion of Black workers from labor unions. Immigration practices transformed from decade to decade to facilitate the entrapment of laborers, reflecting gradually shifting definitions of whiteness and relations of imperialism with different nations around the world. Under contemporary Empire, US American involvement in exploitation is largely through the incarceration system and corporations with origins in the United States or significant US presence. Such corporations engage in extraction of natural resources across the globe, outsource and subcontract jobs through exploitative labor practices, coordinate flows of migrant labor that expose millions of laborers to unsafe conditions, and even persist in the enslavement of workers around the world.

White supremacist violence is as prominent as exploitation in the colonial history of the United States. The industrialized violence of chattel slavery existed alongside the wholesale genocide of Indigenous nations across the continent. Displacement of Indigenous Americans through military power was compounded by efforts to erase Native cultures through the theft of children from their families, compulsory education in English, and forced indoctrination into Christianity. US American imperialism took the form of outright colonization in the Pacific and Caribbean, as well as covert subversion of governments during the Cold War. Contemporary US American participation in the violence of Empire is most prominent in the ongoing impact of US American militarism on the globe—and through the associated targeting of specific racialized populations within the borders of the United States as potential terrorists—as well as the ecological violence committed by corporations.

Without diving deep into these histories and contemporary realities of violence and exploitation, we can nonetheless offer a meaningful answer to the question with which I opened this section: What's going on when it comes to race in the United States? What's going on is that we continue to be confronted by white supremacy and anti-Blackness—colossal, systemic evils grounded in centuries of injustice and empowered by their integration into global systems of economic, political, and military power. White supremacy and anti-Blackness, in their overwhelming power, vast reach, and disturbing coherence, demand an equally empowered, widespread, and coherent opposition to dismantle them. And to be perfectly clear, US churches have indeed responded to what's going on with race by taking up the work of confronting white supremacy and anti-Blackness as the twin evils they are. Sadly, that work falls short of what is required.

WHAT HAS GONE WRONG WITH US CHRISTIAN ANTIRACIST WORK?

Why, in other words, are books offering significant critiques of US Christian antiracist work even necessary? The short answer is while what is required is a sustained, coordinated antiracist movement, what we have are deeply compromised, fragmented efforts to resist white supremacy and anti-Blackness.

"Wait a minute," you might say. "You *just* said the problem is US Christians' failure to understand enmity!"

Well, it turns out that quite a bit has gone wrong with antiracist work in US churches. While this book focuses on a particular problem that requires attention if we're going to turn things around, there is a broader set of diagnoses in relation to which this book will best be understood. Among the various texts that have offered such diagnoses of US churches' struggle to engage in effective antiracist work, two stand out as particularly helpful and appropriately bold: Jennifer Harvey's *Dear White Christians* and Chanequa Walker-Barnes's *I Bring the Voices of My People*. If US churches have not generated a sustained, coordinated antiracist movement but have instead offered deeply compromised, fragmented efforts, Harvey and Walker-Barnes offer important, complementary insights into why this is the case. Taken together, their books highlight five problems with US Christian antiracist work and offer corresponding correctives that can address these problems.[15]

The first problem with much US Christian antiracist work is a flawed understanding of race and racism. Working from the understanding that race is socially constructed—not a matter of biology but of human meaning-making—race is regularly treated as if it is not real.[16] Racism, in turn, is reduced to a problem of social division grounded in biased feelings related to arbitrary distinctions of race.[17] With racism reduced to division—rather than the systematic distribution of exploitation and violence I sketched out in the previous section—the second problem crops up. Rather than keeping the problems of exploitation and violence in focus, a notion of reconciliation as the achievement of unity and togetherness is prioritized as the goal of Christian antiracist work.[18] As laudable as this goal might be, it does not facilitate effective responses to many BIPOC folks' most pressing concerns of addressing exploitation and violence. Rather, it reflects the third problem with US Christian antiracist work. In navigating complex issues of moral responsibility, this work often adopts a universalist posture, prioritizing a sense of our common, shared humanity over meaningful attention to differences of privilege and responsibility.[19] Failing to recognize any distinction in the levels of moral responsibility people of different races bear for racism, this work hits a fourth problem: its tendency to focus on white Christians' concerns (e.g., increasing BIPOC attendance in predominantly white congregations) at the expense of their BIPOC siblings' concerns.[20] So thoroughly led astray by these first four issues, US Christian antiracist work can't help but fall into a fifth problem, the adoption of misguided strategies. Increased interpersonal contact between Christians of different races is pushed without attention to the ways in which white and BIPOC participants do not bear the same responsibility for racial divisions.[21] The pursuit of togetherness regularly devolves into storytelling exercises in which BIPOC participants bear the burden of absolving white participants' guilt.[22] Diversity is pursued through dialogue that excludes BIPOC women, insofar as BIPOC men and white women are each willing to represent BIPOC folks and women more generally.[23]

Against the misunderstanding of race and racism, Walker-Barnes and Harvey each stress the material reality of race and racism. Race is a social construction, but it is nonetheless *real and powerful*. It impacts peoples' lives through legal, economic, and political structures.[24] These impacts must be understood with respect to their historical development through concrete local, national, and global institutions.[25] Racism is not about individuals' feelings but about the modulation of privilege and oppression in relation to a racial hierarchy.[26] Insofar as reconciliation may be the goal of antiracist work, it must be understood as the deeply challenging work of participating in God's mission of bringing wholeness to the world. Such work defies quick solutions and linear progress.[27] It may even be unhelpful to focus on reconciliation as the goal, given the consistent conflation of reconciliation with togetherness. In this light, reparations for past wrongs against BIPOC folks—most notably the enslavement of Africans and the dispossession and genocide of Indigenous peoples—may be a more useful and faithful goal for white Christians in particular.[28] Neither a reimagined goal of reconciliation nor a more immediate goal of reparations can be pursued effectively if guided by a universal notion of humanity that discourages attention to racial difference. Rather, Christian antiracist work must begin with participants' different relations to the distribution of exploitation and violence that constitutes racial injustice.[29] Guided by attention to racial particularity, antiracist work needs to decenter white concerns in recognition that BIPOC folks' needs are more pressing given the reality of structures of racialized violence and exploitation.[30] In particular, BIPOC women's perspectives should be centered, both because they offer deep insights into the inner workings of white supremacy and because it can help facilitate healing and liberation in the context of the routine exclusion of BIPOC women.[31] These shifts in understanding and focus—to a material understanding of race and racism, revised goals of reconciliation and reparations, attention to particularity, and the centering of BIPOC women's concerns—require shifts in strategy as well. Perhaps most obviously, it is important to foreground the pursuit of reparations as central to antiracist work. Racial injustice is a matter of material harm and corresponding debt, and it can be addressed meaningfully through material efforts at repair and repayment.[32] Further, race is intertwined with other categories of identity and requires intersectional analysis that acknowledges the mutual influence of race, gender, sexuality, and the full range of categories that organize privilege and oppression.[33] Given the demands of these strategies and the particular moral responsibility borne by white US Americans for white supremacy in the United States, it is essential for white Christians to come to grips with the fact that the dismantling of structures that favor white people will demand more of white people than BIPOC people.[34]

WHAT MORE NEEDS TO BE SAID ABOUT US CHRISTIAN ANTIRACIST WORK?

Taken together, Walker-Barnes's work in *I Bring the Voices of My People* and Harvey's in *Dear White Christians* present a powerful challenge to US Christian antiracist work, as well as clear directions for more effective work. So why do we need yet another book?

To get to the heart of the matter, fundamentally, the tension between the explicitly political work of antiracism and the emotional dimensions of Christian faith haven't yet been adequately addressed.[35] As those called to love our enemies, we need to be able to both fully claim the reality that we are enemies and wholeheartedly love one another in ways that we can accept as faithfully loving. We need to be able to have enemies without the worry that having enemies is some kind of moral failure,[36] instead embracing the truth that being aware of enmity between yourself and someone else makes it possible to love them more powerfully. In short, we need to examine and reimagine enmity, love, and the relation between them. That's at least enough work for a book.

In this book, my efforts to do this work of examination and reimagination can be summarized in four moves. In chapter 1, I critique the dominant, private understanding of interracial enmity and outline a more helpful alternative: structural interracial enmity. In chapter 2, I examine the role emotions play in white supremacy and anti-Blackness, with particular attention to how love has been distorted by white supremacy, thus undermining antiracist work. In chapters 3–5, I explore the political and theological nature of hope and love by exploring the work of Black theologians and other thinkers. Finally, in chapters 6 and 7, I explore divine and human love and power, laying out a theological foundation for radical antiracist work that embraces the biblical call to love our enemies.

Before I even knew I was headed toward this work, I had a question: How could my grandfather—whose love was so powerful and who was capable of significant change—so cruelly reject his daughter? Such questions regularly come to the surface through antiracist work. I hope this book will help my readers consider such questions as central to Christian faith. They are questions that have been at the heart of our faith ever since Peter turned his back on Jesus in his moment of deepest suffering.[37] We love Jesus, truly. We love our children and parents. We love our friends and siblings in Christ. Too often, though, something gets in the way. Something pulls us apart. Something turns us against those we love so that our love just doesn't seem like it's enough. For Peter, that something was Roman imperial violence, the threat that the crowd would turn him over to the Romans just like they handed over his beloved teacher. For us, that something is often race. It makes enemies of those who should embrace one another as the beloved community. I hope this book shows that even as enemies, we can love one another faithfully and fully.

CHAPTER ONE

Structural Interracial Enmity

Each time I teach my course on loving our enemies, I take some time during the first class session to ask my students a pair of questions: Who are your enemies? Or, if it makes more sense this way, to whom are you an enemy?

Each time I teach that course at the white-dominated seminary where I work, that is, I sit in a room filled—physically and virtually—with people I know to be my enemies and ask them who their enemies are. Most students are uncomfortable answering that question, which presents its own path toward growth and learning. Those who speak up, however, generally offer one of these responses: "Christians shouldn't have enemies," "Christians *don't* have enemies," "*I* don't have enemies."

In six years of teaching, I've heard these claims voiced by students of all races and a variety of denominations. When it comes down to it, many US Christians just don't believe they have enemies, especially when we're talking about race. This refusal to recognize enmity has dire consequences for our capacity to practice transformative Christian love. I'll explore this distortion of love in the next chapter, but for now, I'll state that when Christians dismiss the notion of enmity and settle for a practice of love that amounts to prioritizing togetherness over justice,[1] the command to love our enemies is reduced from one of the greatest challenges confronting us in our lives of faith to self-serving proof that our faith is pure. There is a notion that to admit to having enemies—not to mention prioritizing identifying those enemies—represents a fundamental failure of Christian discipleship and the faith that underlies it.[2] Failing to grasp the nature of the enmity that confronts us, we too often treat enmity and love as if they are mutually exclusive even as we claim fidelity to the command to love our enemies. Constrained by this misunderstanding, our faith compels us to act as though once love arrives on the scene, enmity necessarily evaporates in its warm, brilliant light.

In reality, enmity and love can and do coexist. To love our enemies is not necessarily to make them stop being our enemies or to stop being enemies to them. To acknowledge that our enemies are, in fact, our enemies is not to withdraw our love from them. Rather, our deepest and most intensely loving interracial relationships are—at the same time that they are loving—relationships fundamentally shaped by interracial enmity.

I am not suggesting that people of different races cannot be friends while racial enemy relations persist. Neither am I implying that people in interracial relationships of various sorts are secretly committed to being enemies and only pretend to love one another to assure themselves of their piety or civility. My claim is that interracial relationships of all sorts are inherently compromised, their personal and communal significance hijacked by white supremacy. To point at an interracial couple, friend group, or ministry team as though emotional compatibility, physical attraction, shared purpose, communal acceptance, or even extended mutual care represents proof of the decline of white supremacy is to spread that corruption. This is, to say the least, a challenging reality to confront.

Ultimately, most of this book will be about finding a way to understand love in the context of enduring—even overwhelming—enmity. I begin with enmity in hopes of preparing us to embrace a love that is better equipped to sustain us as we endure white supremacy's insidious infiltration of interracial intimacy. Rather than trying to confine enmity to something that neatly responds to dominant understandings of Christian love, I'm going to look at enmity and work from there to ask how we might better understand faithful Christian love.

The command to love our enemies can be a powerful and practical Christian ethical principle rather than an outdated idea we use to glorify ourselves by implying its irrelevance to those of us who claim to have no enemies. To live out this key element of Christian discipleship, however, we must avoid the temptation to rely on an idea of enmity that doesn't fit the reality in which we live or foster the kind of love that can sustain long-term antiracist work. In other words, if we want to faithfully follow that challenging command to love our enemies through our antiracist work, US Christians need to recognize that interracial enmity exists, understand the nature of that enmity, then question our notions and practices of love in relation to the reality of the enmity within which we live.

In hopes of facilitating the first two of these tasks, this chapter will establish and explore a distinction between two ideas of enmity: private enmity and structural interracial enmity. Private enmity is the mode of enmity that comes to mind most often when we're reminded of the command to love our enemies—and for good reason: it's the kind of enmity that is likely referenced in Matthew's Sermon on the Mount and Luke's Sermon on the Plain. Private enmity refers to a relationship in which one party has wronged another, resulting in a reciprocal, escalating conflict. Structural interracial enmity, by contrast, describes an antagonism woven into the structure of our society. Rather than emphasizing harmful actions between individuals, the notion of structural interracial enmity portrays enmity as a matter of racial groups being positioned against one another by the various structures (e.g., economics, law, politics, culture, faith) that organize society itself. Structural interracial enmity does not necessarily involve parties who feel badly toward each other or wish each other harm. Instead, it often pits us against precisely those people we most fervently wish to treat well and for whom we desire justice. This structural understanding of enmity is surely not what Jesus or the evangelists had in mind in proclaiming those famous sermons. Nonetheless, as I will show later in this chapter, structural interracial enmity is a concept with biblical grounding that can orient that challenging command to love our enemies in Christian antiracist work.

WHAT IS PRIVATE ENMITY?

Why do committed Christians like my students so often struggle to imagine themselves as people who have enemies? In short, Christian understandings of enmity have been shaped decisively by a private model of enmity. Consider how Martin Luther King Jr. explains why Christians should love their enemies in his 1957 sermon "Loving Your Enemies":

> I think the first reason that we should love our enemies, and I think this was at the very center of Jesus' thinking, is this: that hate for hate only intensifies the existence of hate and evil in the universe. If I hit you and you hit me and I hit you back and you hit me back and go on, you see, that goes on ad infinitum. It just never ends. Somewhere somebody must have a little sense, and that's the strong person. The strong person is the person who can cut off the chain of hate,

> the chain of evil. And that is the tragedy of hate, that it doesn't cut it off. It only intensifies the existence of hate and evil in the universe. Somebody must have religion enough and morality enough to cut it off and inject within the very structure of the universe that strong and powerful element of love.[3]

King stands at the heart of US Christian antiracist work for good reason, his life of courage representing some of the finest theology in US church history. Nonetheless, his characterization of enmity in this sermon points us toward the problem that plagues contemporary Christian antiracist work. In this passage, King describes enmity in terms of the unjust actions of individuals: "I hit you and you hit me and I hit you back and you hit me back." Unjust actions link one to another in a "chain of hate," to which the Christian response is powerful, transformative love.

This represents a powerful response to private patterns of harmful action. Returning hate with love not only has the possibility of helping the one who chooses to love to avoid the spiritual and emotional harm that comes from harboring hate within oneself but also opens the door to their enemy's transformation and the collapse of that hateful cycle. For most of the sermon, King raises relevant examples (e.g., unfair coworkers, dangerous drivers, people motivated by jealousy) in which one person has wronged another person, and the danger of retaliation looms. Toward the end of the sermon, however, King builds on this biblical insight to promote nonviolent resistance as a loving response to racist hatred.

King makes what seems like a natural connection between practicing love to defuse a cycle of mistreatment with an aggressive neighbor and practicing love to undermine the manifestation of hatred that is white supremacy.[4] He takes the command to love one's enemy and applies it to a situation in which there is clearly enmity. In doing so, however, he glosses over the crucial distinction between private enmity and structural enmity. This error—represented here by King but certainly not exclusive to him—leads Christians committed to antiracist work to insist that they have no enemies even as they seek to follow the command to love their enemies.

Beyond demonstrating this fundamental mistake regarding interracial enmity, "Loving Your Enemies" also points us toward a key source for the prioritization of private enmity in Christian antiracist work: Matthew 5:43–48.[5] This passage reads as follows:

> 43You have heard that it was said, "You shall love your neighbor and hate your enemy." 44But I say to you: Love your enemies and pray for those who persecute you, 45so that you may be children of your Father in heaven, for he makes his

> sun rise on the evil and on the good and sends rain on the righteous and on the unrighteous. 46For if you love those who love you, what reward do you have? Do not even the tax collectors do the same? 47And if you greet only your brothers and sisters, what more are you doing than others? Do not even the gentiles do the same? 48Be perfect, therefore, as your heavenly Father is perfect.[6]

King's sermon faithfully responds to Jesus's sermon in encouraging those to whom it is proclaimed to love those who would do them harm. To understand the notion of private enmity that structures this call to love our enemies, however, we must recognize that Jesus's sermon is itself in conversation with an older biblical source—Leviticus 19:18—and the private understanding of enmity that is at the heart of that older tradition.[7]

Before moving forward from Matthew 5:43–48, then, it will be helpful to go further back, exploring Leviticus 19:18 and the broader tradition of biblical law to which Jesus responds in the Sermon on the Mount. More specifically, I will now turn to the work of biblical scholar Klaus-Peter Adam to lay out the understanding of private enmity that guides Leviticus 19:18 (along with other passages that can be categorized as biblical law) and explain how Leviticus 19:11–18 portrays and responds to private enmity.

To understand private enmity as it influenced those key biblical texts, it is important to recognize that—somewhat like race is today—enmity was a social construct active in the communities in which those texts were written. Neither a natural state nor a wholly private opinion, enmity was a socially constructed relationship that organized how private individuals would act out their disputes with one another within local communities structured primarily by kinship rather than centralized government.[8] Analogous to marriage, parent-child relationships, or enslavement, the social construct of enmity made sense of a certain kind of relation within or between families, allowing for the development of legal traditions outlining how God's people should act toward their enemies.[9]

Adam lists five qualities that structure the social construct of private enmity: "It (1) implied a form of public declaration or overtly acting out enmity. Furthermore, (2) it included acting out enmity in ways that allowed for flexibility and variation, i.e., opponents could act out their enmity in various ways. In addition, (3) acting out enmity was a reciprocal process and (4) the reciprocity between the enemies usually escalated and could reach its climax in one party's attempt to kill their foe. Finally, (5) private enmity was transitive: a person at enmity with another would naturally expect their friends' solidarity."[10]

Leviticus 19:11–18—the passage to which Jesus likely refers in Matthew 5:43–48—is a biblical response to private enmity, as described by Adam. It reads as follows:

> [11]You shall not steal; you shall not deal falsely; and you shall not lie to one another. [12]And you shall not swear falsely by my name, profaning the name of your God: I am the Lord.
>
> [13]You shall not defraud your neighbor; you shall not steal; and you shall not keep for yourself the wages of a laborer until morning. [14]You shall not revile the deaf or put a stumbling block before the blind; you shall fear your God: I am the Lord.
>
> [15]You shall not render an unjust judgment; you shall not be partial to the poor or defer to the great: with justice you shall judge your neighbor. [16]You shall not go around as a slanderer among your people, and you shall not stand idly by when the blood of your neighbor is at stake: I am the Lord.
>
> [17]You shall not hate in your heart anyone of your kin; you shall reprove your neighbor, or you will incur guilt yourself. [18]You shall not take vengeance or bear a grudge against any of your people, but you shall love your neighbor as yourself: I am the Lord.[11]

Broadly speaking, this passage lays out expectations for how one should treat another member of one's community "in a potential, an emerging, or an ongoing conflict."[12] It rejects a range of actions that would bring harm to the community—flatly rejecting vengeance, which could have a destructive impact on the community, given the tendency of private enmity toward escalation[13]—and offers a practical alternative to long-term enmity.

Delving into the Hebrew used in this passage, Adam points out that the language of verses 17–18 encourages enemies to resolve their conflicts rather than escalating them.[14] Against the mutual destruction toward which cycles of revenge tended, Adam argues that this passage promotes the kind of "mutual legal *instruction*" that would be expected within a family at peace.[15] When conflict arises, Leviticus 19:17–18 teaches, God would have God's people treat one another with the love one owes one's kin, not with the hatred their cultural context deems appropriate to direct toward one's enemies.

In pointing toward a notion of fictive kinship—treating as kin those to whom one is not biologically or legally related to any meaningful extent—Leviticus

19:17–18 offers the community justification for its practical alternative to vengeance. The cycle of retaliation and escalation that characterized private enmity was driven by categories of honor and shame that provided structure to such kinship-oriented societies.[16] In contrast to honor and shame, Leviticus 19:17–18 grounds its proposal of peaceful conflict resolution in a divine preference for fictive kinship as the community's organizing principle. Love—understood as the kind of mutual benevolence expected of family—rather than enmity, would be the response to conflict with one's neighbor.[17]

This articulation of fictive kinship brings us back around to the ministry of Jesus, its recollection in the Gospel of Matthew, and Jesus's command to love our enemies. By rejecting any sense of a distinction between neighbor and enemy in Matthew 5:43–48, Jesus doubles down on Leviticus 19's establishment of fictive kinship, asserting that it includes those who mistreat or persecute oneself and one's community.[18]

Crucially, in promoting this practice of loving enemies, Jesus makes no promise that they will cease to be one's enemies. This is an important divergence from the understanding of private enmity as applied in Leviticus. To be someone's enemy in this sense—to be caught in a reciprocal, likely escalating pattern of hostile acts—was to suspend the relations of "mutual benevolence" that should otherwise prevail among members of the same community.[19] Urging his followers not to accept this apparent limitation, Jesus encourages them to be "perfect" in the manner of God, who blesses the righteous and unrighteous alike. In treating their enemies as kin, Jesus's followers are afforded a practice of piety that imitates divine perfection.[20] In loving their enemies—in withstanding what would seem to be an irreconcilable tension between enmity and love—they live as children of God.

WHY DOESN'T PRIVATE ENMITY WORK AS A MODEL FOR INTERRACIAL ENMITY?

Private enmity is the understanding of enmity that informs Jesus's command to love our enemies. Unfortunately, key qualities of private enmity simply do not apply when we consider what it means in the twenty-first-century United States to call people of different races *enemies*.[21] Specifically, three of the five qualities of private enmity laid out by Klaus-Peter Adam do not correspond to the reality of race in the United States. What's more, those disconnects between private enmity and interracial enmity facilitate some of the most insidious problems plaguing US Christian antiracist work.

First, private enmity implies "a form of public declaration or overtly acting out enmity."[22] In other words, "private" enmity—the kind of enmity to which Jesus responded in the Sermon on the Mount—is necessarily public. Such enemies openly acknowledge that they are enemies and act intentionally to harm one another. For example, in Matthew 5:44, Jesus references persecutors who are actively seeking to harm his followers (and, of course, urges his followers not to engage in the cycle of retaliation expected in private enmity). While overt racism has hardly disappeared from the United States, the ongoing mistaken belief that racism is fundamentally a matter of overt action and stated prejudices represents one of the greatest challenges faced by contemporary antiracist work.[23] In short, private enmity fails to account for both the insidious influence of white supremacy in the lives of those who reject any kind of overt enmity toward people of other races and the capacity for white supremacy to cause harm apart from any localized and personal mistreatment or persecution.

Second, the private enmity model frames enmity as a "reciprocal process,"[24] in which both parties act against one another in a cycle of retaliation. When it comes to race, however, there is no such reciprocity. Consider the historical relation between Black and white people in the United States. Far from a cycle of mutual hostility, there are the originating events of the kidnapping and enslavement of Black people, followed by a centuries-long pattern of unprovoked white aggression, met by Black resistance that almost never takes the form of aggressive retaliation, and white backlash to Black resistance. The originating events and nuances of the stories of other BIPOC folks' historical relations with white people vary, but all have in common the reality that there is no reciprocity to the violence that defines interracial enmity in this country. Enmity among BIPOC folks of different races also lacks the quality of reciprocity. Rather, such enmity is something more like intense competition than any kind of cyclical pattern of mutual hostility, with different marginalized groups routinely falling short of forming a lasting coalition with others who are targeted by white supremacy.

When we search for such reciprocal harm in our communities, we can fall prey to a dangerous error. Searching for back-and-forth hostility in our community and failing to find it, we might mistakenly conclude that race is not a real problem in our community. We may witness the beautiful interracial friendships in our community—or at least the lack of open aggression from any side—and compare them to the murders, brawls, and hateful rhetoric we see in the news or online. It becomes easy to believe that race is a problem "out there" but that *we* are steadily moving past it.

Interracial enmity in the United States simply has not arisen from a reciprocal pattern of retaliation. Rather, it has arisen from—and is perpetuated by—global, generalized histories of injustice. Slavery, land dispossession, genocide, discriminatory immigration policies, and internment camps are not discrete events in various cycles of private enmity. Rather, they are manifestations of enduring structures of interracial enmity.

Third, compounding the fact that interracial enmity is not a reciprocal process, it does not display the escalating quality of private enmity, in which aggression takes more and more intense forms over time, potentially resulting in the attempted murder of one party by the other. Death looms on the horizon for *both* parties engaged in private enmity. When it comes to interracial enmity, however, some bodies are much more vulnerable to death's touch than others. Whether we want to discuss the personal murders brought about by state violence or the depersonalized death-dealing violence of systemic inequities, death is not a danger that arises from a gradual escalation of mutual hostility. Rather, under the conditions of interracial enmity, vulnerability to death is an enduring experience of those who cannot shelter beneath the protection of whiteness.

Private enmity, then, does not accurately capture the dynamics of enmity that pertain to race in the United States. Consequently, the biblical responses to private enmity discussed earlier don't function well as responses to interracial enmity. Specifically, the strategies of extending fictive kinship to enemies and practicing perfect piety in the face of hostility fall short as antiracist practices, given their basic purpose as responses to private enmity.

Extending fictive kinship to people of other races has certainly proven to be an attractive approach to antiracist work. This is essentially what we do when we prioritize common humanity over racial difference. The transformative potential of this fictive kinship strategy, though, is what Jennifer Harvey rejects when she critiques the "universalist ethic" at the heart of the reconciliation paradigm.[25] Whatever truth there might be in referring to all people as part of a single human family, the effect of this universalizing approach is to obscure precisely the differences we need to engage in order to dismantle white supremacy.

Offering love to enemies as a practice of piety in imitation of God's freely offered benevolence, in turn, is flatly inadequate as an approach to antiracism. There may be some role for considerations of personal piety in antiracist work insofar as antiracist work is challenging for individuals, and some degree of spiritual endurance is necessary to follow through on the work in the long term. Personal piety, however, does little to impact the systemic, depersonalized evils that characterize interracial enmity.

Should we follow King in taking the logic of Matthew 5:43–48 a step further—accepting the idea that extending love to our enemies with no demand of mutuality is not simply a matter of piety but also opens the door to their future transformation[26]—we still face a problem when confronting the reality of interracial enmity. In short, changing the hearts of individual enemies cannot be the strategic focus of our antiracist work when the enmity we confront is not primarily a matter of private individuals' moral character. There is surely an important role for personal transformation in antiracist work. Unjust systems do not exist without the cooperation of individuals, after all. However, insofar as we must strive to change the systems that structure white supremacy rather than focusing primarily on individuals' attitudes and actions—as argued by Chanequa Walker-Barnes and Jennifer Harvey—the model of private enmity simply does not equip us to maintain that structural focus.

Before moving on to lay out a structural understanding of interracial enmity, I will acknowledge that something like private enmity regularly crops up in situations marked by racial tension. In workplaces, families, and churches across the United States, people of different races can find ourselves in cycles of escalating retaliation in which race plays a significant role. Parents and children share harsh words because of the children's romantic partners, coworkers undermine one another's careers because of stereotypes and implicit bias, and siblings in Christ fight bitter battles over hymns and electric guitars. The reason private enmity is not ultimately helpful in addressing even these seemingly private instances of enmity is that these private conflicts take root in the social soil prepared over centuries by larger structures of white supremacy. When parents and children fight over romantic partners, coworkers make assumptions about one another's ill intentions, and siblings in Christ squabble over music, the lines of battle *precede* these particular conflicts. The key here is that our analysis of enmity must frame these seemingly private conflicts as consequences of a more foundational mode of interracial enmity—the structural understanding of enmity to which we will turn shortly—rather than as the primary mode of interracial enmity in themselves.

Resolving such small-scale conflicts is important work in itself. Individual families are worth preserving, every laborer deserves a safe work environment, and Christians should strive to address disagreements in ways that work toward beloved community. This work of conflict transformation, however, is not the work that will be central to dismantling white supremacy and transforming society. If we confuse that conflict transformation work for the work of dismantling white supremacy at the systemic level, then our peacemaking efforts can only serve to foster friendships that can endure under the conditions of white supremacy and help to preserve our capacity for kindness in a context hostile to the fullness of our very existence.

I believe that the idea of loving our enemies is sufficiently compelling and sufficiently foundational to the best parts of Christian faith that it can empower socially transformative antiracist work. To do so, however, it must also be sufficiently flexible—and we must be sufficiently creative—to translate beyond the cultural context of private enmity from which it originated. In other words, if the concept of loving our enemies is to play a central role in our antiracist work, we must articulate and practice something beyond what's immediately offered in Matthew 5:43–48. To orient the ethical and theological foundation of our antiracist practice—that we might faithfully and powerfully love our enemies—we must accurately understand the kind of enmity that confronts us.

WHAT IS STRUCTURAL INTERRACIAL ENMITY?

When I claim that race in the United States is best understood in terms of structural interracial enmity, I mean that to be racialized in this country is to have your material interests—financial prosperity, personal safety, political power—set in opposition to the material interests of people of different races. US Americans[27] of different races find ourselves as enemies to one another not because we have somehow *personally* wronged one another through participation in unjust systems. We are not caught within an incredibly complex, generational web of private enmity that has somehow coalesced into discernible systems. Rather, we are enemies because those systems of inequity define us as enemies from birth through death. Structural interracial enmity is an antagonism built into the basic structure of US society and played out in its many systems and institutions.

Structural interracial enmity is what comes to our awareness when we confront white supremacy in its concrete forms and dare to imagine that the world might once have been different and could be different again. Structural interracial enmity is what takes shape when we explore the past in search of the historical development of white supremacy or imagine how we might dismantle it going forward. Whether considering white supremacy in the present, past, or future, we find that fundamental opposition of material interests along lines of race that marks interracial enmity as structural in nature.

Consider how this structural antagonism is manifested through the five categories addressed in the University of Illinois Chicago (UIC) "State of Racial Justice" reports referenced in this book's introduction—housing, economics, education, justice, and health—in relation to the present, past, and future. In examining these systems' contemporary forms, we find mutually reinforcing structures of racial inequity. Inequities in education reinforce both low wages and high incarceration rates for Black and brown folks. Incarceration practices—and the lack of just reentry policies—contribute to unemployment, which, together with wage inequities, compounds already unfair mortgage lending practices and rent costs. Poor housing availability and poverty, combined with exploitative work environments and harassment by police, contribute to higher rates of heart disease and obesity among Black and brown people. These health challenges are exacerbated with inequities in the availability of both health-care services and healthy food in the segregated neighborhoods in which Black and brown folks make up the majority of residents. In relation to all of those systems, BIPOC folks not only suffer varying degrees of heightened exposure to exploitation and violence compared to white people but also find ourselves compelled to compete with one another for the limited resources made available to keep society from imploding under the weight of inequity. Even in this quick summary of just a few of this society's key systems as they have operated in the first quarter of the twenty-first century, it does not take much to recognize the opposition of material interests along lines of race—exploitation and violence consistently reinforcing the moral and economic value of whiteness—that characterizes structural interracial enmity.

It is when we follow the past and future trajectories of these systems, examining the roots of these unjust systems and imagining what it would take to bring about equity, that it becomes clear that this opposition of material interests along lines of race is not simply unjust but also fundamental to US society. Segregation in housing and education, unfair lending practices, disparities in wages and unemployment rates, inequities in policing and incarceration, discrepancies in chronic health conditions and health-care services—all of these are generational injustices. Studying this country's history, we can find atrocity after atrocity—medical experimentation, forced sterilization—to say nothing of the daily, unrecorded injustices through which white supremacy has structured relations of enmity among people of different races. And when we trace these inequities back to the point that terms like *inequity* and *injustice* don't quite seem to apply, we don't come to a utopian past from which we have fallen. Rather, we find that the inequities we confront today—segregation, poverty, police violence, injustice overlapping with injustice—pale before the horrors of this country's history of race. We find that today's inequities have their historical origins in slavery, dispossession, and genocide. From the founding of the United States through the present, the material interests of different racial groups have been opposed to one another. The form changes. The antagonism does not.

With the deep roots of these systems of inequity in mind, we can turn to the future and imagine a society in which justice is the norm and white supremacy has been torn down. Should we dare to imagine such a future, we must cast our imaginations past some kind of fundamental break with the systems we navigate in the present. In such a future, race—that social construction that is real only insofar as people's lives are impacted differently by these societal systems because of race—would lose its reality except in our proud stories of resistance and cautionary tales of injustice. En route to that future in which whiteness is no longer propped up by an entire societal network of violence and exploitation, we must realize that change is going to cost white folks in ways that it simply will not cost BIPOC folks. There are certainly important ways in which we can say that white folks stand to gain more through the dismantling of systems of injustice, especially since those systems quite often harm individual white people and are gradually destroying the global ecosystem on which all people depend. However, *under the conditions of the systems we have and what counts as prosperity under those systems*, white people will lose a great deal if we dismantle white supremacy and all its systems, while BIPOC folks will find ourselves freed from many of the obstacles we face today and the state of competition in which we struggle to form widespread solidarity. The material interests of people of different races are fundamentally opposed in the society in which we currently live. To long for a society in which we are not enemies is to desire an apocalyptic shift in which some weep with fear, while others cheer with joy before the coming of justice.

While I hope you are persuaded by the basic idea that a structural model of enmity better suits the transgenerational reality of racial inequity than a private model, important details yet remain hazy. Toward the end of this section, I will offer a set of qualities that characterize structural interracial enmity. Before doing so, however, there are two important ways in which I need to flesh out this notion of structural interracial enmity: how this structural model of enmity maps onto the social construction of race in the United States and how it accounts for the complexities of our varied lived experiences of race.

Structural interracial enmity is oriented by a fundamental binary between Black and white, as frustrating as that notion may be to those of us who are aware of the diversity and complexity of people's experiences and identities. We can imagine the social construction of race in the United States as laying out people's lives in relation to a line with two endpoints: Black at one end and white at the other.[28] The space in the middle is defined by competition and navigation of the antagonism between those endpoints.

white ◄————————————————————► Black
(idealized) ├———— lived experience of competition ————┤ (idealized)

These endpoints—the two positions that define the entire line—neither correspond to any individual's lived experience nor represent some kind of averaging of individuals' lived experience. Rather, they are idealized positions associated with the mutually exclusive absolute qualities that make sense out of the social construction that is race and justify the material consequences of that social construction's enactment. These unattainable racial absolutes arise as answers to two questions that were asked in the interest of justifying the brutal practices that shaped the colonization of the Americas: Who is human? Who is saved?

The absolutes that orient this Black/white racial binary are expressed powerfully in the work of Frank B. Wilderson III. Wilderson's theoretical work and the term *Afropessimist* that Wilderson and others use to describe it tend to inspire strong—often negative—reactions among Christian theologians. However, it is precisely its boldness in considering the antagonism that lies at the heart of the world race imposes on us that makes Wilderson's Afropessimist thought so helpful when we consider interracial enmity.[29] In outlining the distinction between human and nonhuman as a racialized distinction, Wilderson emphasizes the absolute, irreconcilable quality of the Black/white binary.

As a political and moral category, Wilderson explains, humanity is defined by reference to whiteness and against the state of enslavement. To imagine a white person is, in effect, to imagine a person unbound by any limiting racial markers.[30] If we put this in Jennifer Harvey's terms, whiteness presents itself as universal humanity.[31] To imagine a Black person, by contrast, is to imagine someone who is fundamentally bound by race in ways that echo the physical, economic, and social bondage of enslavement. To be white is to embody the fullness of human life; to be Black is to embody the exclusion from humanity represented by the slave.[32] To be white/human is to be associated with the open-ended possibilities of human life, while to be Black/slave is to be assigned intense, sustained closeness to death given one's unending vulnerability to gratuitous violence.[33] To be white/human is to be empowered to possess other things, as well as to consent—or refuse to consent—to how one is treated. To be Black/slave is to be unable to possess other things because one exists to be possessed and, consequently, for consent to be an irrelevant category in one's existence.[34] Moving beyond the specific contrast between human and slave, it is hardly uncommon for Black people to be characterized as animals or—as Michael Brown was named by the police officer who unjustly killed him—demons.[35]

The absolute racial positions of white and Black that correspond to this human/nonhuman distinction are ultimately grounded in the historical relations of slavery. The mutually exclusive absolutes that define race and interracial enmity find their basic form in the relation between those who can be enslaved and those who absolutely cannot. Importantly, this absolute distinction between white and Black persisted past the US Civil War and the abolition of chattel slavery, as recounted by Isabel Wilkerson. Structured by the development of a "labyrinth of laws to hold the newly freed people on the bottom rung ever more tightly," and intellectually justified through pseudoscience, the Black/white binary was reinforced through the systematic withholding of necessary economic and educational resources from Black communities.[36]

The reality of the space between these endpoints as a space for competition and navigation of the antagonism between whiteness and Blackness was secured through the distinctive interplay of two competing forces at work in the Indigenous nations of this land. On the one hand, US American campaigns of genocide—both the forced removal of Indigenous people from their nations' lands by the US government and the attempted cultural genocide carried out by US churches' boarding school programs—clearly distinguish Indigenous people from the subject position of whiteness, given their intense vulnerability to violence. On the other hand, the coherence within US law of Indigenous claims to sovereignty, despite the limited impact of their formal acknowledgment by the US government, clearly distinguishes Indigenous people from the subject position of Blackness and its absolute lack of capacity to possess or consent.[37] This centuries-long tension between genocide and sovereignty marks out the between space into which people from around the world have entered through the processes of immigration and US American colonization. Different groups of people from around the world have found themselves navigating the Black/white racial binary. Often contrasting themselves as fully as possible with undesirable Blackness, people of many lands and cultures have worked over the course of decades to enjoy the privileges associated with whiteness, though many have found themselves consigned to Blackness or caught in between.[38]

Alongside the question of humanity, a second key question arose through the colonization of what is now the United States: Who is saved? In light of this question, consider again a killer's claim that Michael Brown was like a demon. That invocation of the demonic with reference to a Black body points to how the Black/white binary not only involves the construction of a biological or legal distinction between human and nonhuman but also involves a theological distinction between election and reprobation. That distinction—between those who are assured of their salvation and those whose salvation is perpetually in doubt, if not denied outright—is highlighted in Willie James Jennings's work on the impact of Christianity and colonialism on one another.

The exaltation of whiteness to a state of assured salvation is grounded in supersessionism, Jennings argues. Supersessionism is the widely accepted and deeply corrosive belief that the church, in its most expansive, ontological sense, has replaced Israel as God's chosen people. Carried within the logic of supersessionism was the identification of Christian identity with European identity. As European identity became racialized as whiteness, European Christians lifted up whiteness as a marker of divine election.[39] Further, the identification of whiteness with the status of election developed into an association of whiteness with spiritual maturity. For colonized people to more fully perform whiteness—to dress, eat, farm, speak, and worship more like Europeans—through participation in colonial institutions was to become more spiritually mature under the terms of European Christianity.[40]

The flip side of this racialized theological development—the assignment of reprobate status and perpetual spiritual immaturity to Blackness—is connected with a practical expression of supersessionist logic: the suspicion of Jewish and Muslim converts to Christianity associated with institutions such as the Spanish Inquisition. As European Christians assumed the role of God's elect, Jewish and Muslim converts were closely associated with the status of reprobation—the active rejection of a sinner by God—casting serious doubt on the possibility of their salvation. Established in relation to Jewish and Muslim converts in Europe, a hierarchy of salvific possibility became available for use in European colonization. Europeans found themselves needing to make sense of who among the peoples they colonized could be saved and thus might deserve more humane treatment.

To this end, the theological association of whiteness with election was complemented by the theological association of Blackness with reprobation.[41] The association of Blackness with reprobation was not new during the era of European colonialism. Rather, there is a long history of Christian theological anti-Blackness, going all the way back to association of Ethiopians' Blackness with inferiority, sin, and demonic forces.[42] The demonization of Blackness was put to a new purpose in the fifteenth century, however, through a series of papal bulls that established the theological and legal justification for enslavement and dispossession by European Christian powers. Combining theological anti-Blackness with the logic that justified the Crusades as wars on "enemies of Christ" and allowed the dispossession of nonbelievers, Black Africans were designated as enemies of Christ to be rightly dispossessed of their land and enslaved by Christians.[43]

Other groups of people—primarily those East Asian peoples with whom European colonial powers had the most contact and the Indigenous people of the Americas—were arranged in hierarchies that filled the space between white election and Black reprobation with varying degrees of doubt regarding the relative likelihood of their salvation.[44] Importantly, as with the human/nonhuman distinction, this elect/reprobate distinction served to justify colonial practices of enslavement and dispossession by framing them as practices of rigorous instruction into spiritual maturity (i.e., whiteness).[45] The horrors of colonialism were theologically justified as benevolent acts of spiritual care on the part of white Christians.

These distinctions—human/nonhuman and elect/reprobate—make sense of whiteness and Blackness by providing a deeper meaning and structure to the very idea of race as it exists in the United States. In our everyday lives, however, people tend not to experience the fullness of either of these racial absolutes. Broadly speaking, we can say that those whose bodies and behavior are perceived by others to be closer to whiteness enjoy a greater degree of access to the variety of resources provided by our society's various institutions (e.g., education, housing, health care, jobs), while those who are perceived to be closer to Blackness more consistently experience obstacles as they seek to access those resources. This only scratches the surface of the complications that characterize people's differing experiences of race, not to mention the complexity brought on by the fact that both oppression and privilege are intersectional. Sticking with this narrow discussion of the internal logic of race, though, two key dynamics can help gesture toward the way in which this structural binary relates to the complexities of individuals' lived experience.

First, it is helpful to consider the fundamental instability of races other than white and Black as they exist in relation to this Black/white binary. As noted above in relation to Indigenous claims of sovereignty and the racialization of immigrant groups, those who are neither granted the status of whiteness nor consigned to Blackness find themselves in a liminal, in-between racial state. Theologian Choi Hee An discusses this marginalization of other racial groups in relation to a native/alien binary. This binary works to limit the consideration of US race relations to those groups understood as native: white and Black US Americans. All other groups are framed as outsiders who are making claims on resources that rightfully belong to natives of this land. Asian and Latine folks—as well as *Native* Americans, whose exclusion from the notion of birthright is fundamental to US American land claims—find themselves both excluded from whiteness and placed in conflict with "native"

Black US Americans.[46] Complicating matters, a broad range of questions of hierarchy and identification—which people from which part of the world might be considered "Middle Eastern" rather than "Asian," the extent to which people might be Latine *and* white or Black by virtue of their distant ancestry (as opposed to having parents of different races)—as well as the overall question of the relative status of these different racial categories over against the extremes of whiteness and Blackness vary with time and geographical region. The Black/white binary stands as an absolute scale of racial existence, but enfleshed racial existence is vastly more complex.

Second, it is important to acknowledge the degree of agency that individuals have in negotiating the simultaneously unstable and absolute binary that is race in the United States. As it relates to those things over which we have limited control—our skin tone or facial features, for example—racialization limits or enhances an individual's ability to attain those resources most easily accessible through the performance of whiteness. There are, however, a number of racial markers (e.g., speech, mode of dress, or attention to body odor) that are very much within most people's control. To the extent that they alter these mutable racial markers, a given individual may exceed or fall short of the prosperity that might be expected given those racial markers over which they have little control. The means of exerting control over these racial markers is what many BIPOC folks are taught by our parents in hopes that we will succeed, thrive, or perhaps just make it out of our hometown or neighborhood. I still recall the attention my father paid to teaching my sibling and me to speak "properly."

The longevity and consistency of the two poles of the US Black/white binary are compatible with a great deal of fluidity when it comes to both the status of other racial groups and the outcomes of racialized individuals. A wide range of socially constructed categories complicate individuals' capacity to navigate this binary. Gender, class, and sexuality are perhaps most often cited in the context of antiracist work, but the list of ways in which humans translate difference into structures of inequity is long. Broadly speaking, though, the compatibility of a rigid binary with relatively diverse outcomes is facilitated by the inherently competitive nature of white supremacy. George Lipsitz describes the work of white supremacy as, in part, the protection of white privilege "by denying communities of color opportunities for asset accumulation and upward mobility." Whiteness, in effect, exerts a downward pressure on all those who are not perceived as being white. In the face of such pressure, BIPOC folks are pressured to get ahead by participating in the exclusion of other BIPOC folks from the resources mediated by whiteness.[47] Insofar as a group or individual works to reach toward the prosperity secured by whiteness—rather than working to fundamentally overturn the inequitable systems that structure our society and the interracial enmity at its heart—such efforts come at the cost of others.

Attending to the nuances of how individuals and communities have navigated this Black/white binary is a source of great difficulty even for those who are deeply committed to antiracist work. Generally speaking, it's hard to get folks to stick with antiracist work past basic education on race, its historical roots, and its broadest contemporary structural realities. It's particularly hard to get white folks to even provisionally entertain the idea that they're responsible for systems they may even openly and explicitly oppose. Still, some folks make it through that work and take steps to dig into the complexity of the stories in their community.

What makes this work of exploring how we navigate the Black/white binary challenging even for those who can make it through those first stages of education is the simple truth that what we do—what our ancestors have done—to navigate the tension between white and Black is often a matter of survival. When we approach these dynamics of navigation with a critical edge, we find ourselves confronting deeply painful and precious stories of immigration, of people working hard and attaining their taste of the American Dream, or of being excluded from whiteness despite their best efforts to be "professional," to work hard, to dress and speak "properly." Feelings of bitterness and resentment arise in response to competition between BIPOC folks, and moral judgments are leveled about compromises communities or individuals have made with the demands of whiteness. Folks find themselves questioning their own families' values and the decisions they or their parents have made out of the desire for security or prosperity.

Even for those who are committed, this work is emotionally, spiritually, and socially challenging. And this is precisely why the power of love is needed—not to rescue us from this work by deeming it unnecessary as long as we have love and not to encourage us to present a sanitized, cheerful, abstracted version of ourselves to one another. Simply put, love is what can sustain us through this work, driving us toward encounter with the fullness—the full beauty and full ugliness—of each other's struggles and setbacks, pains and joys, hopes and desires.

No matter how many times I insist that I am motivated by love, though, there are concerns that regularly come up when I raise the subject of the Black/white binary. This is certainly the case in my courses, and those are folks who know me personally! I imagine that many readers also find themselves wrestling with the idea of so wholeheartedly accepting the reality of a Black/white binary. So, before offering a list of qualities that can help us move from conceptualizing structural interracial enmity toward imagining a love that can meaningfully respond to this enmity, I will address the most common form these concerns take.

In one way or another, students often express that this Black/white binary contradicts their experience of race. Black and white students alike express concerns about being trapped in categories that capture neither their particular struggles nor the fullness of their holistic selves. After all, most Black folks hardly see ourselves in the negative ways associated with Blackness—certainly not explicitly, and many of us wage our battles against internalized racism quite successfully. Most white folks don't see themselves as so exclusively exalted over against others, even if they acknowledge the reality of systemic racism. Other BIPOC folks, for their part, rarely experience themselves as truly existing in the space between two coherent racial identities; regardless of the extent to which themes of in-betweenness, liminality, dispossession, or alienation might characterize their experience in the United States.

Broadly speaking, these concerns are grounded in both real problems with the Black/white binary and real historical and cultural trends. These trends include Black folks' long histories of being stereotyped and conceptually stripped of agency. They include other BIPOC folks' long histories of being excluded from the privileges of whiteness and yet pressured to relinquish their cultural heritage in order to compete with Black folks and one another. They include white folks' general discomfort with being made to confront their whiteness.

These common concerns are grounded in these complex dynamics and others besides, but my two-part response is fairly simple. First, I affirm that the Black/white binary does not accurately convey the experiences of almost anyone of any race. That is not because this binary is a poor model for understanding the structure of race in the United States. Rather, it is because race is not about accurate *description* at all. Instead, race is a matter of distributive *prescription* and the justification and normalization thereof.

In other words, this Black/white binary absolutely does not capture the wholeness of our experiences as people who have been racialized. Instead, it provides a framework that justifies the enmity that exists at the core of this country. It grounds political, moral, and theological explanations for why the descendants of slaveowners and settlers so consistently enjoy greater wealth and health than the descendants of those enslaved and dispossessed. The Black/white binary normalizes the consistent truth that the surest pathway for an immigrant to attain prosperity and safety in the United States is by performing whiteness as fully as possible.

My description of race as organized by the Black/white binary is not a description of any particular racialized person's life but instead of the forces of racialization that box us in or box us out as we try to live into the fullness of our being. As such, we feel tension with the Black/white binary not because it is inaccurate but because it is the source of a great deal of the tension race inspires in us. Isabel Wilkerson expresses this point powerfully when she articulates an analogy between race and stage performance: "When we are cast into roles, we are not ourselves. We are not supposed to be ourselves. We are performing based on our place in the production, not necessarily on who we are inside."[48] The Black/white binary is accurate *in its description of how race captures and constrains our efforts to flourish*, and dwelling on it is appropriately unpleasant.

When it comes down to it, race does not function in this binary structure because it provides the most holistic way to understand people. Rather, the inherently competitive function of whiteness seems to require a contrast against which its concentration of privilege and power can be justified so that it might make sense as an organizing principle for society. Race could have conceivably been organized differently—though inequity does seem to tend toward binaries that obscure the broad diversity of human experience—but the Black/white binary is what our history has passed down to us. Ultimately, race has been socially constructed to preserve white supremacy, so it should not be too surprising that its binary structure does not reflect the fullness of our individual and collective experiences.

The second part of my response is more pragmatic in nature: denying the existence of this binary simply does not help us to confront it. For Black folks, denying the existence of this binary—perhaps out of an admirable desire not to be painted as a helpless victim—does not change the fact that race is a reality that works to victimize us, however successfully we defy those pressures.

For other BIPOC folks, rejecting the reality of this binary because it excludes you does not eliminate the competitive dynamics that link resources to the successful performance of whiteness and punish deviation from whiteness with closer alignment with Blackness. And for white folks, denying the fundamental anti-Blackness that sustains the advantages of whiteness is to play into the Black/white binary's normalization of white supremacy. Rejecting the Black/white binary does not get rid of it; it mistakenly minimizes the racializing forces that work on all of us without requiring our consent.

If, at this point, you are convinced there is merit to this Black/white binary model of race, it is important to avoid at least three possible pitfalls, each of which can and does arise in the context of antiracist work. Christian ethicist Ki Joo Choi points toward the first such error, arguing that "white racism is about the violence against black bodies; it always has been and always will be. But such a point in itself does not necessarily preclude the realities of white racial violence against other persons of color."[49] In confronting the Black/white binary structure of race, then, we must not allow it to limit our concern to those two abstract absolutes or the people who most clearly seem to embody them. Whiteness is fundamentally contrasted with Blackness, but the effects of that binary antagonism corral people into a range of other racial categories and impact every person in this country. To address race, we must both understand the Black/white binary and attend to the ways in which that binary affects people of all races.

Second, we should avoid the tendency to treat any racial category as if it is interchangeable with the experiences of particular people assigned to that racial category. It is a grave mistake, for example, for a person to believe that they understand a given Black person because they have some understanding of Blackness as a racial absolute or that they understand Blackness as a racial absolute because their neighbor, coworker, friend, or partner is Black.

Third, we must not carry out antiracist work as if every Black person suffers the material effects of racism more intensely than every other BIPOC person. Race—as much as I focus on it in this book—is an intersectional reality. Gender, ability, sexuality, class, nationality, and many other categories of identity, privilege, and oppression constitute a person's location along with race. Blackness provides coherence to racial inequity by grounding and directing its exploitative and murderous aspects. Black people, however, individually and collectively navigate the Black/white binary structure of race in much the same way as everyone else. Sometimes we do so to our advantage and to the detriment of other BIPOC folks, and the cause of dismantling white supremacy is not served well by minimizing the impact of white supremacy on others.

Having covered at least some common concerns and important qualifications, I can finally provide a clearer description of structural interracial enmity. To do so, I will lay out five qualities that characterize structural interracial enmity and that we must therefore take into account in striving to love our enemies through antiracist work.

Structural interracial enmity (1) exists as an irreconcilable antagonism founded on a basic binary between Black and white and is not a resolvable conflict (such as those relevant to private enmity).[50] This enmity is structured through (2) inequitable racialized distribution of exploitation and violence that is a primary condition of possibility for the promises of prosperity inherent to whiteness. Structural interracial enmity is (3) an inherently competitive system, rewarding with resources those who most fully perform and approximate whiteness while ensuring that others will always be pulled toward the deprivation associated with Blackness. Structural interracial enmity is (4) not simply about what any particular person *does* but also about what race *enables them to do* (or refuse to do).[51] It is about who can reasonably expect to speak in a discussion and have their voice acknowledged, who can enter their home without being suspected of breaking and entering, and who can reasonably expect the agents of their government to respect the sanctity of their body. Finally, given the structural nature of interracial enmity, (5) its local expressions are not reducible to local relationships and histories but inextricably influenced by national and global histories and systems.

With these qualities of structural interracial enmity in front of us, we can make corresponding claims regarding what we need from an account of faithful love of the enemy. We need a love that can (1) persist in the context of irreconcilable interracial antagonism and (2) navigate its manifestation in the consistent, inequitable racialized distribution of exploitation and violence. We need a love that (3) undermines competition even as it (4) fosters the capacity of both lover and beloved to strive for flourishing, freedom, and fully acknowledged dignity. And we need a love that can (5) simultaneously respond to local relationships and their national and global contexts, neither erasing the particular nuances of a friendship between two people nor insisting that such friendship—however authentic, long-term, or grounded in shared faith—is inherently free from the those "outside" influences. In short, we need a love characterized by commitment to one another even as the world continually compels us to be one another's enemies.

Though the social, economic, and political specifics of what such enmity entails do not neatly align with those addressed in Matthew 5 and Luke 6, we truly can understand the work of antiracism as a matter of loving our enemies—if we understand that in relation to race, enmity is structural. This affective and spiritual challenge of remaining committed to life together with those with whom we're trapped in this structural antagonism truly is captured well by the charge to love our enemies. This irreconcilable interracial antagonism gets in the middle of caring relationships and strains them to the breaking point, even in communities in which there is no explicit prohibition of friendship or romantic attraction across lines of race. Loving our enemies, then, is not the most radical edge of antiracist work. It's the basic requirement of antiracist work and—in a racialized society—a basic requirement of meaningful efforts toward building faithful Christian community.

WHAT BIBLICAL SUPPORT IS THERE FOR STRUCTURAL INTERRACIAL ENMITY?

Perhaps you've been paying attention throughout this chapter, and you recall my claim that interracial structural enmity is "not what Jesus or the evangelists had in mind" in urging those who would be faithful to love their enemies. And perhaps you find yourself asking—either out of personal concern or because you know folks in your community will ask—whether the idea of loving a *structural* enemy has any meaningful biblical support. Fortunately, there is indeed biblical support for the idea of loving a structural enemy. What's more, it can be found in the book of Galatians, where one of the most influential verses in Christian antiracist work is located.

Galatians 3:28—"There is no longer Jew or Greek; there is no longer slave or free; there is no longer male and female, for all of you are one in Christ Jesus"[52]—has a long history of being cited in support of the idea of racial reconciliation. Readings of this verse that suggest Christians should focus on our shared faith when seeking fellowship across lines of race risk guiding the faithful into the trap of universalism against which Jennifer Harvey warns us and the disavowal of enmity, against which I've spent this entire chapter arguing. Read with careful attention to the historical and political context of

Roman Galatia, however, this verse and the letter in which it is found offer biblical grounding for the possibility of recognizing structural enmity and faithfully striving toward a love that can thrive in such a hostile environment.

As a guide in reading Paul with such careful attention to his context, I turn to Brigitte Kahl, who finds in Paul a formidable critic of the Roman Empire, if necessarily a subtle one, given the gruesome consequences of openly opposing Rome. Through attention to historical documents and careful analysis of the monuments that more often informed most Roman subjects' understandings of their political and religious world, Kahl paints a clear picture of the Galatian context Paul addresses.[53]

In his letter to the Galatians, Paul addresses people of faith living in the context of enmity between Romans and Galatians, between Romans and Jews, and between Jews and Galatians. In my terms, this context was one of structural enmity along lines of national identity and kinship, which were analogous in function to race in our contemporary context. In fact, it is possible to demonstrate that the enmity between nations in this context exhibits each of the five qualities of structural interracial enmity outlined in the previous section.

1) Structural enmity in Roman Galatia existed as an irreconcilable antagonism founded on a basic binary between barbarian and Roman and was not a resolvable conflict (such as those relevant to private enmity). To read race—as it exists in the contemporary United States—into Paul's first-century context would be anachronistic. However, the binary between conquering Roman defenders of civilization and chaotic barbarians (a category that included the Galatian people) served much the same function as the racial binary we deal with today.

Two historical dynamics can help us make sense of this barbarian/Roman binary and its relevance in the Galatian context. First, through its influence over law, culture, and religion, Rome's superiority over those deemed barbarians was grounded affectively in a widely accepted binary between superior male and inferior female,[54] embodied politically in a brutally enforced binary between victorious Romans and conquered nations,[55] justified theologically through reference to the victory of the gods over the rebellious mythical giants who strived to topple the gods and destroy the world,[56] and codified in religious practice through the exaltation of Caesar as a singular quasi-divine being who benevolently sheltered the masses of humanity.[57] Second, the people of the Roman province of Galatia were framed as the prototypical barbarian contrast to Roman civilized virtue. The Greek word translated as *Galatians* (*Galatai*) can also be translated as *Gauls*,[58] referring broadly to nations of Celtic origin that were widely portrayed as barbarians and whose defeat by Rome ensured the victory of civilization.[59] In short, the imperial project of exalting Rome above all other nations was carried out by casting the people of Galatia—and the wider array of nations that collectively represented a primeval threat to civilization—as the polar opposite of Roman virtue.

This enmity between barbarian and Roman could not be resolved under the terms of the Roman imperial order. Rather, as that imperial order depended on this enmity for its very justification, escape from this structural enmity could be found only in the destruction of those structures. This is what Kahl argues Paul is proclaiming in his letter. Considering Galatians 1:1–9, for example, Kahl suggests the following: "Paul's gospel of Christ confronts the gospel of the idol(s), most notably the gospel of the one primary idol, the divine Caesar, whose proclamations are labeled 'good news' and who is hailed as the ruler of the best of all possible worlds—but from Paul's viewpoint, of 'this present evil age.'"[60]

In Paul's letter to the Galatians, the only escape from the relations of enmity imposed by Rome was in escape from "this present evil age" and the displacement of Caesar by Christ: in other words, a wholesale theological and political overturning of the Roman imperial order.

2) Structural enmity in Roman Galatia involved an inequitable distribution of exploitation and violence that was a primary condition of possibility for Roman promises of prosperity. The characterization of the Romans as victors above all else supported the notion that the quasi-divine Caesar was triumphant even over nature.[61] Wealth and abundance were, in effect, taken to be the natural consequence of Roman victory. Of course, as in the contemporary United States, wealth and abundance were not enjoyed by all.

Roman victory did, in fact, serve as the foundation for Roman prosperity but only insofar as that prosperity was grounded in violence and exploitation. While it grew in part due to technological and economic innovations, Roman wealth was built on the exploitation of the nations Rome conquered. Roman economic practices concentrated wealth in the hands of landowning elites,[62] whose wealth was inflated by the spoils of war.[63]

These spoils of war included not only gold, ivory, and spices but also human captives. Rome was a slave society, through and through, its economy dependent on the labor of those enslaved.[64] Scholar of early Christianity Jennifer A. Glancy describes enslaved Roman subjects as "legal nonpersons" with bodies vulnerable to their masters' violence—particularly to sexual violence—and no claim to their children.[65] By Paul's time, relatively few enslaved persons were taken as war captives, with the pool of enslaved laborers being repopulated primarily by children born to enslaved women. It is quite likely, however, that these women and their children were the descendants of war captives,[66] firmly grounding the Roman institution of slavery in that Roman victor / conquered barbarian binary.

Roman wealth was not only founded in the colonial extraction and the violent enslavement of the conquered but also protected through various extreme forms of violence, of which I will focus on two. First, Roman conquest, and thus Roman prosperity, was justified through categorization of the conquered as feminine. The foundational elevation of masculine over feminine in Roman society was enforced not only through social codes but also through mythological, metaphorical, and physical sexual violence. Conquered nations were characterized as feminine in Roman texts and on Roman coins, justifying their defeat by the violent masculinity of Rome and the rape of conquered people of all genders by violently masculine Roman soldiers.[67]

Second, Roman prosperity was defended against potential rebels and revolutionaries by the brutal violence of crucifixion. Crucifixion—the very form of capital punishment enacted on Jesus of Nazareth—was a form of humiliating and dishonoring punishment Rome reserved for violent criminals, rebels, and those enslaved.[68] In a Roman Empire defined by the binary between Roman and barbarian, the function of public, brutal crucifixion was to demonstrate "not just the execution of a criminal but the elimination of a rebellious, transgressive other and the restoration of the proper order of the world."[69]

For those cast in the role of barbarian, such as the Galatians, becoming recognizable as Roman subjects "meant accepting their place at the bottom of the Roman order with obligations in terms of subjugation, or servitude, including the duties of paying taxes and military service."[70] Galatians lived under the ever-present threat of crucifixion, their awareness of this threat being refreshed through the close ties between crucifixion and the violent spectacles in the arena that provided entertainment to the masses.[71] With crucifixion as the reward for revolution, those at the bottom found themselves compelled to embrace subjugation and willingly participate in the structures of violence and exploitation that secured Roman prosperity.

3) Structural enmity in Roman Galatia was an inherently competitive system, rewarding those who most fully performed and approximated Roman identity with resources while ensuring that others would always be pulled toward the deprivation associated with barbarism. In Paul's time, Rome was supreme by right of conquest from one side of the Mediterranean to the other. In its military supremacy, Rome unified all nations under its sway within what Kahl refers to as "the imperial logic of combat, an order that turns Self against Other in endless spirals of violence, competition, and oppression."[72] Kahl argues that the "law" Paul opposes in Galatians is not Jewish Torah but imperial law, grounded in Rome's competitive order.[73] For the wealthy, even "good works" of charity and public beneficence represented a competitive means of demonstrating one's proximity to Roman virtue through one's emulation of Caesar's own good works.[74] Over time, these various practices would result in the formation of children from a young age to imagine a successful, prosperous future in terms of the attainment of Roman virtue and citizenship.[75] For the Galatians, then, to climb out of "barbarism" and poverty, they had to stop being Galatian and become as Roman as they possibly could.

Enmity between Jews and Galatians that we might mistakenly attribute simply to religious difference was grounded in the competitive order that reserved resources for those who performed Roman identity.[76] As the Roman approach to imperial rule forced conquered nations to orient themselves in relation to the binary between victorious Romans and defeated barbarians, even the distinction between Jew and Gentile was impacted.

For Jewish subjects of Rome, performance of Roman identity was a complex issue. By virtue of their monotheistic religion, they could not worship Caesar or allow their own God to be depicted alongside Caesar. At times, this rejection of Roman religion caused Jews to be branded as atheists, whose refusal to worship the gods deemed responsible for the care of the city and empire was a threat to civilization. Nonetheless, Rome extended a fair—and seemingly unique—degree of toleration to Jewish monotheism and allowed Jewish corporate worship to continue, dependent in part on a sacrifice on behalf of Caesar in the Jerusalem temple and paid for by taxes sent to Jerusalem by Jews throughout the empire. Jewish subjects of Rome found themselves dependent on Roman toleration for the continued practice of their religion.[77]

In this context, the ancient distinction between Jew and Gentile was reframed into a hostile relation between conquered nations. Jews could not fully assimilate to Roman ways and could only depend on Roman authorization of their religious practices—practices that included separation from Gentiles like the Galatians, including Galatian Christ-followers. Galatians' traditional ways had no such authorization by Rome and could find security only through the adoption of Roman names, embrace of Roman modes of government, practice of Roman religion, and service in Roman legions.[78] Under Roman rule, the distinction between Jew and Gentile became a distinction between conquered nations competing for Roman protection while dreading the judgment that their people may be irredeemably barbaric.

4) Structural enmity in Roman Galatia was not simply about what any particular person *did* but also about what their place in the Roman/barbarian binary *enabled them to do* (or refuse to do). Consider what's been stated above from a different angle. Within the Roman order, those deemed barbarians could do nothing meaningful but rage against that order, threaten to bring about chaos, and die before Roman might. Jews, for their part, were fundamentally incompatible with Roman law and religion.

For both Galatians and Jews, the capacity to act politically with any legitimacy and to exist safely with any degree of personal coherence was to be found in undertaking a path that was acceptable *within* the Roman order. For Galatians, that path was marked by assimilation through military service and adoption of Roman ways. For Jews, that path was quite narrow, involving Roman toleration of Jewish monotheism and iconoclasm that could be, and ultimately was, withdrawn at Caesar's whim. As established above, each of these paths—Galatian and Jewish—was fundamentally oriented to the Roman/barbarian binary.

5) The local expressions of structural enmity in Roman Galatia were not reducible to local relationships and histories but were inextricably influenced by imperial histories and systems. It is hopefully clear at this point that enmity among Jews, Galatians, and Romans in Roman Galatia was woven into broader imperial dynamics of conquest and occupation. Jews were a diasporic people, spread across and beyond the lands of the Roman Empire. The Galatians were not understood simply as a local people but as a local manifestation of a foundational and empire-wide Gallic/Galatian barbarian threat. As such—as much as Paul responds to local conditions in his letters, including his letter to the Galatians—it should be clear that the dynamics of enmity to which Paul responds in this letter were not simply a matter of local histories of violence and exploitation. Enmity was fundamental to Roman rule and influenced what went on throughout the lands conquered by Rome.

In his letter to the Galatians, Paul was responding to structural enmity, and his response was centered on the practice of love in the context of such enmity. I will take a different approach when I turn more fully to a discussion of love in later chapters. For now, I offer two brief notes by way of establishing that there is indeed biblical support for the idea of loving a *structural* enemy.

First, in response to this complex, structural enmity between Rome and conquered nations, in which those conquered found themselves pitted against one another, Paul directs his readers to "love your neighbor as yourself" and "bear one another's burdens."[79] Second, regarding Galatians 3:28, which might seem to outright deny the relevance of the enmity that seem so prominent in the Galatian context, I defer to Kahl's careful reading of this letter. Kahl takes seriously Galatians 2:4, in which "Paul refers—explicitly and probably not accidentally—to 'spies' and 'false brothers' who obviously serve as informants."[80] Paul's letter would be read in a context in which the consequence of sedition could be crucifixion—particularly, we might imagine, for those gathering in the name of a crucified savior. As such, Paul's offer of an alternative to the Roman competitive order—any holy imagination he might offer that would undermine and overturn Roman structural enmity—had to be couched in language that would not condemn its readers. With this in mind, consider Kahl's understanding of Paul's political and religious argument and the place of Galatians 3:28 in that argument: "It envisions the rebirth of creation, when human is made (again) in the image of God, not as a human self that consumes the other as commodity, but as commonality of one and other, male and female, Jew and Greek, free and slave (Gen 1:26–27; Gal 3:28). Only in this messianic community that embodies the *other* law can God be truly worshipped and served as the singular one God who is other than Caesar and thus reconciles self and other in a noncompetitive and nonhierarchical body of 'new life.'"[81]

Jesus may not have had structural enmity in mind when he called those who would follow him to love their enemies. Hopefully, for those to whom this is a pressing concern, Galatians serves as a biblical example of love being offered as a key directive in a situation of structural enmity. It is not only faithful but biblical to love our *structural* enemies.

CONCLUSION

We began this chapter, as so much Christian antiracist work begins, with a misunderstanding: the idea that "loving your enemies" requires that you have a private enemy to love, that someone has wronged you personally, or that you have, in turn, wronged another. I argued that this private notion of enmity—marked by reciprocal, escalating conflict—fails to account for the reality of racism in the United States for three reasons: (1) racism often involves no overt claims or acts of hostility, (2) racism more closely resembles intense and unfair competition than reciprocal hostility, and (3) racism involves a steady, deadly threat to BIPOC folks over centuries rather than a mutually escalating dynamic that moves toward lethality.

It is understandable how this mistake was made. For one, private enmity was what Jesus was talking about when he proclaimed the call to love one's enemy. Returning to Jennifer Harvey's critique, it's compatible with a reconciliation-oriented framework in which friendly togetherness marks the cessation of enmity. And, to anticipate next chapter's consideration of the nature of white supremacy, private enmity and the distorted understanding of racism it supports are easier for white folks to disavow—thus protecting their sense of their own goodness—than structural understandings of enmity and racism. This combination of overly narrow biblical interpretation and the corruptive influence of white supremacy even in our efforts to do the right thing has undermined the usefulness of enemy love as a guiding principle for antiracist work.

Rather than discarding the notion of enemy love, however, I have also argued there is an understanding of enmity that can empower antiracist work: structural interracial enmity. Associating prosperity with whiteness and suffering with Blackness, this antagonism built into the basic structure of US society positions people of different races in a zero-sum competitive struggle with one another regardless of personal relationships. In this context, we can acknowledge that we form deeply meaningful interracial relationships of all sorts without mistakenly believing those relationships represent proof that we have overcome interracial enmity. If we can accept the coexistence of love and enmity—the reality that we can love our enemies deeply *while white supremacy continues to position them as our enemies*—we can recognize that the persistent tensions and trials that plague interracial relationships are not failures of love but instead evidence that enmity endures despite personal closeness.

Finally, I demonstrated that while Jesus may have been addressing matters of private enmity in the call to love our enemies, Paul was writing to a region marked by structural enmity in his letter to the Galatians. Paul encouraged the Jews and Gentiles of Galatia—positioned against one another as enemies in the competitive, divisive order of Rome—to love one another and bear one another's burdens. In the face of structural enmity, Paul proclaimed the power of love.

US Christian antiracist work has been burdened by an inadequate understanding of enmity and thus a flawed understanding of enemy love. In the back half of this book, I develop a theological and practical understanding of love that takes structural interracial enmity into account. For now, though, there is more digging to do. Namely, it is important to understand this flawed understanding of love so that we might move past it. In the next chapter, I ask what's gone wrong with love while we've been working with an inaccurate understanding of enmity. I ask what has gone wrong with love, not simply as the theological and ethical principle at the heart of our faith but as an emotion that flows through our individual and collective bodies.

CHAPTER TWO

Love Distorted by White Supremacy

Interracial enmity is not about personal feelings. It is a matter of structural antagonism. Different racial groups' economic and political interests are opposed in ways that expose BIPOC folks to violence and exploitation for the benefit of others while even leading some white people to embrace exposure to violence and exploitation themselves for the sake of a continued belief that their interests lie with the wealthy class that exploits them. Structural interracial enmity is about dollars and cents; votes and voter suppression; food deserts; overpoliced neighborhoods; underfunded schools; and poisoned soil, water, and air.

Yet, paradoxically, interracial enmity is deeply about personal feelings. Racialized structures of violence and exploitation propagate and reinforce themselves by shaping individuals' feelings. The continued existence of these structures depends ultimately on how communities and the individuals within them are organized—or not. Individuals' feelings of rage, helplessness, pride, hope, fear, and love amplify or dampen their willingness to participate in or oppose the structures of violence and exploitation that comprise structural interracial enmity. Eager participation in unjust systems, the rise of resistance, and the lingering malaise of complacency all depend on the complex internal emotional lives of individuals in communities across the United States.

So interracial enmity is not only about personal feelings. Christians err when we reduce racism to a matter of individual attitudes about people who have different skin tones. When it comes to the failure of communal efforts to challenge white supremacy, however, we must understand the role played by feelings. And as we seek to understand why Christians so frequently fail to love our enemies—even as we exhaust ourselves trying—we must make a particular effort to understand love and its distortion by white supremacy.

THE PRODUCTION AND CIRCULATION OF EMOTION

As with so many dimensions of our lives, our emotions are intimately connected to the world around us through complex networks of relationship. One way to conceptualize the complex web of emotions and relationships is through an economic metaphor. Love and the other emotions that sustain structural interracial enmity are things that do not simply burst forth spontaneously from individual racists any more than the food most of us eat springs forth from isolated home gardens or the clothes we wear are sewn by our hands from cotton grown in our own fields. Our labor and our needs are integrated into a complex, global web of production, transport, and exchange of goods and services. Similarly, the emotions that sustain structural interracial enmity are produced and circulated in a vast network of relationships and encounters that includes even those who have no particular ideological investment in white supremacy.

Feminist scholar Sara Ahmed introduces and fleshes out this economic understanding of emotion, referring to such networks as "affective economies."[1] Affect, as discussed by Ahmed, represents the mutual influence between activities at the societal or communal level (e.g., entertainment, politics, religion) and seemingly private, individual feelings. Economy, as she uses it, loosely adapts Karl Marx's critique of capitalism and focuses on how human labor produces value, which is then circulated along with the objects that have been invested with that value.[2] Affective economies, then, are patterns of exchange within which objects invested with emotional value circulate among people and through institutions. These objects include, along with more abstract entities, both physical objects (e.g., flags, guns, people in the flesh) and reports of physical objects (e.g., "I think I saw a suspicious person running through our neighborhood").[3]

Ahmed devotes whole chapters to this concept of affectively sticky objects and their circulation,[4] but I will briefly illustrate this concept by examining a case that has stuck with me for over a decade: the 2013 murder of Jonathan Ferrell by a Charlotte, North Carolina, police officer.

Around 2:30 a.m. on September 14, 2013, twenty-four-year-old Jonathan Ferrell wrecked his car in a suburban Charlotte neighborhood after dropping off a friend. Injured, he went to a nearby house and knocked on the door. The woman who opened the door panicked at the sight of Ferrell and slammed it shut, set off her house alarm, and called 911. After she informed the dispatcher that "a Black man" was breaking into her home—the dispatcher specifically confirmed that this was, indeed, a *Black* man—three police officers were sent to the scene. In under twenty seconds, one officer fired a taser at Ferrell, Ferrell ran into the darkness toward another officer who had his gun drawn, and Ferrell was shot ten times by that officer. He was then handcuffed and soon died of his wounds.[5]

As a Black man, Jonathan Ferrell was an affectively sticky object. In the narration above, we can track the sense of fear and danger that was passed from homeowner to emergency services dispatcher to police officer. That fear prevented any attempts to ask Ferrell what he wanted or—more to the point, given his injured state—needed. That sense of danger resulted in the murder of an unarmed person in need of medical attention by someone whose role was ostensibly to protect and serve that injured, unarmed person. Allowing ourselves a bit of imaginative room, we can speculate about the kinds of family stories, news reports, TV shows, and political rhetoric that may have shaped the perception of Jonathan Ferrell by this homeowner, dispatcher, and police officer.[6] Fear inspired by sources that had little to do with Ferrell surely "stuck" to him as he sought aid.

This high-profile—but frustratingly routine—example helps illuminate what Ahmed means when she writes about the circulation of affectively sticky objects. The particulars of Jonathan Ferrell's situation seem to have had little to do with how those around him responded in his time of need. The series of people who caused Ferrell's death did not perceive a wounded person in need of aid. Rather, they responded to the affectively sticky object that is the Black man, in accordance with the feelings that were stuck to that object. Stepping from the wreckage of his car, Ferrell was hounded to death by an affective economic process that bound his individual situation to the structural reality of interracial enmity.

PAIN, HAPPINESS, AND THE BOUNDARIES OF BODIES

The impact of affective economies goes far beyond the inspiration of individual acts of violence (or kindness, for that matter). Affective economies shape individual, communal, and national bodies at a fundamental level.[7] Through emotions shaped by these processes of production and circulation—especially pain and happiness—we develop a sense of our bodies and their boundaries. Understanding the role of pain and happiness in our bodies is crucial to understanding how white supremacy distorts the love that should sustain Christian antiracist work.

Consider our individual bodies. As we experience painful sensations on our skin, we develop a clear sense of where our bodies end and the rest of the world begins.[8] We bump into each other, we bang our knees on that miserable corner of the bed in the middle of the night, we get a shot at the doctor's office, and our perception of the borders of our body sharpens. Importantly, our awareness of our skin lapses. Between experiences of pain or pleasure, we lose track of our bodies, focusing instead on our phones, our friends, our hopes and worries.[9] For many of us, ordinary life is defined by the relative absence of pain and, thus, the relative absence of bodily awareness.[10]

Much the same is true for communal bodies—neighborhoods, churches, nations—and their self-awareness. Like individuals, communities come to have a sense of where they end and the rest of the world begins by bumping into things. Communities come into conflict with one another or feel the world transgressing their boundaries. A community's sense of ordinary life, like an individual's, is defined by the relative absence of such painful bodily awareness. The clear boundaries of a community can slide from its members' awareness when things are going smoothly.

In communal bodies such as nations or churches, boundary-defining pain is often more a matter of debate than an individual's stubbed toe or a surgical scar. What truly counts as painful for a community is largely determined by the ability of various people and groups within a community to impose their claims of communal injury on others in that community. Stories of pain[11] can be told in different ways, to paint one party or another as the cause of injury or the injured party.[12] As an example, the September 11 attacks created an enduring sense that the US American body was wounded and that Muslim "terrorists" / all Muslims were the cause of injury and thus outside the US American body regardless of their citizenship status. By contrast, ongoing police violence against Black people, increased pressure applied by Homeland Security against immigrant families, and widespread legislation depriving trans folks of their rights are not so widely understood as causing pain to the entire US American body. Rather, these stories of pain serve to define smaller injured communities against those segments of the US American population that do not acknowledge that pain as their own.

The key to understanding the distortion of love by white supremacy lies in the function happiness serves in communal bodies. Through the complex, contested experience of pain, communities are compelled to develop a sense of their boundaries. Happiness, in turn, makes it possible to regulate the activity of the individuals who make up communal bodies. Generally, we want to be closer to those objects we associate with happiness and distance ourselves from those we perceive to be obstacles to happiness. One might strive for a happy family or a safe home and retreat from abrasive kin or menacing strangers. Our sense of an object as happy or unhappy even extends to the object's context, such that we seek out the conditions we associate with a happy object and avoid those we associate with an unhappy object.[13] In working to become that happy family, for example, many US American parents will go to great lengths to ensure that their children go to "good schools" (schools where most students are white and relatively affluent). Insofar as the promise of happiness can be a social promise, it can make social norms (e.g., respectability, "professional" dress and speech) into the kind of affectively sticky objects discussed above. Those social norms become so closely associated with the life we desire for ourselves that we come to feel that conforming to those norms is a way to secure our happiness.[14]

Crucially, when the promise of happiness becomes a social promise, it grounds certain moral distinctions, distinguishing those who are worthy and capable of being happy in the right way from those who are not. Insofar as an individual or community's happiness seems threatened, this is not only because the "right" people are failing to attain the fruits of its promise but also because the "wrong" people may appear to be happy. Consider narratives about mythical "welfare queens" or "illegal immigrants" who are rewarded with a carefree lifestyle and easy money for their subversion of the social ideals of hard work and responsibility.[15] While conformity to social norms is a matter of discipline—of being taught and of practicing such conformity, assuming one has had the opportunity to receive such teaching—such conformity and the happiness associated with it are assumed to be matters of choice that reflect one's moral character.[16]

Pain defines the boundaries of a community, while happiness regulates who manages to comfortably remain within those boundaries. Appearing to be happy about the right things and because of the right choices brings one securely within the affective bounds of a communal body, while the failure to seem happy properly alienates one from that community.[17] Consequently, happiness is not simply a matter of personal fulfillment but also imposes a form of emotional labor, in which one's work is "making others happy by appearing happy."[18]

Jennifer Harvey notes a relevant dynamic in her critique of US American churches' reconciliation-focused antiracism efforts. In such work, the pursuit of togetherness represents the pursuit of a promise of ecclesial happiness. That happy togetherness, however, is not associated with demands for white repentance but rather with the possibility of BIPOC forgiveness and consent to white forgetfulness.[19] In order for the church body to collectively lift up some kind of progress toward togetherness, BIPOC church members are routinely pressured to give a performance of happiness, contentment, and forgiveness. In churches, as well as other spaces, the social promise of happiness places a much greater burden on some than others.

"Happiness is how we can end the conversation about why it is that we desire what we desire," Ahmed states powerfully. It is "a way of stopping an answer from being a question."[20] Employed as a means of social control, happiness undermines challenges to affective economies. We might wish to contest the common association of fear and pain with Black men or Muslims (presumed to be menacingly brown). We might attempt to question why football games are expected to be free of political protest or why we are expected to "support the troops" and respect the police, regardless of the consequences of the violence they wield. We might ask why our pastor keeps calling God "he" or why condemning white supremacy from the pulpit is "too political" and "doesn't feel like church." We might like to overturn the system with our questions and queries, but happiness always stands ready to defend the national or ecclesial body from threats, whether those threats arise from within or outside the communal body.

Taken together, happiness and pain shape individual and communal bodies in ways that reinforce structural interracial enmity. Happiness serves as the simultaneous smoke screen and justification for the reinforcement and propagation of white supremacy even in spaces that openly claim—and genuinely desire—to resist white supremacy. Objects of happiness that are circulated at a societal level (e.g., happy families, joyous churches) are placed in opposition to the very forms of critique and disruption that might reveal structural interracial enmity for what it is. Those who offer such transformative gifts of critique and disruption are rejected as sources of pain that do not truly belong inside the community. Across the United States, pain and happiness shape individuals and fracture communities in ways that align with the structural interracial enmity that is a foundational reality of this nation. In extreme cases, such as Jonathan Ferrell's, this affective economic work has lethal consequences. Its subtler work, however, undermines and corrupts antiracist work on a daily basis. The subtler work of happiness, in particular, is felt most powerfully in US churches through the distortion of love by white supremacy.

THE NATURE OF DISTORTED LOVE

Love is the theological and ethical heart of any Christian church, given the love between God and creation that is embodied in the birth, ministry, and death of Jesus. Churches committed to antiracist work, however, tend to make the centrality of love particularly explicit in their striving toward that theological imagination offered by Martin Luther King Jr.: beloved community. Though it is at the heart of churches committed to antiracist work, love—like all of God's wondrous gifts— can be distorted by evil.

White supremacy corrupts the power and beauty of love by aligning love with the promise of happiness. Distorted love results from an unswerving theological and ethical orientation toward happiness. The promise of happiness, the sense that happiness is guaranteed to those who direct themselves toward the right objects, is a promise of security from pain that threatens the community. As such, the promise of happiness is also a refusal to permit conditions that might make happiness unattainable,[21] a refusal to permit people whose actions interfere with the pursuit of happiness.

Displacing the presence of God at the center of our lives, the promise of happiness turns our feelings against us. Where white folks might feel drawn to repent that they might truly embrace their BIPOC siblings, they instead recoil when BIPOC folks refuse to allow them the pretense of piety. Where BIPOC folks might feel drawn to build meaningful relationships with white folks, we instead downplay our feelings to maintain a shallow illusion of harmony. The promise of happiness is the theological and ethical foundation of a distorted love that takes good feelings as a sure sign of good relations and that blames bad feelings for the bad relations that cause those bad feelings in the first place.

In a context in which the affective economic operations of structural interracial enmity so deeply influence how we feel about people of different races, good and bad feelings should not be assumed to offer reliable ethical guidance. Love misguided by the promise of happiness leads white Christians to confuse BIPOC folks' critique of whiteness with hatred for white people. Love misguided by the promise of happiness confuses white Christians' desire for affirmation and absolution with a desire to live with BIPOC people in relations of mutuality and intimacy. Love misguided by the promise of happiness blames discontent with white supremacist violence and exploitation for white fear and shame. Love misguided by the promise of happiness imagines rejection in the call for repentance that is the invitation to a more faithful love, a love that can bring forth the healing sought by churches that engage in antiracist work.

This distortion of love is powerful not simply because of the theological and ethical importance of love in Christian churches but also because of the work love does in enabling communities to constitute themselves as coherent bodies. Much like pain and happiness, love distinguishes an insider from an outsider. Love marks the line between acceptable difference and threatening difference. For example, a nation is granted cohesion through its status as a "shared object of love" for its many members.[22] Insofar as the nation is fundamentally white—as is the case with the United States—this community-binding love is, then, at least partly a shared love of whiteness.[23] For white people, love of their nation is a matter of embracing an ideal image of themselves and projecting it on those with whom they share that nation as the basis of their love for them.[24]

Jennifer Harvey highlights two important ways in which this distorted love oriented toward whiteness arises in churches committed to antiracism. First, much antiracist work assumes that what is needed is greater inclusion of BIPOC Christians in predominantly white churches.[25] White churches work to continue to be white churches, centering the emotional and spiritual needs of white Christians while pointing to the racial diversity of their membership to defend the virtue of whiteness they struggle to recognize as whiteness. Second, antiracist work is often carried out without consistently critiquing the way in which whiteness does not simply sit alongside other forms of racial identity but instead constitutes the "moral crisis" that is investment in the very systems of exploitation and violence that constitute structural interracial enmity.[26] As such, the love of a "reconciled" church that is at the heart of much antiracist work is a love that embraces the root of the very problem it purports to strive against.

I draw deeply on Sara Ahmed's work in this chapter. There is a key difference between her work and mine, though: where I hope to articulate a faithful, reliable love in contrast to distorted love, Ahmed opts for a more reserved evaluation of the possibilities of love.[27] Ahmed's cautionary stance toward love is important and has been influential in shaping my understanding that not all love is faithful. Distorted love, with its formation by white supremacy and contribution to structural interracial enmity, is love nonetheless.

Love is powerful yet morally ambiguous. The fact that we *feel* love does not mean we are *acting* in a way that will promote a loving justice. Such a conflation of good feelings with just relations is a key aspect of the distorted love that undermines antiracist work in US churches. The kind of critique and call to repentance that BIPOC Christians offer in love can hardly be expected to evoke good feelings, nor will it always be offered out of good feelings, and yet it is essential to transformative, faithful antiracist work. Feelings, bereft of a critical account of their formation, cannot guide us well. We must work to understand what is shaping our love and discern whether that formation is faithful.

Not everything that draws on love for its sustenance is necessarily good. If love is reduced to a feeling, an affective resource to be harnessed by any political and/or religious movement that comes along, then Ahmed is correct to reject love as central. Rather than taking love from the center, though, I argue that we must account for the distortion of love by white supremacy and counter that distortion with a constructive theological imagination of faithful love. Love is the beating heart of the melancholic hope that has sustained the Black radical politics that inform transformative antiracist work and is no less vital to Christian theology.[28] Faithful love is neither a privatized feeling that exists to satisfy a moral test nor a foundation on which white churches might build a sure sense of piety and righteousness. Rather, faithful love is the power of God's presence itself, woven into committed relations of mutuality and reinforced by practices that can help achieve and preserve such relations. Fleshing these ideas out is the work of chapters 6 and 7, however. For now, I continue the work of accounting for love's distortion.

DISTORTED LOVE'S SUPPORTS: FEAR, SHAME, AND OPTIMISM

I have suggested from the start of this book that I do not believe Christian antiracist work fails because those who claim a commitment to it are disingenuous or deceitful. Rather, their work falters because they have *been* deceived. They embrace love, as they ought, but the love to which they cling betrays them. Three other feelings support distorted love in turning those who commit to antiracist work against that very work: fear, shame, and optimism. These three feelings prevent those who have been captured by distorted love from recognizing that their love is twisted, that it serves the subtle workings of white supremacy even as it steers them clear of the overt forms of white supremacy and anti-Blackness they might more easily recognize. Fear, shame, and optimism defend distorted love by securing structural interracial enmity and projecting the illusion that distorted love is both necessary and good.

Sara Ahmed explores fear in the context of US American responses to the September 11, 2001, attacks. The fear of individual US Americans toward those who looked to them like Muslims or Arab immigrants was not understood by those individuals to be a matter of personal fear or prejudice. Rather, they interpreted their intense feelings as love for the nation and the desire to protect the United States from threats. The effect of their fear was to intensify these supposed threats. This created a distinction between those who felt threatened and those who supposedly presented a threat.[29] This distinction became distance as those who were afraid withdrew from the "source" of their fear.[30] Such withdrawal—white people withdrawing from brown people who *may* be Arab Muslims (themselves undeserving of such fear)—was not recognized as a failure of love because it was *experienced as patriotic love*. Much the same happens in the context of antiracist work, in which white people sit anxiously, worried about "angry outbursts" from their BIPOC siblings. In turning away from that which one fears—withdrawing from the imagined Arab terrorist or Black thug—it feels as though one turns toward the object of one's love: one's nation.[31]

Where fear defends distorted love largely by identifying future supposed threats to the nation, shame protects distorted love from evidence of its past failures. Shame drives us to expose failures of love, trusting that our experience of shame is itself a sign that we truly are committed to love. Insofar as a given failure of love is judged to be temporary and in the past, exposing it can be interpreted as an expression of love. By expressing shame for a past act of injustice, the nation—or a given individual who identifies with the nation—testifies to a past failure of love in order to promote present pride. The ability to recognize that a past action was shameful is presented as proof of love's success in educating a misguided heart, whether or not present actions contribute to the same kind of injustice that marked the past failure in question.[32]

Like fear, shame defends distorted love by securing structural racial enmity. However, where fear serves as a means of reinforcing this enmity by distancing people from those who are frighteningly unlike themselves, shame more directly conceals structural racial enmity. To the extent that one is implicated in the nation's past wrongs, shame confines those wrongs to the past and discourages acknowledgment of their connection to present systems of injustice. Even the apologies that shame provokes can work to preserve distorted love. Providing passage from shame to pride, these apologies routinely fail to focus on the wrong that was done and instead emphasize the presumed present moral status of the one who loves strongly enough to recognize the past as shameful.[33]

Shame secures structural interracial enmity by confining it to the past and refusing to acknowledge its meaningful persistence. For example, white US Americans routinely express their shame at the nation's history of slavery without committing to effective action to redress slavery's generational legacy of systemic anti-Blackness. The expression of shame allows the white person to feel like a person who loves their Black fellow citizens, even as their inaction perpetuates anti-Blackness. We can witness this each year on Martin Luther King Day, when the same people who condemn protests against police violence express their shame at how the United States "used to be," failing to connect past and present injustice.

Fear and shame often work much the same in church as they do in relation to the nation. If we substitute beloved community for the beloved nation in Ahmed's analyses, we can consider how fear positions BIPOC Christians who express their anger with structural racial enmity as threats to the love that binds the church. Rejection of BIPOC congregants' anger is not presented as the defense of whiteness but rather as a loving defense of the possibility of reconciliation. Blame for the rejection of BIPOC congregants—whether through overt church discipline or not-so-subtle social segregation and isolation—is assigned to those BIPOC congregants' supposed faltering faith in Jesus and lack of belief in the value of antiracist work. Individual white congregants' fear of their BIPOC siblings' anger can be understood as commitment to doing antiracism right rather than as a failure of love. And while such fear is perhaps most obvious in its impact on white Christians, I've certainly witnessed BIPOC Christians pulling away from others. White and BIPOC Christians alike can find themselves distancing from those who show their anger too readily for the comfort of the white folks in the room or refuse to quit bringing up hurtful and unresolved incidents. Believing that they are protecting their beloved community, both white and BIPOC Christians can find their love led astray by the fears formed by interracial enmity.

Shame, in turn, arises in prayers and lament services that express dismay at the persistence of systems of injustice and particularly visible or local events that are shockingly evil. Such shame does not necessarily confine white supremacy to the past but may instead acknowledge that injustice continues in society while enforcing a distinction between the society and the church. Such lament for evil in the world is often paired with praise for God's grace in empowering the work of antiracism that is being done in the church—the very work of antiracism that stumbles in the presence of unfiltered anger toward the church's part in perpetuating white supremacy. The expression of shame at love's failure defends the persistence of distorted love.

Fear and shame pave the way for the embrace of optimism, which reinforces the deceptive connection between distorted love and the promise of happiness. Distorted love infects those who chase the perpetually deferred promise of happiness and traps its hosts in a relation that Lauren Berlant describes as "cruel optimism." Berlant defines optimism as a force that draws you closer to "the satisfying *something* that you cannot generate on your own but sense in the wake of a person, a way of life, an object, project, concept, or scene."[34] Fundamentally, optimism involves the drive to return repeatedly to that which promises satisfaction—a "happy object," in Ahmed's terms—and that drive to return can be "cruel" insofar as that promise undermines the possibility of attaining satisfaction. Workers routinely grind in hopes of a promotion only to find themselves trapped in their position, deemed too productive as workers to risk promoting but ensured that loyalty to their company will be rewarded. Survivors of intimate partner violence regularly remain with those who harm them. Seeking stability, they find themselves caught in life-threatening situations with partners who promise things will get better. Cruel optimism, then, describes an attachment to something that promises some form of fulfillment and betrays its own promise *without ceasing to make a convincing promise.*[35]

Like fear and shame, optimism secures structural interracial enmity in US churches. The relation of white Christians to distorted love is cruelly optimistic insofar as what distorted love promises is the whitewashed version of beloved community—security, relief from shame, connection with others who are different but not too different, and, ultimately, happiness—but all it delivers is a perpetual defense of love's failure to transform community. Cruel optimism leads white Christians to tune out critique as so much unfaithful bitterness while sharpening their ability to identify those BIPOC Christians who can offer them the affirmation they crave. BIPOC Christians are caught in this cruel optimism insofar as we accept our role in that whitewashed imagination of beloved community, offering forgiveness without calling for repentance and shying away from conflict. We can find ourselves believing that if we are just patient enough—if we can survive long enough in relatively friendly spaces structured by white supremacy—our white siblings in Christ will come around, repent on their own, and work for the transformation of our society. Trapped in this cruelly optimistic attachment, BIPOC Christians find ourselves striving toward a saintly, compromised patience or learning to disguise our anger with humor.

Through fear, shame, and optimism, love itself is ensnared in the service of structural interracial enmity. These feelings encourage white Christians to seek physical distance from those they fear, temporal or institutional distance from the systems of injustice in which they're shamefully entangled, and proximity to whiteness and its cruelly optimistic promise of happiness. BIPOC Christians are placed in a position where we are called on to alleviate white fear, assuage white shame, and share in white optimism, all in the name of long-suffering Christian love. Through the work of fear, shame, and optimism, a distorted love that confuses good feelings for good relations is protected from the very critique that could expose its failure to ground faithful antiracist work.

EXHAUSTION, ENDURANCE, AND WHITE FRAGILITY[36]

Christians' cruelly optimistic attachment to an imagination of beloved community warped by distorted love is poisonous to antiracist work insofar as the proper goal of such work is the development of relations of mutuality and the dismantling of structural interracial enmity. The alignment of emotions in defense of white supremacy is overwhelming, and it's no wonder that it has a particular impact on white Christians. When it comes to antiracist work, white Christians who have been captured by distorted love are not only deluded about what antiracism is; they lack the emotional and spiritual endurance necessary to withstand BIPOC folks' calls to repentance and have even developed a set of skills that help them to remain in the grasp of distorted love. Before moving on from analyzing distorted love, it will be helpful to understand both white Christians' lack of endurance and the patterns of thinking, feeling, and acting that derail attempts to inspire their growth in this area.

Elizabeth A. Povinelli offers important insights into what I've called *emotional and spiritual endurance*.[37] For decades, Povinelli has lived and done ethnographic research among a group of North Australian Indigenous people. This group was driven from their community because they failed the Australian government's standards for having a claim on their land and thus endangered the claim of their entire community. Povinelli shares a particularly powerful story about a resource-gathering trip some of her colleagues in that precarious community made across a bay in a barely seaworthy boat. In relating this story, Povinelli emphasizes the extent to which the community's mutuality and resistance to exploitative economic systems are in defiance of the economic systems that govern "the late liberal and neoliberal regime" that sets the terms for existence in our world:

> No one is going to kill us or lock us up for trying to succeed, though many of this group will be locked up for using illegal resources; they are just going to let us exhaust ourselves. They are making a wager that few people will be able to be like Stan or the group on our boat, so few that the otherwise we represent will never be able to sustain itself, let alone extend, thicken, and become dominant. Late liberalism[38] knits together internationally a careful weave of sovereign killing (capital punishment and assassinations), criminalization of life staples such as certain food, drugs, and forms of protective gear, and self-righteous neglect.[39]

Povinelli uses this experience to offer the reader a view of the kind of resistance faced by those who seek to sustain communities that live in defiance of the systems of exploitation and violence such as those that structure Australia or the United States. Such efforts not only demand the difficult work of living in community but also require that community members be willing and able to persist as that difficult work is made more taxing by the weight of the societal pressure that opposes it. This pressure does not necessarily take the form of violent force. Rather, creative and life-giving community-building is routinely undermined by the sheer weight of the work, done without support from societal structures that are designed to reproduce relations of structural enmity.

Now, when Povinelli discusses her North Australian friends and family, she writes about pressures that push their community to the brink of plague and famine. When I write about white US American Christians who claim a commitment to antiracism, I am discussing a wildly different context. As such, some translation will be required with respect to two concepts that Povinelli helpfully theorizes: alternative social projects and the abandonment of those who would bring such projects into being.

Povinelli stresses that her North Australian family and friends' way of life is not intended to be a revolutionary project. Rather, simply by virtue of its existence, this community threatens the ability of late liberalism to present itself as the only viable way in which society can be organized.[40] Political and economic systems of exploitation and violence do not abide challenges. They do not encourage competition in the hopes that a better system might be found. Rather, they are perpetuated through the widely accepted assertion that there are no true alternatives, that these systems (e.g., inherited wealth, policing, national borders) are the pillars of human civilization itself. As such, even small, marginal, and seemingly nonthreatening Indigenous communities cannot be supported in meeting their needs should they seek to persist in living otherwise but must be steadily strangled through neglect and indirect criminalization.

The challenge antiracist work in churches presents to white supremacy may be obvious. To make that challenge perfectly clear, however, Frank Wilderson's Afropessimist thought is once again helpful. The exclusive identification of humanity with whiteness is dependent on the commodification of Black flesh, which in turn justifies the constant vulnerability of Black bodies to legal and extralegal violence.[41] The equation of whiteness with humanity is fundamentally dependent on the culturally produced inability of white people to respond meaningfully to Black suffering. Projects that threaten to shape white people to not only claim that Black people are human[42] but also to deeply *feel* that Black people are human and to respond to that feeling with action are dangerous alternative social projects. A white person who can take the suffering of Black folks as seriously as their own is a threat to the structural interracial enmity that is dependent on white numbness to Black suffering.

Antiracist work, when it brings about even individual repentance, gestures toward ways of being together that are fundamentally incompatible with structural interracial enmity. However, it is unlikely that a white person who engages in antiracist work through their church is going to find themselves struggling to feed themselves[43] or threatened with jail time because of it, even indirectly.[44] Though they will not face the same kind of abandonment as that described by Povinelli, they will court abandonment in other ways.

White people who bite the hand that feeds them and repent of white supremacy often find themselves abandoned on multiple levels, even in their first steps toward living otherwise. Repentance demands that they disavow a defining, if obscured, feature of their identity. Repentance requires accounting for privileges that almost certainly factor into the successes and accomplishments that provide the material for their life stories, then divesting themselves of attachment to and reliance on those privileges. Repentance compels them to face family members who feel rejected, creating distance between themselves and the people who raised them, who taught them to be the very people who might have a chance of responding to God's love by loving others. Repentance demands that they turn toward BIPOC folks who may not offer comfort to replace the illusion of security afforded by whiteness but may instead offer further critique interspersed with what surely feel like rare moments of encouragement. White folks who persist in challenging white supremacy find themselves abandoned culturally, emotionally, and spiritually, set adrift within the very structure of interracial enmity that had sustained them from their first moments in this country.

While this kind of abandonment is not materially comparable to that described by Povinelli, white people nonetheless face crushing exhaustion if they attempt to truly accept Black people as fully human, much less work to bring about societal transformation. Antiracism teams in churches don't fall apart because white folks are just acting in bad faith or pretending that the work is too hard. Antiracist work really does burn white people out. This is not because the challenges faced by antiracist white folks somehow strain the absolute limits of human endurance. Rather, the challenges faced by antiracist white people and the abandonment leveled against them by white supremacy are specifically beyond the endurance *of people weakened by white fragility.*

The concept of white fragility provides an explanation for why white people generally lack the emotional and spiritual endurance to withstand BIPOC folks' calls for repentance, however gently they are articulated. Robin DiAngelo,[45] who draws on both her own qualitative research and a wide range of literature on whiteness and education, describes white fragility as follows: "White Fragility is a state in which even a minimum amount of racial stress becomes intolerable, triggering a range of defensive moves. These moves include the outward display of emotions such as anger, fear, and guilt, and behaviors such as argumentation, silence, and leaving the stress-inducing situation. These behaviors, in turn, function to reinstate white racial equilibrium."[46]

White fragility is a consequence of the environment in which white people in North America live. Insulated from race-related stress, white people come to expect comfort in relation to race, to the extent that it is even an actively engaged feature of their lives. As such, they develop a stunted capacity to endure race-related stress.[47] Absent sustained work to expand this capacity, white people find themselves lacking the endurance required to persist in the challenging personal, interpersonal, institutional, and societal work of antiracism. This does not only lead white people to perceive antiracist work as challenging, however. Rather, this condition of white fragility also leads white people to confuse comfort with safety and respond to race-related stress as if a challenge to their dominance in the dynamic of structural interracial enmity is a threat to their safety.[48]

DiAngelo provides an extensive list of situations that can cause race-related stress, thereby exposing white fragility, and hints at the patterns of thinking that support white supremacy:

- Suggesting that a white person's viewpoint comes from a racialized frame of reference (challenge to objectivity)
- People of color talking directly about their own racial perspectives (challenge to white taboos on talking openly about race)
- People of color choosing not to protect white people's feelings about race (challenge to white racial expectations and need for, or entitlement to, racial comfort)
- People of color not being willing to tell their stories or answer questions about their racial experiences (challenge to the expectation that people of color will serve [them])
- A fellow white disagreeing with [their] racial beliefs (challenge to white solidarity)
- Receiving feedback that [their] behavior had a racist impact (challenge to white racial innocence)
- Suggesting that group membership is significant (challenge to individualism)

- An acknowledgment that access is unequal between racial groups (challenge to meritocracy)
- Being presented with a person of color in a position of leadership (challenge to white authority)
- Being presented with information about other racial groups through, for example, movies in which people of color drive the action but are not in stereotypical roles, or multicultural education (challenge to white centrality)
- Suggesting that white people do not represent or speak for all of humanity (challenge to universalism)[49]

Each of these triggers can disrupt "white racial equilibrium," the default state for white existence, in which energy need not be spent on dealing with race, whether physically, intellectually, emotionally, or spiritually.[50] When white racial equilibrium is disrupted by these triggers, a range of responses aimed at reestablishing that equilibrium can occur. These responses to events as innocuous as acknowledging the relevance of racial segregation to educational access range from crying and walking out to arguing and withdrawing emotionally.[51] Austin Channing Brown refers to one particularly insidious response as the "relational defense." Rather than responding to critique with repentance, a white person might instead point to their family or their BIPOC friends as witnesses who can verify that eyeroll-inducing claim, "I don't have a racist bone in my body."[52]

The behaviors scripted by white fragility are precisely the sorts of behaviors that routinely undermine and derail antiracist work in US churches. They are reinforced by two patterns of thought that justify white supremacy even as they hide it from white people's awareness. First, race is only consistently perceived by white people in spaces in which BIPOC people are present. If BIPOC people are not around, white people can just be "people." Racism, in turn, is presumed to be irrelevant—or even nonexistent—in spaces in which BIPOC people are not present rather than the rule that creates such racially segregated spaces.[53]

This selective perception of race is facilitated through racially coded language (e.g., *urban*, *disadvantaged*) even in the very settings in which white people are working to purge themselves of white supremacist patterns of thinking.[54] The unacknowledged equation of *white* with *good* in reference to schools, neighborhoods, and other institutions and communities is particularly effective in preserving segregation and thus white fragility.[55] Those who confront race while under the influence of white fragility struggle not to understand the very encounter with a BIPOC person—functioning within structural interracial enmity as the embodiment of race itself—as a sign that their formerly good/white space has been contaminated. Their "good" neighborhood is starting to feel dangerous. Their "good" school seems like it has lowered its standards. Their "good" church is losing its focus on God's love and getting too political.

This shaping through racially coded language is implicitly aided by a second pattern of thought: the interchangeable invocation of universalism and individualism. Like Jennifer Harvey, DiAngelo notes that white people are taught to see themselves as "universal humans." Believing their personal experiences represent a broader human experience, they often fail to acknowledge the weight of structural interracial enmity and its differential impact on the lives of white and BIPOC folks, whether dealing with matters of access to resources or perception of social settings.[56]

Such universalism is paired with an individualism that denies the relevance of other white people's behavior to an individual white person's. Even as a white person rejects a BIPOC person's experience and knowledge of white supremacy on the basis of a supposedly universal human experience, that white person may, with their next breath, assert their status as a wholly unique individual who cannot be held accountable for the flaws of others. White supremacist individualism plays an important function within structural interracial enmity, making it possible for well-meaning white people to reconcile whiteness with their personal sense of justice and integrity.[57] Such individualism is not extended to BIPOC people, who are consistently associated with our racial groups. Further, universal humanity tends to only apply to BIPOC folks insofar as it allows white folks to dismiss claims that contradict their own universalized understanding of reality (e.g., "I've never felt scared seeing a police car near my kids' school"). Ultimately, this combined invocation of universalism and individualism obscures the position of whiteness in relation to structural interracial enmity and discredits the notion of interracial enmity itself.

For the purposes of this book on antiracism in US churches, then, what is white fragility? White fragility is the condition that makes individual white people depend on distorted love and defend it from attack.[58] It is a personal manifestation of the cruelly optimistic relation between white people and a whitewashed version of beloved community. White fragility results from the failure of white people to develop the ability to endure race-related stress and taps into the behavior patterns of white supremacy to equip them with skills to preserve their fragility and avoid the challenging experiences that would build their endurance. Pushing white people to engage in behaviors that shut down creative encounters, white fragility prevents them from developing the ability to approach encounters with BIPOC people as simultaneously challenging and nonthreatening.

White fragility is the personally manifested condition that makes the preservation of distorted love the path of least resistance for white people. Primed by white fragility to avoid race-related stress and led by distorted love to conflate good feelings with good relations, white people can easily believe that their refusal to engage in encounters they wrongly perceive as hostile is a sign of their own commitment to good relations. They come to believe that the path of least resistance, provided to them by structural interracial enmity, is the *right* path. In taking that path of least resistance, white people preserve their fragility and fail to develop the endurance that would make taking a more demanding, faithful, and just path viable in the future.

White fragility is an affective malformation, an emotional and spiritual weakness that enables and is reinforced by the circulation of racially charged objects.[59] Consider the impact of white fragility in this everyday example: Asking for prayer about how the neighborhood around their church is less safe (more Black) than it used to be, a white person may be criticized for this racially coded language by a Black female church member. Having been left unable to handle such an encounter by white fragility, this white person might simultaneously employ five strategies to preserve their fragility: rejecting the Black woman's perspective as incompatible with their own "universal" view of reality, relying on individualism to deny the possibility that such anger could rightly be directed at them personally, perceiving race as a problem that the Black woman "brings with her" into the confrontation, refusing to discuss the matter further, and relying on the image of the "angry Black woman" to explain away her legitimate critique. That white person could then complain to their white family and friends about this angry Black woman, reinforcing the affective power of that stereotyped image. When those family and friends next encounter Black women in other contexts, they already perceive them as angry Black women™, regardless of immediate context.

The effects of white fragility become particularly disastrous in churches when they are amplified by the embrace of distorted love in relation to antiracism. When love distorted by white supremacy is closely associated with divine love, white Christians' comfort becomes a nonnegotiable criterion of the peace and justice that are at the heart of God's beloved community. Insofar as BIPOC critique disrupts white racial equilibrium, then, what is disrupted is not perceived by white Christians as a set of white supremacist affective expectations but instead as a divinely mandated order. The defensive reactions dictated by white fragility are recast as attempts to protect beloved community itself. BIPOC critique is not just a threat to white emotional comfort but is a bitter or hateful rejection of divine love. Under the sway of distorted love, antiracist work in churches takes white fragility as its guide and can therefore do little but preserve white supremacy in an ecclesial guise.

These are precisely the kind of unambiguous, critical claims that can easily be read as motivated by hatred or bitterness. However, in discussing white fragility, I am not deriding white people. Rather, my point is that white Christians genuinely face a great deal of difficulty as they strive to perceive Black humanity and respond faithfully. The odds are heavily stacked against white Christians who would respond faithfully to God's love. I do not highlight white fragility to claim that white people are inherently flawed—as if I trade in some kind of laughable "reverse racism"—nor do I wish to absolve white people of their responsibility for the perpetuation of white supremacy. Rather, I want to stress that white Christians are born with one foot in a socially structured snare that can capture even their best impulses, leading them to derail antiracist work because their very ability to imagine God's love at work in human community is compromised by white supremacy.

Before moving on, I should emphasize that white fragility does not lead all white people to happily conspire in the defense of white supremacy. After all, this book is interested primarily in understanding the missteps of those white Christians who try to oppose white supremacy. In such Christians, however, white fragility engages the operations of shame described by Ahmed. DiAngelo describes the way in which white fragility rears its head among such actively antiracist white people, arguing that "white moral objection to racism increases white resistance to acknowledging complicity with it." In response to perceived attacks on their "moral reputations," and in lieu of acknowledging the accuracy of the critiques leveled against them, white people who identify as progressive often portray themselves as the victims of the antiracist work to which they claim to be committed. In doing so, they serve their interests in relation to structural interracial enmity and center their emotional needs as the focus of the antiracist work they are, in fact, undermining.[60] As long as white Christians fail to understand white fragility and its relation to structural interracial enmity, they will not only lack the endurance to persist in antiracist work but also co-opt such work to reinforce white supremacy.

CONCLUSION

I turned to this investigation of distorted love to illuminate the inability of many white Christians to perceive love in the critique and call to repentance offered by BIPOC Christians. My hope was that I might be able to offer an explanation of how white Christians committed to antiracism could fail to do the work necessary to reckon with structural interracial enmity yet still burn themselves out in efforts to love their enemies. In other words, I wanted to answer the question that led me to this project in the first place: What is wrong with these white people?

It is not enough, however, to settle for examining the distortion of love by white supremacy as a problem narrowly related to white Christians' participation in antiracist work. Given the centrality of love as a theological and ethical concept in Christianity, the distortion of love represents an existential threat to Christian faith. At the close of this chapter, then, I want to stress that the distortion of love by white supremacy not only undermines antiracist work in churches—however central or marginal that work may be in a given church—but also degrades churches at a fundamental level.

Too often, white folks' happiness is accepted as the criterion by which we judge the loving character of an act or a word. When white folks' happiness stands as the true end goal of corrupted antiracist work—work that, in churches, is ostensibly about realizing love as a theological and ethical principle—love is distorted. Distorted love demands that white people receive uncritical forgiveness and affirmation from BIPOC people. It works in both white and BIPOC people, deluding us into thinking that this demand for forgiveness and affirmation is nothing less than the holy demand of love. Grounded in the conflation of good feelings and good relations, distorted love leads those ensnared by it to blame bad feelings on the BIPOC folks with whom those bad feelings are unjustly associated. Love of the enemy becomes twisted, taking the form of an active refusal to acknowledge structural interracial enmity, imposing a mode of friendship that disregards the exploitative and violent context of interracial friendships.

Through the distortion of love, the theological and ethical heart of Christian faith is turned against the possibility of its social, economic, and political realization. Distorted love directs churches' energy and effort toward the protection of good feelings and the elimination of sources of bad feelings rather than the repair of bad relations and support for the repentance needed to make that repair. Fear, shame, and optimism are summoned in defense of distorted love's good feelings and are misinterpreted as faithful virtues. Fear of BIPOC anger is mistaken for righteous anger at bitter breaches in the pious purity of "peaceful" antiracist work. Shame is mistaken for repentance, as though the acknowledgment of past failures excuses the refusal to cease one's ongoing service to white supremacy. A cruelly optimistic attachment to corrupted antiracist work is mistaken for a steadfast belief in the transformative power of love.

Distorted love is further reinforced by the widespread phenomenon of white fragility. Racial stress, regardless of context, consistently results in bad feelings for white people. Given the misorientation of love toward white happiness, these bad feelings are perceived as indicators of bad relations precisely when antiracist projects enter the kind of difficult work that could transform the truly unjust relations that reflect structural interracial enmity. White fragility saps the endurance white Christians need to recognize and respond faithfully to their BIPOC siblings, in direct defiance of the structural interracial enmity they struggle to even perceive. To the extent they can accept bad feelings as potentially productive, then, white Christians have few resources for dealing with them.

To put it bluntly, this is a bleak picture. If my account of distorted love is accurate, many US churches have embraced the promise of white happiness as if it is the gospel, the good news of divine deliverance. The gospel, in other words, has been set aside for the sake of white supremacy and the structural interracial enmity in which it is manifested. It should be no surprise, perhaps, that churches in a nation born from slavery and genocide would struggle to be faithful to a message of salvation from bondage and death when they have yet to truly account for the effects of this nation's sin on their ecclesial formation. In failing to respond faithfully to the loving challenge of the gospel, US churches have facilitated the distortion of love by white supremacy, contributing generously to the maintenance and mystification of structural interracial enmity. It may feel overwhelming to confront this daunting reality. Yet there is no shame in feeling overwhelmed when recognizing the challenge presented by an overwhelming evil so insidious that it has compromised the very love on which we depend for our spiritual and ethical guidance.

I close out this chapter by offering a pair of promises, with a bit of guidance on how we can reimagine faithful love of the enemy sandwiched in between. My first promise is one I regularly make to my students when the crushing weight of white supremacy truly bears down on their faith and sense of call: that I seek to expose the true horror of the sin-distorted love in which we are entangled that we might more fully embrace the power of the grace-filled, liberative power of faithful love.

To that end, I offer five further requirements for an account of faithful love of the enemy to the list I began in chapter 1. We need a love that (6) decenters whiteness and deprioritizes white folks' happiness as a criterion of love. We need a love that can (7) disentangle good feelings and good relations while (8) holding together love and acknowledgment of enmity. We need a love that (9) has a healing impact on our other emotions. And we need a love that (10) encourages the development of emotional and spiritual endurance. In short, we need a love that can both unravel the affective web of distorted love and foster emotional and spiritual healing among Christians who would pursue that exhausting work of loving our enemies.

Finally, my second promise: after this challenging examination of our churches' deepest failures, I will spend an entire chapter exploring the possibilities of a hope that can survive a full awareness of structural interracial enmity and US churches' entanglement in that enmity.

CHAPTER THREE

Hope(s) in the Midst of Enmity

Confronting enmity is the challenge before us. Love is the power that Christian faith proclaims is up to that challenge. The rest of this book will explore what it means to love our enemies, but first we must pause and take a breath. It may seem like love is precisely the subject that needs to be addressed at this point, given the weight of the previous two chapters and the dismal picture of our society they paint. If you're feeling that impulse to grasp for love in search of comfort and reassurance, let me offer a caution and an encouragement.

First, the caution: don't reach too quickly for love as an antidote to the overwhelming pressure of enmity as the awareness of what *faithful* love demands is no less weighty than a clear perception of enmity. As discussed in chapter 2, there are certainly notions of love that offer simple comfort in the face of enmity, precisely because they represent love that has been distorted by white supremacy. A faithful love that has the potential to empower us to confront the overwhelming evil of structural interracial enmity, however, is demanding in the way that following Jesus so often is. Recall that Jesus warned his disciples, "If any wish to come after me, let them deny themselves and take up their cross and follow me. For those who want to save their life will lose it, and those who lose their life for my sake will find it."[1] Love—and certainly this book's exploration of love as a response to structural interracial enmity—presents its own challenges. In other words, love is hard work.

Now, the encouragement: there is no need to grasp for love in immediate response to enmity as the resources of Christian faith are abundant. In my experience, Christian communities do better transformative work when we work out of abundance rather than scarcity, out of hope rather than anxiety and desperation. So while love is surely the heart of Christian antiracist work, it is not the only one of God's gifts for which we can reach when confronted by the overwhelming evil of white supremacy. We can ground ourselves in a powerful, faithful hope.

In this pause for breath, then, let's allow ourselves to ask whether it is truly possible to believe that there is hope if we take seriously the idea that structural interracial enmity is a foundational reality of this society. Let's ask whether we can believe the words of twentieth-century Catholic Worker organizer—and Black Chicagoan—Arthur Falls, who said, "When you work for justice, you don't always lose."[2] And let's give ourselves the chance to answer yes, not simply because we feel we must but confident that we do so out of a deep, abiding sense of hope and with a rich appreciation of the abundance of resources available to us.

IS THERE ANY ROOM FOR HOPE IN AFROPESSIMISM?

The first two chapters of this book draw heavily on intensely academic theory, with relatively little reference to Christian theological texts. As I've framed this chapter as a pause for breath, you might assume that this is where I'll turn fully to Christian theology, demonstrating how Jesus offers us hope over against the hopelessness of "secular" theory. But while I'll certainly turn more toward Christian theology in the latter half of this chapter—and believe there are particularly powerful resources of hope offered by Christian faith—I want to be clear that we don't have to overly simplify or explicitly spiritualize our analysis of interracial enmity to find hope in its midst. Put differently, I want to demonstrate that meaningful antiracist work in churches is an everyday possibility, and not something that lies only at the end of time, that can only be enjoyed in some heavenly realm, or that requires supernatural power to take the place of the gifts with which we have already been blessed.

To find such an accessible hope in the midst of enmity, however, we must resist the temptation to seek hope by embracing a narrative of progress. As folks drawn to antiracist work, we might be tempted to echo those voices that point to emancipation, to the civil rights movement, to the Obama presidency, to other moments of triumph and reform. These voices tell the story of the United States as a narrative of progress: confronting its original sin of slavery, this nation has gotten better, is getting better, and will continue to get better. There are no shortage of politicians, preachers, and pop culture icons who invite to place ourselves in that narrative as those who are poised to continue this march of progress.

To be clear, this is not a narrative that can be dismissed as a simple or selfish evasion of the truth. After all, it would be foolish to disregard the real differences between chattel slavery and contemporary anti-Blackness. Further, many do not wish to be ungrateful to those who gave up their time, their energy, their safety, even their very lives to strive for freedom. So if some degree of realism and a great measure of gratitude inspire people to embrace this sacred narrative of progress, what's wrong with grounding our hope in it?

Scholar of religion Joseph R. Winters offers a distinction that can help highlight the danger of relying on progress for our hope. Winters draws a clear distinction between hope and progress-dependent optimism, offering a critique of much antiracist political struggle. Winters critiques the concept of progress that encourages us to "assume that Americans are situated on a progressive trajectory that continues through time" and will culminate in the irrelevance of race. He argues that when the optimism that sustains and is sustained by this notion of progress is conflated with hope, it fosters the expectation of a better future at the expense of those memories and feelings that suggest otherwise.[3] Progress-dependent optimism, in other words, leads us right into those affective traps discussed in chapter 2—cruel optimism, the promise of happiness, and white fragility—by telling us that everything will be okay and steering us away from addressing painful histories and their deadly legacies.

When it comes down to it, progress-dependent optimism is not a hope that can withstand the reality of structural interracial enmity as I've laid it out in the first two chapters of this book. Its narrative of progress only tells half the story about this country's history of interracial enmity, highlighting forward motion while downplaying or outright erasing those many demoralizing and deadly steps back. In search of a hope that can persist in full awareness of structural interracial enmity and is responsive to the changing reality of the church, we will start by returning to Frank Wilderson's Afropessimist thought[4] before building on the insights we find to offer some possibilities for powerful hope in the midst of enmity.

In further engaging Wilderson's Afropessimism, I am well aware that I'm taking you right back into what might be the clearest sign that my understanding of enmity is mired in despair: my insistence that interracial enmity is a matter of irreconcilable antagonism and that people of different races will be enemies until society as it currently exists is completely overturned. If your impression of Afropessimism is that it is fundamentally despairing—whether you've never seen that term before opening this book or have done some reading yourself—you're not alone. Hopelessness and negativity are common criticisms of Afropessimism and Wilderson's work in particular.

Consider, for example, the critique offered by Kelly Brown Douglas, whose work on hope we'll turn to later in this chapter:

> Afropessimism argues that anti-Blackness is so pervasive and deeply ingrained, not simply within systems and structures but in the very psychic framework of the world, that the affirmation of Black humanity is impossible. Frank Wilderson describes Afropessimism as a "meta-theory" that is "pessimistic about the claims theories of liberation make when these theories try to explain Black suffering." This would include Black faith claims and the Black theologies of liberation that flow from them. Wilderson says that Black people must face the stark truth that when it comes to Black suffering, "there is no imaginative strategy for redress—no narrative of social, political or national redemption." For Afropessimists there is no hope for a future where Black lives will ever matter. The best option, therefore, is for Black people to accept the reality of Black suffering and to stay alive and sane while trying to navigate it.[5]

Douglas's critique highlights a crucial nuance that we need to keep in mind in working with Frank Wilderson's Afropessimist thought and that it is easy to pass over amid Wilderson's unrelenting and fundamental critique of our society. Douglas is right that for Wilderson, there is indeed no hope for redemption in this society. There is no possibility that this nation will be able to respond adequately to Black suffering. However, Douglas and others incorrectly make the leap to pronounce that this means Wilderson allows no possibility of a better future. Wilderson insists that there is no way to fix what we've got, no way to a more just world *short of overturning the entirety of this society.* We return to Wilderson's Afropessimism, then, because it is my contention that the critical stance of Afropessimism is not a matter of hopelessness. By extension, neither is the account of enmity that I have offered in the first part of this book. By finding what room there is for hope in Afropessimism—what hope Christians might find beyond the boundaries of the world as it is—we can find room for hope in the midst of enmity.

It takes some digging to find space for hope in Afropessimist critique. For assistance, I turn to the "Black optimist" work of Black theorist and poet Fred Moten, who understands Afropessimism as the study of the impossibility of the love of Blackness. Afropessimism, from Moten's perspective, supports us as we refuse to look away from the meaningless void that is the place of Black life in a world structured by white supremacy.[6] In terms of this book, then, Afropessimism empowers Black folks who have been condemned to unending enmity to do two things: (1) take seriously the place of Blackness in the Black/white racial binary and (2) pursue as full an understanding of the place of Blackness in that binary as possible.

Moten helps us find hope within the work of Afropessimism by stressing the necessity of an additional task: (3) sustaining the belief that Black people are something more or something other than that place of vulnerability to exploitation and violence to which we've been assigned. To my knowledge, Frank Wilderson himself doesn't undertake this third task—in my estimation, the first two tasks are challenging enough on their own, and it's unclear if he's interested in the third. Nonetheless, Moten makes it clear that Wilderson's Afropessimist work is extraordinarily helpful in taking on that empowering, hopeful work of finding beauty and dignity in Black life.

Relating his Black optimist thought to Afropessimism, Moten explains that "if pessimism allows us to discern that we are nothing, then optimism is the condition of possibility of the study of nothing as well as what derives from that study."[7]

As my beloved high school Latin teacher Ms. Steppe would ask, "Clear as mud?"[8]

I promise I'm not dragging you through the world of heavy theory for no good reason. In this single quote, Moten points us toward the path from Afropessimism to hope, and he does so in three quick steps.

First, Moten states that "pessimism allows us to discern that we are nothing." In making this claim, Moten highlights that crucial insight of Afropessimist thought: in a world structured by anti-Blackness, Black people are nothing. To whatever extent we operate under the rules that structure the world as it currently is, we accept that Blackness is devoid of value, of purpose, of life itself. According to the rules of the world as it is, Black people are nothing.

Second, he names optimism "the condition of possibility of the study of nothing." Moten asserts that the exploration of this hideous truth does not demand Black thinkers' acceptance of our nothingness. Rather, the effort to seek a fuller understanding of Black people's position in this world reflects a kind of optimism. To be clear, this is not the progress-dependent optimism critiqued by Winters but a basic commitment to the idea that we are not truly nothing. The optimism woven into Afropessimism—the belief that we have value, purpose, and vibrant life that are incomprehensible in terms of an anti-Black world—is necessary for the sustained study of what's been done to us.

Third, Moten stresses that the "study of nothing" enabled by this distinctly Black optimism makes something further possible. Crucially, it makes it possible to actively seek out those spaces and times in which the anti-Blackness that would make us into nothing fails in its work, the points at which Black life stubbornly exhausts the death-dealing power of anti-Blackness[9] and powerfully demonstrates that "nothing is not absence."[10] In other words, it is possible to seek some other way of being by fully acknowledging the dreadful state of the world and refusing to retreat into wishful thinking or demand faith in a promise that everything will be okay.

Moten's "study of nothing" presents a fundamental challenge to whiteness's demand that we justify ourselves on its terms. Moten argues that whiteness highlights the importance of having the capacity for agency and meaning in one's own right, then implicitly defines Blackness as that which lacks the capacity for agency and meaning, obscuring the fact that attempts to assert such agency and meaning on terms other than those of white supremacy will meet deadly resistance.[11] To briefly connect this discussion to chapter 1, we can say that Black people can achieve such agency and meaning in an anti-Black world only by performing whiteness. That is, the sanctioned path to agency and meaning is for Black people to present ourselves as respectable people (dressing, speaking, and engaging in political action "properly"). The acknowledgment of our agency and meaning is only ever provisional, always under threat of being overshadowed by the recognition of our Blackness. This dynamic is reflected in the history of colonialism and slavery that is so thoroughly woven into the history of the United States.

In rejecting justification by whiteness, Moten is clear that Blackness is not created by whiteness, though naming it "Black" is an artifact of white supremacy. Rather, Blackness—understood as that which does not fit into the model of capacity for agency and meaning promoted by whiteness—precedes whiteness and the demands it makes on us. Whiteness does not create Blackness, a mode of life together that fails to live up to its promises.

Rather, whiteness attempts and fails to fully capture Blackness, a form of life together that does not require justification by whiteness to breathe and move.[12] Black life finds room to breathe where whiteness fails to find a meaning or value and thus fails to exert control.

To find an everyday example of this, we need to only consider the rapid evolution of Black culture in the United States. Black culture often blossoms and thrives in spaces deemed unlivable by whiteness (e.g., "bad" neighborhoods, as discussed in chapter 2). Dances, phrases, humor, music styles, and so on grow in darkness, then wither and lose their vibrancy when co-opted and commercialized by white-dominated market forces. What can't be readily commodified is deemed distasteful or low-quality, often to be rehabilitated at such time as it *can* be packaged for mass consumption. The story of US American culture has always included the story of Black creativity outpacing and eluding complete capture by white capitalist desire.

In light of the conceivable refusal by Black people to justify ourselves on whiteness's terms, Moten offers yet another mind-bending question: "What if the thing whose meaning or value has never been found finds things, founds things?"[13] What if, in other words, that which escapes definition by whiteness is able to sustain life in the absence of the agency and meaning provided by whiteness?[14] What if there are things we assume to be necessary for life—security, self-determination, and order as defined under white supremacy—that trap us in structural interracial enmity but are not truly necessary for life because we can find alternative ways to sustain life together? These questions are crucial because if we are to ask where hope can be found in a world structured by interracial enmity, it is possible that we must seek such hope in what Moten describes as owning our "dispossession,"[15] in somehow embracing the denial of rights that are seemingly fundamental to human life.

To be clear, Moten is not suggesting that Black people should actively seek to forfeit what protections we manage to make use of in the face of a world that is designed to kill us, whether through the sharp crack of a police officer's pistol or the slow progress of stress-related heart disease. Rather, Moten—along with Wilderson and other Afropessimist thinkers—rejects the idea that any lasting salvation is to be found in taking advantage of anti-Black systems. We are to look for hope not in structures that kill us, even as they claim to offer us life, but *in the openings revealed by the death dealt by those structures.*

In seeking hope, Moten points Black folks toward homelessness and the hold of the slave ship, toward those spaces and ways of being that leave us no doubt that this world simply will not suffer us to live. Moten describes an existential homelessness as a persistent reality of Blackness. Blackness never finds itself at home in this world but is always forced into a fugitive flight from the powers that seek to secure it as the negative reflection of a perfect white world and thus stabilize the Black/white binary. Moten argues that this recurring homelessness is a gift that can be embraced by those who live in Blackness. It is not an unambiguous blessing, to be sure, but Moten is confident that we can study "what it is to own one's dispossession" and find something in homelessness that cannot be found in the poisoned ground of the home one might secure through one's justification by whiteness.[16] That something, found only in the flight from a home that one has been refused, is life shared with others in openness and in common dispossession.[17]

What enables the sharing of life in homelessness is what Moten finds revealed in what he calls the "fantasy in the hold of the ship."[18] The hold of the slave ship was, for Moten, the place where it was made most clear that to be Black is to be nothing in this world. And yet life continued in the nothingness of the hold.[19] Stripped of any sense of coherence in relation to time and space, enslaved Africans in the hold were forced into a way of being that did not rely on the conferral of agency and meaning by the performance of whiteness. Even in the context of the horror of the Middle Passage, the embrace of deep and life-defining intimacy and renunciation of power over others by enslaved Africans in the hold suggests to us what is needed for an escape from the trap of justification by whiteness.[20]

Though it's certainly not the focus of his work, Wilderson himself points toward the possibility of an escape from this trap in a 2010 interview. Responding to a question about his stance on the importance and possibility of reparations to Black US Americans, Wilderson offers the following thoughts:

> Reparations suggests a conceptually coherent loss. The loss of land, the loss of labor power, etc. In other words, there has to be some form of articulation between the party that has lost and the party that has gained for reparations to make sense. No such articulation exists between Blacks and the world. This is, ironically, precisely why I support the Reparations Movement; but my emphasis, my energies, my points of attention are on the word "Movement" and not on the word "Reparation." I support the movement because I know it is a movement toward the end of the world; a movement toward a catastrophe in epistemological coherence and institutional integrity—I support the movement aspect of it because I know that repair is impossible; and any *struggle that can act as a stick up artist to the world,* demanding all that it cannot give (which is everything),

> is a movement toward something so blindingly new that it cannot be imagined. This is the only thing that will save us.[21]

Wilderson rejects outright the idea that repair is possible. There is simply no basis on which things might be made right between Black people and the society that seeks to confine our existence to nonexistence, to make our life into death. Enmity cannot be resolved while leaving intact the world structured by that enmity. Wilderson does, however, leave open the possibility that the reparations movement is "a movement toward the end of the world."

Wilderson's Afropessimist thought truly is not hopeless, though the hope it offers is thoroughly apocalyptic. Such hope, in that sense, is a hope to which it seems Christians could be particularly open. Inextricably woven into our faith is the claim that this world is not as it ought to be, that death reigns but will not have the final word, that the mighty exalt themselves but will be cast down, and that the end of this world will be both terrifying and glorious.

Stark as his picture of the world is, Wilderson does not go out of his way to deny any hope in the possibility of justice and life together. Rather, he strives to demonstrate that our world goes out of *its* way to deny that hope. This world, defined by anti-Blackness, works to reduce to nothingness any possibility of life together by making the fullness of white people's lives dependent on the denial of such fullness to Black people.

Understood through the lens of Moten's Black optimism, Wilderson's Afropessimism closely examines the apparent ubiquity and overwhelming power of anti-Blackness, rejecting any easy path toward a better world. Nonetheless, it does not foreclose all possibilities of resistance and renewal. Wilderson does not make hope easy, but working with his analysis of anti-Blackness does not crush hope entirely. In theological terms,[22] we could say that their work suggests there is no way to a just world short of the coming of the Kindom of God. This is a far cry from saying that there is no way to a just world.

WHAT HOPES CAN WE FIND IN BLACKNESS?

Taking seriously the reality of structural interracial enmity—much like the Afropessimist thought I turned to in order to articulate that reality—does not foreclose all possibilities of hope for justice and mutuality. In fact, within the space of thought and belief bounded by the evil of enmity, there are infinite possibilities for hope. Writing on the power of precisely the kind of "Black Study" embraced by Moten, scholar of religion Ashon T. Crawley argues that such study can enable us to recognize in Blackness a powerful gift: the power to imagine and live into "otherwise possibilities," any number of alternatives to the way things are and seem as if they must be.[23] Crucially, Crawley stresses that "imagination is necessary for thinking and breathing into the capacities of infinite alternatives."[24] It is in search of imagination that can find hope—otherwise possibility—in Blackness without dismissing the reality of enmity that we will look at three different thinkers, each of whom envisions hope arising amid the fullness of Black life: Joseph R. Winters, Kelly Brown Douglas, and Keri Day.

Earlier in this chapter, I discussed Winters's critique of progress-dependent optimism. In offering a constructive account of hope, Winters insists on the value of the very attachments and memories that are marginalized by progress-dependent optimism. In short, he argues that we will not find an empowering hope by "getting over" past injustices, downplaying the severity of ongoing evils, and relying on progress-dependent optimism.[25]

Rather, Winters stresses the value of a "melancholic hope," a hope that does not let go of the hurts of past generations but instead appreciates their connection to the present. A melancholic hope does not primarily make us feel more optimistic about the world, help us to easily generate alternatives to our current situation of structural interracial enmity, or inspire belief that the future *will* be better. Rather, it "potentially allows the past to disrupt, unsettle, and rework our sense of and relationship to the past."[26] A melancholic hope "opens up spaces for contestation, tarrying, revision, and reimagination,"[27] making room for the slow, weighty work of overturning a society structured by enmity. A melancholic hope, in other words, refuses to accept the deceptive guarantee of a better future and guides us toward uncertain—but real—otherwise possibilities.

Beyond serving as a pragmatic alternative to progress-dependent optimism, Winters's notion of melancholic hope has practical implications for the work of communal and societal transformation. Rejecting the notion that change comes through unqualified unity, Winters argues that while change certainly requires the coming together of different communities to seek common goods, it also depends on "introducing and heightening tensions, conflict, and dissidence that are concealed by the tendency to privilege or assume unity."[28] The affective conformity critiqued by Sara Ahmed—that pressure to mirror the good feelings of others as a sign that you fit in, that you're willing to preserve the illusion that everything is okay—is simply unnecessary to antiracist work if we can relinquish progress-dependent optimism in favor of a melancholic hope. Ultimately, refusing to forget past suffering can inspire a "heightened capacity to remember, contemplate, and be unsettled by race-inflected violence and suffering,"[29] enabling us to work through the tensions that arise in the course of antiracist work and evade the affective traps of cruel optimism, the promise of happiness, and white fragility.

A second conception of hope that thrives without disregarding the depth and breadth of evil in our world is offered by Episcopal womanist theologian Kelly Brown Douglas. Douglas builds an account of resurrection hope in relation to the tension between two sets of demands: her son Desmond's demands for a way forward in the face of ongoing anti-Black violence and the demands of her role as an Episcopal priest.[30] Where Winters grounds hope in the space created by melancholic attachment to the past, Douglas's resurrection hope balances attention to the past and the future, encouraging Christians to orient ourselves toward the future while remaining rooted in the faith of our Black ancestors.

On the one hand, Douglas understands faith communities as fundamentally accountable to the just future God desires for our world. Discussing the relation faith communities should have to the movement for reparations, Douglas writes of this accountability as a matter of faith. She insists that "inasmuch as faith is about partnering with God to mend an unjust world and thus to move us toward a more just future, then faith communities, by definition, are accountable to that future." For Douglas, orientation toward a just future enables both the possibility of believing in a world free from white supremacy and the opportunity to invite the nation to embrace that belief as a core moral tenet.[31]

On the other hand, Douglas finds that this orientation toward the future does not sustain us on its own as we confront overwhelming anti-Blackness in the present[32] and, as her son stressed, recognize that such anti-Blackness more closely mirrors past injustices we so deeply wish we would never have to endure again.[33] Hand in hand with an orientation to the future, therefore, Douglas urges the careful stewardship of our Black ancestors' faith. Responding to her son's concern with the seemingly cyclical nature of anti-Black violence, Douglas invokes one such ancestor:

> I answered by telling him about his great-great-grandmother. We called her Mama Mary. Mama Mary was born into slavery. She died when I was around six years old. Every time I think about Mama Mary, I think of those Black people who were born into slavery, died in slavery, and never drew a free breath. In fact, they never dreamt that they would ever breathe a free breath. Yet, they fought for freedom anyhow. They fought for a freedom that they knew they would never see, but still believed that it would in fact one day be. They fought for a freedom that was nothing less than the freedom that is the justice of God. This was their hope—a hope that was found and lived out in their struggle for freedom—for it was in that struggle that they met God, even in the midst of slavery. Theirs is a resurrecting hope, because when I think of them and their fight for freedom, I cannot give in to that which would destroy Black life. It is because of their hope that I am here writing this book.[34]

Douglas's hope relies neither on a narrative of progress nor entirely on a promised just future. Rather, this resurrection hope is strengthened by a keen, deeply grateful awareness that Black people have indeed confronted lethal, degrading anti-Blackness throughout our centuries in this country and *that it has not stopped us from struggling for freedom and meeting God in that struggle.*

Douglas describes her hope as a resurrection hope, presenting resurrection as the theological connection point between our painful, precious past and God's just future. After all, our past is not ours alone. It, too—in its tragedy and its beauty—is God's. Drawing on the richness of James Cone's Black liberation theology, Douglas understands the cross as the clearest sign of "Jesus' utter identification with the oppressed." This identification is not only with their suffering, however, but also with their "struggle to survive and thrive in the face of the crucifying realities that threaten and destroy their lives." After all, while the cross is the instrument of Jesus's death, it is followed by the resurrection. And if Jesus was not ultimately destroyed by the cross, Douglas insists, we can believe that his "ministerial vision"—womanist theologian Delores Williams's term for Jesus's gift of showing the path toward survival and quality of life in even the worst circumstances—outlasted the cross too. Thus, for Douglas, the cross "is not the end, but a revelatory point on the way to new life, new reality."[35]

In light of God's resurrection power, past struggles and the promise of a just future come together to empower a politically empowering hope. Douglas highlights the political relevance of resurrection hope in considering the continued work of the Black Lives Matter movement. Describing moments of transcendence in which God's presence can be felt in the midst of protest and witnessing to the gloriously contagious spread of an affirmation of Black life in response to widespread anti-Black violence, Douglas offers resurrection hope as precisely the kind of hope that can thrive in the midst of enmity.[36]

Where resurrection power binds past, present, and future together in Douglas's hope, Pentecostal womanist theologian Keri Day describes a similar temporal synthesis in terms of eschatology, the area of theological study devoted to consideration of the relation between the world as it is and the Kindom of God to come. Day articulates a notion of "realized eschatology," a hope that "points to the possibilities for rebirth, renewal, and 'becoming' in the present as the seeds of hope have already been planted in the past that await to be actualized." Roving across and even beyond time, this kind of hope finds no conflict between human activity and divine activity outside the bounds of what we perceive as human history. Instead, hope for the transformative power of each kind of activity is productively held together with hope for the other.[37]

Day turns to womanist theological and ethical works for inspiration and finds that the realized eschatology woven throughout them empowers its bearers to imagine not only a better future but also the conditions of possibility of that future.[38] Hope as realized eschatology maintains a tight connection between the world as it is and a better world to come, imagining a just future in concrete terms, as a "new socio-economic order, governed by ideas of love, solidarity, and hope."[39] As such, the imagination stemming from a realized eschatology does not require us to project a perfect future in order to maintain hope. Rather, she argues, what is most needed is an imagination that is closely connected to our own social worlds yet points beyond them to "alternative worlds *located in the present.*"[40]

Grounding her reflections on hope in reflection on the religious and political action of the Argentinian movement Madres de Desaparecidos, Day argues that hope as realized eschatology is not an abstract virtue but a concrete practice of commitment to "liberative projects of human flourishing."[41] For BIPOC women who actively lead social movements, Day finds that this hope embodied in social practice is found in "the ordinary and mundane practices of their everyday lived experience." In their everyday lives, that is, many BIPOC women exercise their faith through practices that help them to "fashion new possibilities toward love, justice, and freedom" amid their present struggles and hardships.[42]

The everydayness of hope as realized eschatology helps it to persist in the midst of the evil we confront every day. Like Winters, Day draws a distinction between optimism and hope. Optimism, for Day, involves imagining transformation under the terms allowed by dominant powers, while hope imagines a new world on the terms of "radical social practices among the vulnerable and disenfranchised." Where optimism "attempts to reform within the hegemony of the visible," hope is a radical activity that "hinges on making visible 'the invisible,' that is the invisible practices of vulnerable, suffering populations who point toward new futures of love and care based on their social practices." As such, it is *only* through attention to the reality of marginalized people's lives, their suffering and their resistance, that we can find some basis for hope.[43] Hope—openness to the alternative worlds that were planted in the past, are already coming to life in the present, and that might transform the world in the future—requires an awareness of the overwhelming evil that is so consistently confronted by powerful social practices of love and care.

Each of the notions of hope I have covered here—melancholic hope, resurrection hope, and realized eschatology—offers a distinct understanding of how we might persist in pursuing justice in the midst of interracial enmity. In exploring the idea of melancholic hope, Winters suggests that hope can arise precisely from our awareness of the suffering in the world and specifically from our memory of histories of suffering. Such melancholic hope can open up spaces for critique and reimagination. Douglas emphasizes resurrection hope's ability to orient us to a just future, root us deeply in the powerful witness of our ancestors' faith, and embody resurrection power through present-day political action. Day grounds a radical hope in a realized eschatology, presenting such hope as manifesting itself in the alternative worlds in which vulnerable populations live lives of love even as they resist the dehumanizing structures that surround them. These three accounts of hope make it clear that when we take Wilderson seriously and agree that the world is deeply structured by racial antagonism, we can still hope—and, in fact, may need to if we want to engage in the activity of resistance and the embrace of otherwise possibilities.

CONCLUSION

So far, I hope I've made the case that it is possible not only to find some kind of hope in full awareness of structural interracial enmity but even to find a politically powerful and spiritually enriching hope. Still, I've made my point by proposing a few different accounts of hope, and there are some ways in which they don't necessarily fit together. For example, Douglas and Day are theologians offering distinctively Christian accounts of hope. Winters, however, is a scholar of religion whose account of hope mostly eschews theology in favor of literature, jazz, and critical theory. These hopes do not fit neatly together, and this frustrated me until I looked over at my bookshelf and saw *An Unpromising Hope*.

In this book, Lutheran theologian Thomas R. Gaulke explores the question of hope with a particular group in mind: the many "agnostics, atheists, and belief-fluid folks" who have been present in the churches he's served as pastor and with whom he often identifies (as do I, when I'm able to fully honor my doubts).[44] Writing from that pastoral perspective, Gaulke highlights something weighing on many hearts: a more just world has been promised, but it has not come into being.[45] This promise offers little to those "agnostics, atheists, and belief-fluid folks" who nonetheless need hope just as much as those who more straightforwardly believe. While we might feel that any human requires some source of hope, Gaulke points out that the work of community organizing and movement building, in particular, "depends upon hope and spiritual strength, whatever dogma one does or does not believe."[46] In response to this spiritual and political need for hope, Gaulke declares his commitment to building community in which "where our beliefs remain uncertain, we nevertheless share a hope without belief. Our shared hope shapes our shared community and our shared mission, simultaneously."[47]

In writing of the possibility of sharing hope across lines of belief, Gaulke points toward a powerful possibility: that we need not share *a* hope at all but might instead share a commitment to hope. We might, that is, recognize the importance of hope for our individual and communal lives, committing to supporting and sustaining one another's particular understandings and practices of hope as they empower us to continue in our shared work of communal and societal antiracist transformation. It is clear that not all hopes can sustain antiracist work in the midst of interracial enmity. It is equally clear that there is some essential work we need our hopes to accomplish. I end this chapter, then, not with a hope we can all get behind but with some broad guidelines that might help us to find powerful hopes within that space of a shared commitment to hope.

One the one hand, the scholars discussed in this chapter suggest we avoid hopes that demand that we stifle and silence our doubts, forget past wounds and struggles, or articulate our desires for the future in terms of white supremacy's understanding of prosperity. In a world in which so much of what is considered good, beautiful, and true is defined by white supremacy, doubt, melancholy, and incompatibility with this society can play an important role in promoting the generation of otherwise possibilities. That is, in a world in which evil presents itself as the divinely ordained, inevitable product of sacred progress, we need to leave room to question that which claims to be divine, refuse to celebrate narratives of progress, and reject circumstances that most people take for granted.

On the other hand, there is work that seems essential to the role of hope in antiracist work. There may be many ways to undertake this work, but seven tasks are important for any hopes on which we might rely in the midst of enmity. Our hopes must (1) empower us to resist in the face of persistent injustice; (2) help us to persist in the gap between stumbling, unsatisfying "progress" and the just kindom for which we long; (3) hold open space in which we can honor, process, and share both "positive" and "negative" feelings; (4) reinforce our resistance to the shaping of our sense of what's possible—politically and even metaphysically—by white supremacy; (5) facilitate a connection between vibrant imagination and practical action; (6) grant us at least moments of feeling deeply that Black lives have meaning and value in the midst of an anti-Black world; and perhaps most centrally, (7) sustain our capacity to remain open to otherwise possibilities arising where we might least expect them.

I am confident that many conceptions and practices of hope can accomplish this work, not least those touched on in this chapter. As we engage in antiracist work, then, part of our work is to find ways to hold together the many hopes that sustain us as we do that work in the midst of enmity. Our various hopes might *feel* different, arise from different sources, or have different relations to Christian faith. Nonetheless, we can find ways to witness to one another about the hopes we experience and practice, work to better understand one another's hopes, and mirror those hopes to one another as we engage in our work together. We can, in short, embrace the possibility that our work is sustained by abundant hopes, more than sufficient for the work of confronting the overwhelming evil that pits us against one another as enemies.

CHAPTER FOUR

Black Love as Politically Transformative Emotion

Brutal, intractable enmity and abundant, world-changing love. Demonic problem and divine response. To the extent that this book lays out the interplay between interracial enmity and antiracist love as problem and response, this is the chapter where we turn fully from contemplating this transgenerational problem to reimagining its timeworn response.

Chapters 1 and 2 framed the problem of interracial enmity in relation to two themes: the nature of interracial enmity and the distortion of love by that enmity. Christian antiracist efforts falter when they misdiagnose interracial enmity as private, involving a reciprocal, escalating, and ultimately reconcilable conflict grounded in the wronging of one party by another. However, the interracial enmity to which we are called to respond with love can best be understood as *structural* enmity, which can be resolved only through wholesale societal transformation. Mistaking structural interracial enmity for private enmity has led to ineffectual understandings of love of the enemy, in which love amounts to forgiveness and affirmation of white Christians by their BIPOC siblings in Christ without any firm demand for repentance. For BIPOC folks to demand changed behavior of their white counterparts—not to meekly pray for it but to *demand* it as a just and faithful response to the recognition of the twin sins of white supremacy and anti-Blackness—is routinely misrepresented as hateful or ungrateful.

Love itself has been distorted through the influence of structural interracial enmity. Even in the context of antiracist work, love often serves to reinforce the relations of power, privilege, exploitation, and violence that constitute interracial enmity. Distorted love prioritizes white happiness over Black and brown—or, in fact, *white*—wholeness. Distorted love shapes entire communities and churches, informing their understandings of compassion, justice, and trustworthy leadership. Distorted love truncates our capacity to engage our own emotions by marginalizing "negative" emotions except insofar as they can be manipulated to reinforce the validity of that distorted love. And, ultimately, distorted love falters in the face of difficulty, including that involved in the deeply challenging work of antiracism.

Chapter 3 took the first step toward a response, arguing that even in the context of structural interracial enmity and its thorough distortion of love, we can yet hope. Even if we accept this book's dour diagnosis of the problem we're facing, we can turn toward otherwise possibilities and believe in alternative worlds. But where do we go from here? For Christians committed to antiracist work, we must search for those otherwise possibilities that allow us to turn toward a *faithful* love of our enemies.

After all, love yet remains the theological and ethical heart of the Christian response to enmity, despite its distortion and misuse. Love is a central theme in the scriptural interpretation and powerful public witness of modern Christian figures such as Martin Luther King Jr. Love's importance to addressing interracial enmity has been reinforced through repetition over decades in pulpits across the country. I turn to love, then, because while someone else might be able to imagine a Christian theological response to the enmity that is not grounded in love yet still has some hope of informing the lives of churches in the United States, I cannot. I can, however, imagine a faithful love that challenges, rather than facilitates, structural interracial enmity.

In teaching and speaking on the need to reimagine love, I've encountered a range of concerns and uncertainties. Among these, two stand out as particularly pressing and representative of that broader set of concerns. First, some doubt that love is a realistic basis for work that will function effectively on political and economic levels. There is a suspicion that grounding antiracist work in love amounts to succumbing to optimism of the kind critiqued by Joseph R. Winters,[1] leaving us feeling cheerful about our prospects but failing to empower the hard work of systemic change. Second, some worry that in reimagining love as an antiracist practice, we might betray the biblically grounded, theological dimensions of love, sacrificing the sacred beauty of love for the sake of political power.

These concerns are understandable and important. I will have failed in my task if this book leaves you with a notion of love that can be reduced either to pious sentimentality or to political utility. I will have failed, that is, if I do not leave you with an understanding of love that can empower antiracist work on its emotional, spiritual, and political levels simultaneously. To avoid such failure, I approach the question of love by taking love and its power seriously, without setting aside the context of structural interracial enmity.

To pull off this balancing act, I ground my work of reimagining love in Blackness, that space from which otherwise possibilities can be perceived and conceived. In part, I am simply picking up a thread from chapter 3. I'm following the insights of Fred Moten and Ashon Crawley, each of whom find in Blackness a space in which we might imagine and encounter ways of being that are not distorted by white supremacy.

Beyond Moten and Crawley's compelling theories, though, I am holding fast to my theological roots, engaging in the work of Black theology as I was taught by James Cone, and turning to Black history and Black experiences as central sources for reimagining love. Black history and experiences have much to offer when it comes to taking both love and enmity seriously. After all, the history of Black folks in this country is marked by perpetual confrontation with white supremacy *and* the continual preservation and expansion of the bonds of kinship and care. The experiences of Black folks in this country include simultaneously resisting anti-Blackness *and* thriving in and through that creative resistance. Our history and experiences have much to contribute when it comes to accounting for the nature of life-bringing love in the midst of death-dealing enmity.

I will, then, build my account of loving through enmity on the foundation of a political and theological account of Black love. Black love is love that has flourished through centuries marked by being denied and fighting for freedom, losing and finding family, creating and retrieving culture, forgetting and rediscovering ancestors, and being deceived by and resisting the fragmenting forces of capitalist competition—and that's only scratching the surface of Black history. In turning to Black love, then, my intention is to hold Christian antiracist love accountable to a tradition of love that has sustained hope through the most trying times and in intimate awareness of structural interracial enmity, succumbing neither to despair nor to the temptation of superficial optimism.

In chapter 5, I will discuss Black love in a distinctly theological sense, addressing the second concern listed a couple of pages back. In this chapter, though, I will address that first concern by exploring love's political effects, particularly for Black people in a land so thoroughly shaped by white supremacy and anti-Blackness. I will, in other words, demonstrate that love is not just an idealistic response to enmity but holds up well to the challenges of transformative political action. I will present Black love as a guide toward a mode of love that can empower the work of dismantling structural interracial enmity. Insofar as Black love is *Black*, it is grounded in that space of Blackness from which we can imagine otherwise possibilities,[2] alternatives to the white-dominated world that pits us against one another as enemies. Insofar as Black love is *loving*, it possesses the power to sustain us as we do the challenging work of opening ourselves to those otherwise possibilities.

What, then, is Black love, such that it is capable of all this? Black love is a politically transformative emotion, expressed through politically engaged practices of perception and connection, and grounded in an enduring pride and oriented toward mutual care. Black love sustains communal efforts to strive for a world where whiteness and the evils with which it is entangled no longer constrain Black flourishing. To explore these varied aspects of Black love, I turn to Black thinkers Keri Day and James Baldwin.

POLITICALLY TRANSFORMATIVE LOVE

Centering Black feminist and womanist political thought and practice, womanist theologian and ethicist Keri Day offers a powerful imagination of love as a practice of perception[3] that guides the shaping of alternative forms of community by fostering meaningful connection. Day argues for the importance of an "affective politics" for Black feminist and womanist political engagement. Affective politics captures "the cultural politics of emotions and how emotions work to align political subjects to certain causes and political commitments," particularly insofar as it is "in and through *the body* and its emotions that love and subsequent commitments associated with love become possible."[4]

Day points us toward an insight that many Christians who dive into antiracist work have discovered for themselves: in seeking a society guided by love and structured by ideals such as compassion and justice, we risk emotional, spiritual, and physical exhaustion if we don't have some kind of steady, sustaining support. It's just not enough to believe—however firmly—in the righteousness, faithfulness, or pragmatism of our antiracist cause. Day stresses that if love-oriented political principles are to endure over time, they require ongoing attention to the emotional dimensions of political life. After all, societal structures and individual feelings interact in that space Day, I, and others call *affect*. As such, intolerance and injustice not only shape societal systems and institutional policies but also erode individuals' capacity for compassion and understanding.[5]

Addressing our shared economic life, Day explains that unjust economic structures shape us in two crucial ways that diminish our lives. First, the association of private property with status, influence, and power compels us to rely on our property to confer a "sense of self and identity." We are, Day points out, *possessed* by our possessions, dependent on them and the unjust systems that give them meaning for our own meaning. Second, unjust economic structures draw us into objectifying relationships. With our sense of self tied so closely to property, the relationships through which we make sense of ourselves also become a matter of possession and ownership. Relationships—even our relationship with God—are reduced to struggles for control and ownership. Unjust economic structures fundamentally undermine the development of politically transformative qualities such as compassion, understanding, desire for justice, or trust in the strength of community.[6]

Day's account of the impact of economic injustice on our capacity to love sheds further light on the relations of exploitation that are central to structural interracial enmity. In positioning us as enemies to one another, white supremacy and anti-Blackness organize consistent patterns of possession, ownership, and objectification. Whiteness, at a fundamental level, is about ownership and the capacity to present oneself as a subject, while Blackness is defined as absolute objectification. To strive for a better life through the performance of whiteness—as I discussed in chapter 1—is to find oneself possessed by possession, caught up in what George Lipsitz describes as the "possessive investment in whiteness."[7] To the extent such exploitation allows for love, it is the distorted, controlling love described in chapter 2.

Day certainly helps us understand how the exploitative dimensions of structural interracial enmity erode our capacity to approach one another with a love that strives for mutuality. If nothing else, we can be confident that the hope and love to which she points in her work are hardly uninformed or naive. Still, you have surely noticed that I have not yet gotten to how Day helps us address this chapter's guiding question: Is love a politically transformative response to structural interracial enmity?

Fortunately, Day does not delve into the depths of structural evil simply to bring her readers down. Rather, she outlines the effects of unjust economic structures to draw out ways in which they can be—and have already been—resisted. She emphasizes that the reductive reframing of human connection as possession and exploitation results in the dissolution of attachments. To the extent that they are helplessly trapped in a struggle to reduce others to mere objects, lest they be objectified themselves, Day warns that "people have no deep attachment to themselves or to others, not *because they do not care but because relationships are so thin and empty due to the cultural promotion and celebration of selfishness and narcissism*."[8] But while we might mourn whatever degree of isolation and alienation comes from this diminishment of relationship, what is so *politically* important about attachments?

Given the political and social impacts of feelings, Day argues that reclaiming our capacity to feel for each other, to love one another, is an inherently political activity. It serves as a means of combating the function of soul-crushing structures at their most personal level. This capacity to feel for each other is a function of what Day follows Audre Lorde in calling "the erotic." While this word can cause some discomfort in those who've yet to explore Lorde's powerful writings—and I've certainly seen my share of students and church folks struggle to make eye contact with others while discussing the erotic—to reduce the erotic to sexuality or sexual exploitation is to play along with that broader reduction of human connection to possession.[9] Reaching for something far larger and deeper than sexual desire, Day describes the erotic as "a passionate life force and creative energy that fuels all of our endeavors and loving acts of labor in the world."[10] The erotic is inherently bodily, fundamentally oriented toward mutuality, and in drawing us into community held together by "connection, desire, and freedom," resists discourses and institutions that both devalue the body as somehow incompatible with the pursuit of truth and bind those bodies in nonmutual, hierarchical relations.[11]

The erotic is political in that it is not simply a private feeling, but is "shaped by and in movement toward another person, idea, or object."[12] Such movement is not marked by the assumption of "a naïve 'oneness' or unity" but is "the struggle to respectfully work together toward justice even in the midst of our differences."[13]

The power of connection has turned apparent political impossibility into legal reality in my own community. During my years in Chicago, I have witnessed and—through my work with the Faith Liberation Movement of

The People's Lobby, a Chicago-area power organization—participated in the elimination of money bond through a massive organizing campaign that led to the passage of the Pretrial Fairness Act into Illinois state law. Through the efforts of thousands of people, money bond—a practice that sits precisely at the intersection of racial and economic injustice—has been abolished in Illinois.[14] Ordinary people knocked on doors, texted and called their neighbors, contributed their legal and political expertise, spoke up on social media and in the news, and raised money to make all of this work sustainable for many of those who made this campaign their job. Confronted by large-scale campaigns to prevent the passage of this law or undermine it through amendments, these ordinary people persisted.

At the root of all this organizing work was *relationship*. People got to know one another and helped one another recognize the ways in which the issue of cash bond impacted them. We developed a collective sense that money bond—ostensibly a safety measure—made our communities more fragile, that it was wearing away the fabric of mutuality and care that makes a neighborhood a place filled with neighbors. We could recognize that money bond was contributing to the hostility in our city that makes our churches feel like shelters from an uncaring city instead of spaces of rest and formation from which we go out to do the work to which we've been called.

Again and again across the United States, we are sold the idea that our communities would be safer if cleared of those deemed undesirable, whether or not they have been convicted of a crime. In Illinois, we instead embraced the idea that our communities will be safer if we fight to hold them together. Love was both the goal and the means by which this campaign was won. Love, growing slowly through the formation of relationships and increasing attachment to our communities, overcame a key pillar in the structure of interracial enmity. I have witnessed the power of the erotic in my own community, and I am sure that anyone reading this book can find examples of how ordinary, if organized, people have overcome injustice in their community too.

As politically transformative as the erotic and embracing connection can be, there is more to Day's account of the political power of love. Day warns of the way that the erotic can be misused, as we might expect, given the corruptive influence of white supremacy on love. This transformative power of desire and connection is never free of the potential for consumeristic corruption or restriction to those with whom we most easily find connection. The power that might bring us together can instead be a dangerous source of distrust and disconnection, leaving people to be fearful of those with whom they've been taught they cannot build community and "unable to be vulnerable and 'love big' within their social contexts."[15]

The key to combating this misuse of the erotic, and the distrust and disconnection it breeds, is the way in which loving rightly is perceiving rightly. Day describes the power of love as a mode of perception as follows:

> Love reframes and expands our vision of ourselves and others so that we are able to trust and consider the interests of others. Love is not merely external acts (although there is an external component) but an internal attitude in which one's vision is re-ordered toward what is truly moral and ethical. And this love is not concerned with the results or "fruits" of such love. The task is "loving forth" love in others. For example, when being rooted in love, one can see the possibilities of the good in one's neighbor, even enemy, rather than embracing a radical distrust of others. One can also love without being desirous of something in return. To be certain, this internal attitude sponsored by love is not a naïve acceptance but an open-eyed ethic of right relationships that understands the call individuals have to love others without reservation.[16]

This mode of perception, capable of drawing forth love in others, demands that we shift from focusing entirely on what we perceive in others to how we have been trained to perceive them to begin with. The extent to which each person is shaped *by* love to perceive others *in*—and thereby transform others *through*—love grounds the practice of love in a community.[17] Drawing on Black feminists and her fellow womanists, Day describes love as a "*politics* of claiming, embracing, and restoring marginalized, subjugated subjects (such as Black women) within personal and political relationships." Flowing through individuals and into communities, love is a public and political practice that enables new, alternative forms of community by drawing individuals toward each other through powerful connections that are enabled by the perception of love.[18]

PRIDEFUL LOVE

Love can open up possibilities for living differently, insofar as it is a mode of perception, but it can also sustain the ways of living that are revealed through that transformed perception. Hope, after all, is not self-sustaining in the face of a world that reacts to attempts to live into otherwise possibilities by abandoning them, starving them of resources, isolating them from broader community, and deploying economic, cultural, and armed violence to bear against them.[19] It is because of his ability to articulate the power of a *prideful* love to sustain Black life—ever a way of being otherwise in an anti-Black world—that I turn to the essays of James Baldwin.

Though he died in 1987, Baldwin taps into the ongoing reality that throughout our experiences of joy and connection, day-to-day life as a Black person is a matter of endurance and persistence. Anti-Blackness leaves its mark on Black lives whether we actively oppose the systems through which it works, do our best to achieve success through the performance of whiteness, or simply try to take things one day at a time. Reflecting on the gradual crushing of his father's spirit and its poisoning by increasing bitterness, Baldwin and his glorious gift with words captured this demand for Black endurance and persistence in a single phrase: "the weight of white people in the world." This weight—which we might understand as a common Black perception of the state of enmity in which we live—is a terrible imposition with which Black people in the United States have had to live for generations,[20] and Baldwin illuminates four of the ways it manifests itself in the lives of many Black people.

First, the close association between whiteness and qualities such as competence, reliability, and authority means that Black people's encounters with people in positions of power *are* encounters with whiteness. Whether seeking a loan, applying for a job, seeking medical care, asking a question to a teacher—or, perhaps most obviously, when confronted with a police officer—such encounters with whiteness demand that a Black person has a keen awareness of what whiteness expects of them and, as Baldwin puts it, produce that expected behavior "with disarming artlessness."[21] This performance must, in other words, come across as entirely free of bitterness, resentment, deceit, or manipulation.

In the 1950s, Baldwin had in mind the near ubiquity of white people in positions of power, both petty and grand. Considered in our contemporary context as sketched in chapter 1, however, it is clear that these encounters with whiteness do not only happen when we encounter white people. The most reliable path to positional power is the performance of whiteness, such that an encounter with a Black person in a position of power is still likely to be an encounter with whiteness and its demands. The January 7, 2023, murder of Tyre Nichols by five Black Memphis police officers offers a grim example of the performance of whiteness by Black bodies.[22] The weight of whiteness—not simply white people—in the world presses down on Black people in every encounter with power. It demands that we work to make those in positions of power trust and like us, lest we find ourselves fully captured by the stereotyped images and feelings our skin brings to mind.[23] To be Black in the United States is to live in constant awareness of the ways in which a stray word said in an angry tone, a lingering gaze, or the admission of some measure of self-doubt can cause a carefully constructed life to crumble with terrifying speed. That awareness and the behaviors it inspires are exhausting.

Second, the weight of whiteness in the world forces Black people to struggle for identity and even a sense of our own basic worth. To name this struggle *as struggle* is not to claim that Blackness is continual self-doubt and self-hatred. Rather, it is to stress that whiteness intervenes in the hard work of self-discovery and self-affirmation, actively working to deny the possibility that such pursuits are possible for Black people. This interference takes place not only through the cultural violence enacted through the widespread depiction of Black people as criminals or through the tension created by the encounters with whiteness described above but also through the encounters with well-meaning white people who believe they're offering solidarity when what they truly offer is paternalism.[24] Insofar as a given Black person might adopt a role that helps them to get some breathing room while being hounded by whiteness, Baldwin warns that in playing such roles, we run the risk of accepting those roles as definitive of our identity.[25] Survival, identity, and the basic sense that one has worth are routinely placed in tension with one another as the weight of whiteness asserts itself in Black lives.

The third way in which this weight makes itself known has been woven throughout the previous two: Black parents are placed in the difficult position of preparing our children for a world structured by white supremacy and anti-Blackness. On the one hand, Black parents have to teach our children to survive in a world where being Black is sufficient cause for their state-sanctioned murder. This drive to pass down these lessons of survival is not *only* the result of intergenerational trauma, recalling the threat to enslaved children or the threat of lynching in the Jim Crow decades following emancipation. We cannot dismiss our caution as a collective haunting by the bereaved ghost of Mamie Till-Mobley, mourning her murdered son and warning us to beware whiteness. The threat to our children is real, ongoing, and aggressive.

Police officers still kill our children. A 2020 study that reviewed death certificates from across the United States found that Black children are six times more likely to be shot to death by police than white children.[26] Here in Chicago, the 2014 murder of Laquan McDonald drew national attention when it resulted in a Chicago police officer being charged with murder for shooting someone while on duty for the first time in fifty years. McDonald—seventeen years old at the time of his death—was shot sixteen times as he walked away from his murderer, whose name is as reviled in this city as McDonald's is lifted up with reverence and lament.[27]

My father—a Black police officer himself—took it upon himself to pass on these lessons about the threat of anti-Blackness. One way he imparted these lessons was by playing a pair of games with me during my early teen years.

The first game was played at the mall (Honey Creek Mall, for those in the know). This educational game had two unspoken rules and a victory condition that was only ever confirmed when we shared playful, knowing looks with one another.

> Rule one: Stand behind a white woman who's sitting on one of the mall benches.
> Rule two: Don't do anything aggressive . . . you know, aside from being Black male bodies in relative proximity.
> Victory: The woman draws her purse close, then walks quickly away. (We always won.)
> Lesson: My body is inherently threatening, and the burden is on me to allay the fears of the white people who could make life difficult, even impossible, for me.

The second game was played at various big box stores in our town. It had two rules and a somewhat more explicit victory condition.

> Rule one: Walk around the store.
> Rule two: Do not touch any merchandise unless it is going into our shopping cart.
> Victory: I correctly identify the loss-prevention employee—that is, the person employed by the store to watch for shoplifters—who would inevitably start following two Black males through the store.
> Lesson: Even if I think I'm just going about my day with no intention of causing any trouble, police and their various civilian adjuncts will be watching me closely.

Baldwin lays out the dynamic behind these lessons, or "the talk" that so many Black parents (including my father and me) give our children, in which we explain that if the police accost them, they are not to resist, talk back, or even give them a dirty look. On the one hand, the compulsion we feel to give our kids "the talk" betrays that behind Black parents' authority "stands another, nameless and impersonal, infinitely harder to please, and bottomlessly cruel." This cruel authority demands that however much their parents adore them or know that they are innocent, Black children must learn that they are not allowed to behave as if their innocence can be taken for granted, as white children do.[28]

On the other hand—if we can set aside the reality that parenting feels like it takes ten or twenty hands—even as Black parents must show our children what it is to be despised by the world, we are confronted with the task of creating in our children "a stronger antidote to this poison" than we have found for ourselves.[29] Addressing his baby nephew, Baldwin wrote, "Here you were: to be loved. To be loved, baby, hard, at once, and forever, to strengthen you against the loveless world."[30]

Even as we have to teach our children to respect that the law of this land ever threatens to crush them, we have to grapple with the truth that to teach our children to *truly* respect that law—to accept that it has moral authority over them and deserves to operate uncontested—is to raise them to give up something crucial, to cede their self-respect in the face of anti-Blackness.[31] Baldwin characterizes Black parenting—insofar as it is an awakening of children to the tension in which they will live and, by awakening them, offering them some chance at finding a new way to live in that tension—as being "the custodian of an inheritance." We prepare our children to fight a war for their souls, knowing that our children will have to fight that war long before their parents can lay down our burdens.[32]

I can speak with firsthand experience of this tension and the weight I feel pressing down on me as, for example, my children play in a public park where police cars regularly linger (I wonder if they stay there in hopes of keeping kids safe). I want my kids to grow up free of the worry my father instilled in me. But I see those police officers right there, I see my kids getting bigger year by year, and I can't help wondering when playfighting with sticks will start to look like assault. In fact, I can't help wondering if it already has. Each time my kids play in public, I feel the pressure to constrain their play, to dampen their excitement and joy, to limit their freedom, to go back over "the talk" or have a yet-more-mature version of it, to make it clear that they can't be kids in the same way as the white kids playing in the same park.[33]

The fourth way in which Baldwin describes the weight of whiteness in the world bearing down on Black people is in how it incessantly presses rage and hatred into Black lives, not least as a response to our awareness of how race took something from us even as children. Baldwin presents this rage as universal, leaving us to choose between living with it reluctantly and giving in to it altogether.[34] As this rage—experienced by many, if perhaps not truly all, Black people—is potentially lethal, Black people are left with the need to regularly hide it. However, Baldwin suggests that Black rage is simply too deep to be fully hidden,[35] even as he denies that we ought to simply accept rage.[36] Ultimately, rage is passed down generation to generation[37] as part of the burdensome, trauma-tinged inheritance of which Black parents are sacred custodians.

This discussion of the weight of whiteness in the world is hardly exhaustive. These are, after all, only four ways in which white supremacy and anti-Blackness work to crush Black people. Neither is this discussion—or Baldwin's work, brilliantly insightful as it is—fully representative of all Black people's experiences. Further, while these insights are articulated artfully by Baldwin, they are hardly unique to him. Why, then, do I bother turning to Baldwin at this turning point in my book?

The answer is simple: while delving into the difficulties and injustices that are part of Black lives, Baldwin's work simultaneously identifies and analyzes the powerful presence of love in those same Black lives. It might seem, given Baldwin's career-long preoccupation with these four burdens of Black life, that Baldwin would hardly be able to offer much in the way of hope-sustaining love. Indeed, it might seem that Baldwin could offer nothing more than the scars of intergenerational trauma. However, like Keri Day, Baldwin demonstrates how to hold acute awareness of enmity together with belief in a politically transformative love. Along with Day, Baldwin reveals how we might endure the weight of white people in the world while actively living into the alternative world that is the Kindom of God.

Guided in this search for love by the attentive reading of English professor and Baldwin scholar Ed Pavlić, I turn to a rich passage in which Baldwin muses on his father's funeral and gets to the heart of this tension between awareness of enmity and openness to love: "It began to seem that one would have to hold in the mind forever two ideas which seemed to be in opposition. The first idea was acceptance, the acceptance, totally without rancor, of life as it is, and men [*sic*] as they are: in the light of this idea, it goes without saying that injustice is a commonplace. But this did not mean that one could be complacent, for the second idea was of equal power: that one must never, in one's own life, accept these injustices as commonplace but must fight them with all one's strength."[38]

The need to navigate this tension without giving in to either of these challenging ideas is necessitated, for Baldwin, by twin truths: first, that hatred destroys the one who hates and, second, that love does not come easily when the world is so ready to deal out hate to the one who loves.[39]

Caught in this tension, Black people who would reject the self-destruction promised by hatred are left with a hard choice, once we realize just how poisonous hatred is: "One is always in the position of having to decide between amputation and gangrene. Amputation is swift but time may prove that the amputation was not necessary—or one may delay the amputation too long. Gangrene is slow, but it is impossible to be sure that one is reading one's symptoms right."[40]

Pavlić elucidates the two alternatives Baldwin offers as responses to the weight of whiteness in the world—amputation and gangrene—as follows. On the one hand, Black people can try to cut off any engagement with whiteness (amputation)—even if we might not be able to avoid contact with people committed to the performance of whiteness—and deconstruct the effects whiteness has had on our self-understanding. On the other hand, we can attempt to mitigate the poisonous effects of continued negotiation with whiteness (gangrene) in the hopes that its cultural near-ubiquity and endless efforts to infiltrate our relationships will not undercut our efforts.[41] With these two options before us, even the attempt to free ourselves from the burden of hatred simply adds one of two new burdens to Black life, without eliminating the others.

How, then, are Black people to not only endure under all these burdens but also strive for a world in which we might no longer bear them at all, refusing to hand them over to our children? Pavlić takes Baldwin's amputation/gangrene dichotomy as a point of entry into Baldwin's method of managing the tension between awareness of enmity and openness to otherwise possibilities. Ultimately, Baldwin believed that amputation was an illusory possibility, that "one can, indeed, die from gangrene even in a phantom limb." To attempt amputation is to delude oneself into believing it is possible to cut off engagement with whiteness, thereby ignoring the eventual cause of one's death. Baldwin sought to find a means of tolerating the risks of gangrene in the hope that a viable path to Black flourishing free from the weight of whiteness might be found.[42]

And in the means Baldwin found, perhaps painfully aware of the burdens of Black life and the risks of gangrene, we come to the heart of what he offers us: a powerful notion of prideful love. Baldwin understood pride as the refusal to rely on the world for the social change one believes necessary, paired with a corresponding commitment to work toward such change oneself. Passed down by Black parents along with all the rest of our troubled inheritance, pride is formed deep within an individual, granting autonomy as they work for change. Such autonomy cannot exist in isolation, however, lest it slip into romantic fantasy and lead pride to work only to soothe vain pretensions of heroism. For pride to create the change it enables its possessor to seek, it requires connection.[43] Understood in light of Keri Day's exploration of the erotic, pride comes into focus as an aspect of that relational erotic power, that energy that draws us together in politically powerful networks of desire and mutuality.

Working to endure the weight of whiteness without giving in to hatred for white people, what Baldwin sought was a way to bring together the personal power of individual pride and the sustaining, politically transformative power of human social connection.[44] What he found was that the very change within the depths of an individual's being that enables pride to come to life is itself dependent on interaction with others. Pride draws its strength from the well of erotic power and comes to life in working together with others to build community, sticking together to sustain that community, and having one's gifts and efforts recognized and affirmed by one's community.[45]

The longing to connect with another that is love and the deep, enduring strength that is pride are mutually necessary. Pride without love becomes vain romance, and love without pride is doomed to die in a world in which white supremacy and anti-Blackness ever work to corrupt our capacity for connection. Only a prideful love can sustain us as we endure the burdens of Black life and strive to maintain our openness to otherwise possibilities. Such love could only be—to linger just a bit longer with Baldwin's beautiful words—a miracle able "to outlast death, which can cause life to spring from death."[46]

CONCLUSION

Together, then, Day and Baldwin point us toward a Black love, love that thrives in the imposing, nurturing space of possibility and power that is Blackness. Day's model of politically transformative love casts love as a politically engaged practice of perception that facilitates the formation of meaningful connection. Baldwin's model of prideful love emphasizes how love both strengthens individuals and draws them ever more strongly into connection with others. These two understandings of love share an emphasis on connection and the erotic energy that compels us to seek one another out and form bonds of mutual care. This erotic power of connection and care thrives in Blackness, in the midst of that which anti-Blackness would deem unlivable and worthless, and is thus the space from which we can imagine and live into radical alternatives to a world in which life and worth are defined by whiteness.

So—to more directly address the central concern of this book—is this Black love responsive to the problems we encounter in antiracist work? Let's recall the two central, related problems that drove chapters 1 and 2: that Christian antiracist work has, first, failed to recognize that interracial enmity is structural and, second, accepted as its heart a distorted notion of love.

Where Christian antiracist work has struggled to recognize interracial enmity for what it is—structural opposition of the material interests of people of different races, in the context of an inherently competitive set of systems—Day and Baldwin each articulate their understandings of love directly in response to structural interracial enmity, demonstrating the ways in which Black love thrives precisely in its capacity to respond to the powers that seek to deny us the possibility of a life-giving love. In its fundamental responsiveness to structural interracial enmity, Black love resists the temptation to offer easy comfort by making love and enmity private matters. Like all emotion, Black love flows between the individual and the communal in an affective current of mutual formation and transformation. As such, Black love draws individuals into ever-broadening networks of connection. These networks form the fabric of a community that is not only committed to overcoming the constraints enmity places on our flourishing but is also capable of taking effective transformative action precisely on the basis of the strength of those networks of connection.

Where Christian antiracist work has been hijacked by a distorted love that undermines antiracist work by centering white happiness and comfort, Black love offers a firmer ground for politically transformative antiracist work in three ways. First, rather than reinforcing the relations of privilege, exploitation, and violence that constitute interracial enmity, Black love is oriented toward the needs of *all* in the community and held accountable to the pride that compels each person to seek out transformative community. Rather than promoting practices of forced forgiveness and unceasing affirmation that prioritize white happiness over anyone's wholeness—including the wholeness of white people whose capacity for connection is inhibited by white fragility and moral injury—Black love is capable of sustaining a steady process of critique and adaptation. Rather than reinforcing conformity by fostering fear, shame, and optimism, Black love maintains this process of critique and adaptation by nurturing the steely pride of a community's many members.

Second, love as distorted by white supremacy falters and ultimately fails as the work of antiracism gets hard. Black love, by contrast, draws on pride and connection to promote an enduring network of mutual encouragement and care. It has demonstrated this across generations and in a wide range of political contexts, from the subversive, secretive work of building community under conditions of slavery to the loud, public protest of the Movement for Black Lives. It is not by avoiding discomfort and difficulty that Black love facilitates mutual care but by gathering the community to face discomfort and difficulty together, leaning on one another for strength, courage, and compassion.

Finally, Black love undercuts the marginalization of "negative" emotions demanded by distorted love. This third point brings us to the heart of the politically transformative power of Black love. The power of Black love—politically transformative, prideful love—is a matter of affect, capable of addressing structural interracial enmity by drawing together the political power of connection and the emotional resources required for enduring resilience.

If I might try to capture its power in a single phrase, Black love serves as the foundation for an alternative *affective* world. As we strive to live into otherwise possibilities, living as if we are already entering into alternatives to a world structured by structural interracial enmity, Black love facilitates our access to an entire range of ways of feeling and thinking that are appropriate to those alternative worlds. The rage that is a potentially poisonous response to whiteness, when harnessed by Black love, can be channeled against white supremacist institutions through collective action and practices of communal accountability. The sorrow that we rightly feel in looking on Black suffering can be shared and received with a politically engaged compassion, deepening the relationships on which we depend for politically transformative action. The happiness we find in music or play can similarly serve to strengthen our bonds of love rather than serving as insulation in our attempts to look away from an ailing world or numb our awareness of our own suffering.

Black love is politically transformative. Should Christians, however, consider it *faithful* love? What does this prideful, politically engaged love have to do with God? To satisfy this second pressing concern regarding the theological viability of a love of the enemy that is both politically powerful and faithful, I turn in the next chapter to one of the most significant Christian theologians of love: James H. Cone.

CHAPTER FIVE

James Cone, Theologian of Love

Black love is political, prideful, and powerful. It is capable of thriving in the awareness of enmity, fostering transformative connections in community, and sustaining us through the emotional challenges of confronting white supremacy and anti-Blackness. If anything might make it possible to engage in long-term, effective antiracist work, it seems like Black love can. But, powerful as it may be, is Black love well-suited for *Christian* antiracist work?

For many, it is by no means certain that Black love is theologically compatible with the revelation of our creator, redeemer, and sustainer in Jesus Christ, the revelation that draws us together *as Christians*. Those whose faith is rooted in the traditions of the Black Church may find this politically engaged Black love familiar—though it is by no means a universal constant of Black faith—and may take it for granted that politics and pride are compatible with Christian faith. However, I have found that even Black Christians balk when they are asked to discuss love while also embracing the claim that structural interracial enmity is intractable, that people of different races truly are enemies *even if they all believe in Jesus*. Fortunately, there is a Black theologian who consistently articulated Christian love as politically transformative and deeply rooted in pride while maintaining a clear awareness of structural interracial enmity from his early career until his death: James Cone.

A QUICK INTRODUCTION TO JAMES CONE

James H. Cone was a theologian and ordained AME pastor who is widely acknowledged as the father of Black liberation theology, a theological perspective that draws on and holds itself accountable to Black people's experiences in light of Jesus's presence in the midst of Black communities. He was also a foundational mentor to me, along with many other students whom he taught during his decades at Union Theological Seminary (NYC) until his death in 2018. I'm no biographer—and Cone wrote fairly extensively about his life and the place of his theology within it[1]—so I'll get to the heart of the matter and highlight two theological claims that are both central to Cone's Black liberation theology and essential to understanding his insights into love.

First, Cone proclaims that the God who took on flesh in Jesus Christ is a God of liberation. The God revealed in the Bible, Cone argues, is a God who frees an enslaved people in the exodus and demonstrates a consistent concern for those poor and oppressed via the prophets.[2] Crucially, "in Christ, God enters human affairs and takes sides with the oppressed. Their suffering becomes [God's]; their despair, divine despair."[3] In fact, God so profoundly identifies with those oppressed that God embraces their experience as God's own experience. This is true not only during Jesus's first-century life but in all times. As such, Cone insists that to be able to say that the God enfleshed in Jesus is a God of liberation, we must also say that God is Black, wholly identified with those who are profoundly oppressed here and now.[4]

In describing God as Black, Cone recognizes that "the reality of God cannot be limited to a particular human experience."[5] Cone's insistent declaration of God's Blackness follows his contention that "because God is not less than our experience of the divine, we must speak with an absoluteness that does not compromise with evil, despite the relativity of our claims." For Cone, if Black people encounter God in the midst of God's intimate participation in our lives as we struggle for liberation, then that encounter must definitively shape our proclamation about God. We can and must proclaim that God has taken on our condition as God's own.[6] We must, in other words, proclaim that the God of liberation is Black.

Second, just as Cone proclaims that God is Black, he witnesses to Jesus as the Black Christ. This is not a claim about any possible African ancestry of Jesus of Nazareth. Rather, Cone argues that Jesus is Black because he was born into a first-century Jewish community suffering under Roman occupation. Whatever the specific details of his ancestry, Jesus was fully present to the oppressed people with whom God had made a covenant and is fully present today to those oppressed.[7] As God is Black through God's identification with the oppressed, so, too, is Jesus.

Cone grounds his proclamation of Jesus as the Black Christ in his reading of the Gospels. Jesus was born into an oppressed people. He was baptized to align himself with sinners, then wandered into the desert to refuse the temptations of "oppressive or self-glorifying power." Jesus proclaimed God's "unqualified identification with the poor precisely because they are poor," endured the fullness of oppression through his execution on the cross, and through his resurrection revealed both God's rejection of death's power and God's unending commitment to liberation. When we ask where Jesus is at work today, then, we must look to those among whom we know Jesus chose to spend his life. For Cone, this meant that we could unequivocally proclaim that Jesus was to be found in the Black community, continuing his work of embodying God's identification with those oppressed. This identification is so complete that Jesus not only loves Black people but *is* Black.[8]

Before moving on, I'm going to pause to make a point that's important enough to break the flow of my argument and too important to be buried in an endnote that most folks won't read: Cone's understanding of Jesus's Blackness does not have to mean that Jesus's Jewishness is *only* significant in its relation to oppression. However, Cone certainly should have done more to emphasize that point. Cone's theology lends itself too easily to a kind of supersessionism, though one in which election is demonstrated by suffering oppression rather than by claiming dominion over the world through conquest. I understand Cone's discussion of the connection between Jesus's Jewishness and Blackness in the context of Cone's theological approach as mentioned above: the need to speak with absoluteness—absolutely rejecting the idea that Jesus is not wholly identified with Black people today—while maintaining the humility necessary to recognize that God's reality is always more than we could name, however expansive our efforts. For Cone, Jesus is Black because he was a Jew, but I do not think Cone meant that we must discard Jesus's Jewishness on any level, nor should we do so regardless of Cone's intent.

God is a God of liberation, which means that God is *wholly* identified with those oppressed. Jesus is the Black Christ, the embodiment of God's complete identification with those oppressed in all times and places, including in a US context defined by interracial enmity. These are two core claims in James Cone's Black liberation theology, and they are essential to understanding how his theology is a profoundly powerful theology of love.

They are also why at least some of you are probably asking: Could that theology really be a theology of love? In particular, while we certainly shouldn't center the needs of white people to the exclusion of others', it might seem like Cone's theology could not have any room at all for white people. Before addressing that concern, and as another step toward understanding Cone's theology as a theology of love, I'm first going to turn to the work of Martin Luther King Jr., a theologian who's more readily recognized as a theologian of love.

PRIDEFUL BLACK LOVE IN THE WORK OF MARTIN LUTHER KING JR.

James Cone was clear—in both his teaching and his writing—that his own theological perspective was definitively shaped by two figures: Martin Luther King Jr. and El-Hajj Malik El-Shabazz (most well-known as Malcolm X). In fact, Cone wrote an entire book that used these two giants of Black politics and religion to better understand one another. In *Martin & Malcolm & America*, Cone succinctly expresses the influence of King and Shabazz on his theology: "I am an African-American theologian whose perspective on the Christian religion was shaped by Martin King and whose black consciousness was defined by Malcolm X. In more than twenty years of writing and teaching black liberation theology, I have been attempting to relate Malcolm X and Martin King to Christian living in America, seeking to show that *justice* and *blackness* are essential ingredients in the identity of Christian faith for African-Americans."[9] Cone's basic theological commitments, as highlighted in the previous section, reflect this influence. Crucially, Cone's unshakable belief that God loves Black people fiercely and forever reflects that influence.

I imagine that this acknowledgment of King's significance, specifically—if not the basic topic of this book—spurs some readers to ask an obvious question: Why isn't this chapter about King to begin with? Well, in part it's because I was not King's student; I was Cone's! I met James Cone at an important formative point in my faith journey, and he helped me to bring together the commitment to justice with which my parents had raised me and the faith in Jesus that was a much more recent development. Cone, in short, helped me to understand how my faith could actually deepen my desire for justice rather than constantly working to convince me that things I knew to be unjust were faithful. As Cone now lives on as a beloved ancestor through his words and his students, I both honor his impact on my life and hope to amplify that impact as I am able. As I hope you will agree by the end of this chapter, Cone's theology has much to offer those who would follow Jesus by loving their enemies.

There are two reasons for my prioritization of Cone over King that go beyond my fidelity as a student to my cherished mentor. First, there is a pressing danger in King's understanding of *agape*, self-sacrificial love. Like many others, King takes 1 John 4:8 seriously and proclaims that God *is* love, "the great unifying force of life."[10] Overflowing from God's own being, King proclaims, love is a gift freely given to humanity. That love is properly received through obedience that is enabled by the power of faith to open the human heart to God's transformative power.[11] King famously uses the Greek word *agape* to describe this love that overflows from the being of God and marks the participation of the faithful in God's being. *Agape* is not a matter of affection or romance. Rather, as God's love working in human lives, *agape* "means understanding, redeeming good will for all [humanity], an overflowing love which seeks nothing in return."[12] It reacts to the need of the other—especially the "enemy-neighbor from whom you can expect no good in return"—to be loved and to belong "to the best in the human family." *Agape* will go to any length to restore community, as seen on the cross, "the eternal expression of the length to which God will go in order to restore broken community." King understands this divine, self-sacrificing love as the expression of real and definitive divine power and consequently the source of power for nonviolent political action.[13]

Here is the problem: for King, God is love, and love is *agape*, which leads King to accept *agape* as an unqualified good. For King, that overflowing gift from the very being of God is necessarily pure. However, insofar as we might think of humans' self-sacrificing love for one another as a response to God's love for humanity, this kind of love is far from flawless. *Agape* can harm both the lover and the beloved. Genuine, self-giving love can take the shape of surrogacy,[14] and mutually destructive relations can take the place of mutuality.

To question the purity of *agape* is not to question the sincerity of that love. Rather, as I discussed in chapter 2, it is to insist that love is morally ambiguous. Faith-driven self-sacrifice simply is not proof against exploitation. Thus, even as I lift up love as a practice to which Christians are called, I will insist that self-sacrifice ought not be understood as the essence of that love. Self-sacrifice is, at most, simply one possible practical manifestation of faithful love.

Even if we find a place for self-sacrifice—and thus King's theology—in our own understandings of love, there is a second reason to turn away from King, who is exalted by many as the definitive theologian of antiracist love. Namely, as we work to radically rethink love after its distortion by white supremacy and anti-Blackness, there is value in turning toward one whose ideas about love have largely gone unrecognized *as ideas about love.* After all, when trying to understand the power of love in antiracist work, we turn to King only partly because he preached, wrote, and practiced love in a compelling way. In large part, we turn to King because of his larger-than-life stature and the weight that stature lends to our own efforts to make meaningful progress in our antiracist work.

In the long racial history of the United States, King stands as a kind of messianic hero who demonstrated how love could someday overcome hate, who gave his life so that others might be free. King proclaimed that love fueled the movement that lifted him up as its most prominent leader, and we are right to believe him, *in part.* Love fueled the civil rights movement, but that love was not *agape*, as obvious as the willingness to submit to self-sacrifice was among those who marched, sang, prayed, and sat in.

There was a deeper love at work in the movement that surrounded King. This deeper love not only empowered self-sacrificial commitments and actions but also empowered the day-to-day work of movement-building that made the difference between discrete acts of martyrdom and the building of a movement. That deeper love was the erotic power described by Keri Day,[15] bringing people together and building politically transformative networks.

Tied into this misrecognition of love is the transcendent imagination of beloved community that churches so often center as the ideal toward which antiracist work is directed. Jennifer Harvey points out the danger with this notion in the context of her critique of the reconciliation paradigm—the idea that racial separation is the primary problem of race, with togetherness as its solution[16]—with particular emphasis on the problem beloved community poses among white Christians. To be clear, Harvey rejects the idea that King's beloved community is "a sentimental vision of unity and love," as King could not imagine this community grounded in love coming into being "without the prior actualization of freedom and justice."[17] However, while acknowledging that it is possible white Christians *believe* they are drawn to King's imagination of beloved community in its fullness, Harvey argues that in settling for the flawed reconciliation paradigm, white Christians have spent decades running away from the challenge of Black Power to a greater extent than they've embraced King's theological and ethical imagination.[18]

Between the dangers of *agape* and the perilous insinuation of distorted love into King's legacy—wrongly embracing love that sets white happiness and comfort as the criteria for what is considered loving—the need for an alternative theology of love looms large. And while Cone's theology will ultimately leave us with some more work to do, my contention is that he can get Christian antiracist work closer to a transformative theology of love than it has found by returning again and again to King. So while there is certainly merit in the work of reimagining King's legacy or retrieving what is most transformative in that legacy,[19] clinging too tightly to King's legacy just doesn't get us where we need to go. Rather, that dependence is a trap into which Christian antiracist work keeps stumbling, priming its participants to succumb to distorted love.

Nonetheless, to highlight as clearly as possible Cone's theology *as a theology of love*, it is important to draw out in King's work a core theme that is too often overshadowed by attention to *agape* and beloved community: prideful Black love, grounded in certainty of one's worthiness and oriented toward connection with others. This mode of love comes through with particular clarity in three elements of King's work, as expressed in his writings.

First, King demonstrates a desire to preserve the hearts of Black people from the poison of hatred. His rejection of hatred toward one's enemies is well-known and often emphasized: "Hate is just as injurious to the person who hates. Like an unchecked cancer, hate corrodes the personality and eats away its vital unity. Hate destroys a [person's] sense of values and [their] objectivity. It causes [them] to describe the beautiful as ugly and the ugly as beautiful, and to confuse the true with the false and the false with the true."[20]

In the same sermon, King goes on to lament the impact of hatred on white people who found themselves unable to recognize Black people as their equals. It is clear, though, that his concern is not solely, or even first, with the souls of white folk. Rather, he is preaching as a leader to his own community, warning them that they, too, could succumb to the soul sickness they witnessed at work in white people. Even as King describes love as self-sacrificing, he holds love for white enemies accountable to Black folks' concern for our own well-being. This balance is reflected in his understanding of the nonviolent resistance in which *agape* is to be manifested: "I am sure that many of our white brothers in Montgomery and across the South are still bitter toward Negro leaders, even though these leaders have sought to follow a way of love and nonviolence. So the nonviolent approach does not immediately change the heart of the oppressor. It first does something to the hearts and souls of those committed to it. It gives them new self-respect; it calls up resources of strength and courage that they did not know they had. Finally, it reaches the opponent and so stirs his conscience that reconciliation becomes a reality."[21] Like Baldwin,[22] King wanted Black people to love our white enemies not simply for their sake. He longed to protect our pride and basic capacity to love in the context of overwhelming anti-Blackness.

Further, as shown in that same passage, King strove to combat Black self-hatred by building up Black self-respect. In describing the state of the movement at the founding of SCLC,[23] King praised what he perceived as an ongoing change in Black people since the days of slavery: a rising unwillingness to accept "injustice and exploitation," connected with a growing sense that every Black person is "somebody," a beloved child of God whose dignity demanded the destruction of segregation.[24] And despite his early conviction that nonviolent resistance would persuade white people of Black somebodiness—a conviction that waned as King's disillusionment with US American virtue waxed—King rejected the idea that Black freedom fighters were dependent on white paternalism for their struggle, proclaiming that "the most powerful force that is breaking down the barriers of segregation is the new determination of the Negro."[25]

Second, King's concern for the well-being of Black people was not only spiritual but material. He did not stress the importance of self-sacrifice solely for the sake of Black folks' moral purity. Rather, he understood himself as following the model of Jesus: "Upheaval after upheaval has reminded us that modern [humanity] is traveling along a road called hate, in a journey that will bring us to destruction and damnation. Far from being the pious injunction of a Utopian dreamer, the command to love one's enemy is an absolute necessity for our survival. Love even for enemies is the key to the solution of the problems of our world. Jesus is not an impractical idealist: he is the practical realist."[26]

Beyond this question of human survival at large, King was deeply committed to the material—particularly economic—well-being of Black people, for whom he would come to demand "an economic bill of rights" in the context of the 1968 Poor People's Campaign.[27] King wanted Black people to survive and thrive and believed self-sacrificing love of the enemy embodied in nonviolent resistance was the only way to transform society for the better.[28] For King, love of the white enemy was the slow and exhausting, but sure, path to spiritual and material salvation for Black people. Insofar as King was concerned with the possibilities of redemption for white people, that concern cannot be understood to overshadow his commitment to Black well-being and the prideful Black love in which it was grounded.

Third, King demonstrated prideful Black love through the integrity of his leadership. While King often appealed to the conscience of white US Americans and backed away from violent means of resistance and revolution, he demonstrated a keen awareness of the dangers of working with the white political establishment. Responding to the critiques of Black Power, King lamented that "a glaring weakness in Negro life is lack of sufficient mutual confidence and trust." He attributed this weakness to the skill of white leaders in "flattering and cultivating" Black leaders, who would then change "from the representative of the Negro to the white man into the white man's representative to the Negro." Recognizing an important dimension of the critique represented by Black Power, King expressed the need for "organizations that are permeated with mutual trust, incorruptibility and militancy."[29]

Throughout his ministry, King provided just this sort of incorruptible, militant leadership. In James Baldwin's analysis, King did not manipulate the political will of his followers for his own gain or for the benefit of white "allies." Rather, from the beginning of his ministry in Montgomery, "once he had accepted the place [his congregants] had prepared for him, their struggle became absolutely indistinguishable from his own, and took over and controlled his life." King embodied a prophetic courage that enabled him to follow prideful Black love into deeper connection with others, accompanying his people as he "suffered with them and, thus, he helped them to suffer."[30]

Over the decades, King has been twisted—by both bad-faith actors and well-meaning folks guided by distorted love—into a symbol of the potential for Black people to suffer endlessly while continuing to affirm white folks' innocence. However, even this quick pass through King's sermons and essays reveals the steady presence of prideful Black love in his ministry. And while I have not gone out of my way to demonstrate the politically engaged nature of King's practice of love, I trust that even the distorted image of King has failed to erase that aspect of Black love from his life. In King's life and work, we can recognize the presence of prideful and politically engaged Black love but not their full theological expression. We can now turn to James Cone's theology of love, in which he more fully fleshes out the theological dimensions of Black love.

JAMES CONE'S THEOLOGY OF LOVE

There is a powerfully prideful Black love at work in King—powerful enough to inspire pride in others, perhaps in an entire generation—but it is theologically entangled with his understanding of *agape* and all its dangers. Building on the elements of pride in King's work, James Cone offers a theology of love that situates Black love within an account of divine love without continuing the distortion of love by centering self-sacrifice (which consistently becomes BIPOC self-sacrifice in practice). While I contend that Cone's theology has love at its core, Cone differs from King in that he does not regularly highlight the role of love in his work. As such, we need to consider how love is woven throughout Cone's Black liberation theology and can do so by paying attention to the two key theological claims I outlined earlier.

First, God is a God of liberation, which means that God is *wholly* identified with the oppressed. Cone rejects any notion of a "God who is on everybody's side—which means that God loves everybody in spite of who they are."[31] God's love is inextricably tied to their work of liberation, which means that God's love is concentrated among those who most desperately need liberation from the unjust systems that constitute structural interracial enmity. God's love does not obey the universalist ethic critiqued by Jennifer Harvey, radiating to all people in an identical fashion. Rather, as God pours God's love into the hearts of Black people, this divine love assures us that we have worth in our Blackness "because God imparts value through loving." In return, this outpouring of love requires us to respond in faithful acceptance of God's affirmation, with pride that defies the images imposed on us by white supremacy. That pride demands the acknowledgment of Black worth by others, such that one cannot meaningfully speak of love apart from justice and power. For Cone, love is inconsistent with God's nature unless it empowers Black people to fully value ourselves as children of God. That means we cannot accept the distortion of love by white supremacy and anti-Blackness, settling for paternalism and the demands of white comfort and happiness. Rather, to respond to the love of the God of liberation at work in our lives is to love others as equals who are responsible for their actions, for their attitudes, and for affirming the fundamental goodness of God's Black children.[32]

At this point, we can return to the possible concern that Cone's theology of love is a theology of love that actively excludes white people. This is a concern that was raised early on in Cone's career by Black theologian J. Deotis

Roberts.[33] In the context of his efforts to relate liberation and reconciliation to one another, Roberts critiqued Cone, insisting that "Cone confesses an indifference toward whites" and attributing this unfaithful indifference to the idea that "James Cone is on the fence between the Christian faith and the religion of Black Power."[34]

Holding fast to Roberts's—and, more importantly, King's—language of reconciliation, Cone responds to Roberts's critique as follows: "Roberts opens the door not only for white people to be oppressors and Christians *at the same time*, but also for them to participate in black liberation and to set the *terms* of our reconciliation with them. This assumption is unbiblical and unhistorical. Indeed, in black history, reconciliation and liberation on white terms have always meant death for black people."[35] Cone further insists that Roberts fails to realize that "in his call for reconciliation alongside the theme of liberation, whites would hear *only* the former but completely disregard its connection with the latter."[36]

In this critique of Roberts, Cone demonstrates an awareness not only of the depth of the enmity between Black people and white people but also of the white moral injury described by Chanequa Walker-Barnes: the way in which interracial enmity limits the capacity of white people to even recognize racial injustice.[37] However, given the reality of distorted love, it is difficult to accept the very recognition of interracial enmity and white moral injury as compatible with the love that is at the heart of Christian theology. At least, that is the case if we are trapped within the that distortion of love that so frequently plagues Christian antiracist work.

Cone offers an alternative theology of love. I have already pointed out how Cone accounts for God's special love for Black people and the pride that love empowers within us. That pride, in turn, inspires us to oppose white supremacy. After all, white supremacy stands in the way of Black people pursuing the liberation that is inherent to the very being of the God of liberation. Let's follow Cone's theology of love a bit further now.

Cone imagines what I am calling prideful love—based on the acceptance of God's love for Black people—as a solid ground for the creation of a future for Black people.[38] Crucially, he insists, as King does in his later years, that this future of Black liberation cannot mean "a share or parity in the current American capitalist system."[39] Rather, the future Cone envisions is one in which the beauty of Blackness is accepted not only by Black people but by the entire US American nation.[40]

Far from excluding white people, Cone's Black liberation theology clearly articulates God's powerful love for white people *and holds that love accountable to his articulation of God's love for Black people and the manifestation of that love in Black liberation*. To lay out Cone's understanding of God's love for white people, it is best to work backward from how Black people might faithfully love white people to God's love for white people.

Cone insists that Black people practice love for our white enemies through resistance and the call to repentance.[41] This tight pairing of resistance and the call to repentance reflects the way in which Black love for white people relates to God's love for white people. Denying any sense that God does not love white people, Cone contends "that in a racist society, we must insist that God's love and God's righteousness are two ways of talking about the same reality. Righteousness means that God is addressing the black condition; love means that God is doing so in the interests of both blacks and whites."[42] After all, given God's fierce love for Black people, white people are not simply political adversaries of Black people. In accepting that political arrangement of enmity, white people set themselves against God, who takes the side of those oppressed.

In this society, defined so thoroughly by interracial enmity, Cone calls it "blasphemy to say that God loves white oppressors unless that love is interpreted as God's wrathful activity against them and everything that whiteness stands for in American society."[43] God's love for white people is, without exception, accountable to God's love for Black people and manifests itself in forceful opposition to whiteness and those who embrace it. Insofar as Black people's capacity for love is grounded in God's love for us, we are to extend that love to white people but never apart from resistance to whiteness.

Cone explicitly rejects the idea that such resistance reflects hatred or some spurious notion of "reverse racism."[44] He insists that Black pride does not demand the repudiation of the white would-be "master's human dignity, but only [their] status as master."[45] Even in his earliest work, in which he engages in particularly strong rhetoric condemning whiteness, Cone refuses to "rule out the possibility of creative changes, even in the lives of oppressors," considering such judgment itself oppressive.[46] The gospel, Cone avows, "is available to all—including white people. But the availability of the gospel is exclusively dependent upon a *conversion* experience, wherein one makes an unqualified commitment to the struggle of the poor for freedom."[47]

Total, comprehensive conversion is necessary, Cone argues, because "whites have only one purpose: the destruction of everything which is not white." As such, "blacks live under sentences of death," aware that "whites will kill them rather than permit the beauty and the glory of black humanity to be manifested in its fullness."[48] Under these circumstances, Cone proclaims that "what we need is the destruction of whiteness, which is the source of human misery in the world."[49] To be perfectly clear, Cone is not advocating the death of all white people, even as he refuses to condemn revolutionary violence as a response to systemic violence.[50] Rather, holding open that possibility of complete conversion, Cone believes that white people might "become black," wholly taking the side of oppressed people and working to dismantle white supremacy and anti-Blackness.[51] Cone distinguishes sharply between whiteness and people racialized as white, between birth into a world that offers one the temptation of white supremacy and the embrace of that temptation. There is room for white people in Cone's theology of love. The question is whether white people are interested in love that has not been distorted by white supremacy to lift their comfort and happiness above the very survival of others.

Finally, let's come back around to the second key claim of Cone's Black liberation theology: Jesus is the Black Christ, the embodiment of God's complete identification with those oppressed. What is it that that Black Christ does in the lives of those who believe in him? How does Cone's Black love relate to God in human flesh? The answer to this question lies in Cone's understanding of the significance of the cross and resurrection of Christ.

To sum up Cone's understanding of the cross and resurrection in a single phrase, the cross and resurrection are God's inextricably bound, loving work of judgment, liberation, and reconciliation. Consider what is likely Cone's most definitive statement about the meaning of the cross for US Americans:

> A symbol of death and defeat, God turned it into a sign of liberation and new life. The cross is the most empowering symbol of God's loving solidarity with the "least of these," the unwanted in society who suffer daily from great injustices. Christians must face the cross as the terrible tragedy it was and discover in it, through faith and repentance, the liberating joy of eternal salvation.
>
> But we cannot find liberating joy in the cross by spiritualizing it, by taking away its message of justice in the midst of powerlessness,

> suffering, and death. The cross, as a locus of divine revelation, is not good news for the powerful, for those who are comfortable with the way things are, or for anyone whose understanding of religion is aligned with power.[52]

All that happens though the cross and resurrection is grounded in "God's loving solidarity," that total divine identification with those oppressed embodied by Jesus.

Through the cross and resurrection, God's love levels a judgment against all powers that carry on the legacy of Empire. God is wholly identified with those crucified in all times and rejects absolutely that their crucifixion is compatible with God's will. All those powers that dispossess, enslave, and execute God's beloved children fall under God's judgment. God's wrath is directed against all those individuals who rest comfortably in a world structured by such powers and all those who dare to claim that such exploitation and violence are ordained by God. On the cross, Jesus dies as one of those who are poor, God follows through on their love for those oppressed, and those who align themselves with the powers of Empire find that God's love has nothing for them but an unyielding invitation for them to join those oppressed through repentance and the promise that those powers will ultimately be overcome by God's life-giving power.

God's judgment is inextricably bound to their loving work of liberation. The cross and resurrection stand not only as confirmation of God's condemnation of Empire but also offer the most profound sign that even death cannot overcome God's liberating power. Recall that, for Cone, liberation is found not only in final victory over the powers of Empire but just as potently in our very commitment to participate in tearing down those powers. Liberation, then, is manifested not only in Christ's victory over death in the resurrection but also in his defiance of death in the face of his imperial executioners. God's love is not a prize or a comfort, waiting for us at the end of a long campaign of resistance and revolution. God's love delivers us to freedom with every act of resistance we take, large or small. God insists on being with us *now* as we participate in God's work of freeing their beloved children.

Finally—providing a solid foundation for God's loving judgment and liberation—the cross and resurrection accomplish reconciliation. This healing of relationship through which those who should never have been separated are brought back together is not first and foremost reconciliation between humans separated by enmity. Rather, it is the healing of the bond between God and humanity, as Cone explains through his reading of Ephesians and 2 Corinthians:

> Reconciliation is not a human quality or potentiality, although it affects human relationships. It is a divine action that embraces the whole world, changing our relationship with God and making us new creatures. Formerly we were slaves; but reconciliation means that we are free. Formerly we were separated from God, alienated from God's will and enslaved to the evils of this world. Now we are reconciled; fellowship with God is now possible, because Christ through his death and resurrection has liberated us from the principalities and powers and rules of this present world. Formerly our knowledge of our identity was defined by those who had power over life and death in this world. Now God has redeemed and reconciled us, so that we know that true life is found only in him who conquered death on the cross and was resurrected on the third day.[53]

Displaying the persistence of their love, God reconciles us to themself, condemns the powers of this world to destruction, and liberates us that we might participate in freeing ourselves from those powers and for new life with our true identities.

As work of judgment, liberation, and reconciliation, God's loving work through the cross and resurrection demands a response from us. Further, Cone emphasizes that it makes different demands of—and has different effects on—Black and white people. For Black people, when God offers us new life, we "must accept our new existence by struggling against all who try to make us slaves," committing to "rebel against all white masters, destroying their pretensions to authority and ridiculing the symbols of power."[54] Importantly, reconciliation requires reconciliation *within* Black communities.[55] God's love compels us to love ourselves, embrace each other, and refuse to allow distorted love to lead us to relate to white people in ways that are compatible with white supremacy. God's liberating love makes us into a new and holy people as we accept God's gift of freedom and refuse to define our existence in any way that betrays it.[56]

For white people, the demands of this new life are costly. For those who are have been defined by their performance of whiteness, God's loving work of judgment, liberation, and reconciliation "means *death*, and only those who are prepared to die in the struggle for freedom will experience new life with God."[57] It is no simple matter of sympathy or compassion[58] but requires participation in "God's wrathful destruction of white values" that have promised prosperity and security in exchange for their performance.[59] New life demands the death of the old, liberation from that which God's judgment has lovingly condemned, and reconciliation with God and with all those whom God most fiercely loves. Crucially, this experience of new life must inspire humility,[60] lest the assurance of mastery that is so deeply woven into whiteness continue the distortion of love that plagues Christian communities.

This, then, is the Black love that is woven throughout Cone's Black liberation theology. The God of liberation, the God enfleshed in Jesus as the Black Christ, does not love everyone the same. Rather, God has a special, intense love for those in need of liberation from the powers of this world, which includes Black folks. In response to God's love, Black people are called to embrace our pride. We are called to love ourselves as God loves us—unshakably and in defiance of the many snares of anti-Blackness—always following the pull of that prideful love into politically transformative connection with our Black siblings and all those who embrace God's loving work of liberation. If our love for white people is to be faithful, it must be wholly accountable to that prideful Black love, betraying neither the affirmation of identity bestowed on us by God nor the political work of liberation. For white people to respond faithfully to God's love requires that they accept God's judgment against whiteness and embrace reconciliation to God and those oppressed by wholly committing to the politically transformative work of liberation with humility and accountability to the Black pride that is essential to the love extended to them.

This can be a challenging understanding of love to recognize *as love*—and not only for white folks. After all, the very affective structures within which most US American Christians have been shaped—feelings twisted to fit the shape of distorted love and its prioritization of white comfort and happiness—predispose us not to recognize anything that challenges white mastery or decenters white comfort as loving. Cone captures this dilemma with his characteristically passionate insight:

> When black people emphasize their right to defend themselves against those who seek to destroy the black community, it never fails that so-called white Christians then ask, "What about the biblical doctrine of reconciliation?" "What about Christian forgiveness?" "Can't black people find it in their hearts to forgive us?" White people who ask these questions should not be surprised if blacks walk away in disgust. The difficulty is not with the reconciliation-forgiveness question itself but with the people asking it. Like the question of violence, this question is almost always addressed to blacks *by* whites, as if we blacks are

> responsible for the demarcation of community on the basis of color. They who are responsible for the dividing walls of hostility, racism, and hatred want to know whether the victims are ready to forgive and forget—without changing the balance of power. They want to know whether we have any hard feelings toward them, whether we still love them, even though we are oppressed and brutalized by them, What are we to say to a people who insist on oppressing us but get upset when we reject them?[61]

What *are* Black Christians to say to a people who insist on oppressing us but get upset when we reject them? James Cone suggests that we ground our answer in God's love for us. First, we tell ourselves, individually and collectively, that God loves us so fiercely that God is among us even now as the Black Christ who takes part in our joys and struggles. Then we tell ourselves that God loves us enough to empower us to hold our white siblings accountable to God's love for us. Only once we truly believe that can we turn to our white siblings and faithfully tell them that we love them and that our love is why we cannot stand by as they indulge in distorted love and continue to work—whether unwittingly or eagerly—to reinforce the structures of enmity that are killing God's beloved Black children.

CONCLUSION

In the introduction to chapter 4, I raise a pair of concerns regarding the viability of grounding transformative antiracist work in love. In that chapter, I address the first concern—that love is not a reliable basis for effective, politically and economically transformative work—by drawing a notion of Black love from the work of Keri Day and James Baldwin. This notion of Black love bears two distinctive characteristics. First, it is a politically engaged practice of perception that facilitates the formation of meaningful connection. In learning to perceive one another as deserving of mutuality, rather than perceiving one another as structural interracial enmity trains us, we become capable of transformative, resilient political organization. Second, this Black love is prideful, grounded in a deep sense of our own worth, and oriented toward others so that we might ensure our self-worth is honored even as we honor theirs. This Black love, so thoroughly oriented toward connection and unerringly committed to mutuality, is crucial to the kind of movement-building organizing work that can bring about political change in the context of structural enmity.

In this chapter, I address the second concern: that in reimagining love as an antiracist practice, we might betray the biblically grounded, theological dimensions of love and exchange the sacred beauty of love for cynical political efficacy. To address this concern, I highlighted the theology of love that lies at the heart of James Cone's Black liberation theology. On the one hand, Cone's theology of love is compatible with the notion of Black love developed in chapter 4. It demands that love be politically transformative, grounding that politically transformative potential in God's work of correcting our perception of the worth of those who are oppressed. It grounds love in pride, holding any human response to divine love accountable to participation in the work of liberation and complete acceptance of the worth and beauty of those oppressed. On the other hand, it is biblically grounded, drawing on the defining event of Christianity—the cross and resurrection of Jesus Christ—in the context of the broader story of God's liberating work in creation. Cone proclaims the gospel throughout his career, always lifting up a witness to how God is pouring love into their creation, with particular, powerful care for those who most desperately long for the world to be transformed, for the powers of this world to be cast down, for the many biblical promises of God's loving justice to be fulfilled.

Cone demonstrates the theological potential of Black love. The love that animates his theology certainly doesn't seem like what's usually preached as love in most of our churches, including those that claim and strive to follow through on a commitment to justice. This is the influence of the distortion of love by white supremacy and anti-Blackness. It turns out that when churches are captured by love's distortion—when they try to hold their proclamation of the good news accountable to white comfort and God's love at the same time—being confronted by the reality of God's world transforming love is challenging, if not existentially threatening.

As much as I love Cone and his work, however, his theology does not take us as far as we need to sustain transformative Christian antiracist work. There are three critical ways in which Cone's theology falls short of what we ultimately need from a theology of love. First, Cone's grounding of God's liberative character in the exodus story just is too shaky a foundation, regardless of the historical importance of the exodus story to those who long for divine deliverance. In his final published work, Cone acknowledges the ambiguity of liberation as a biblical theme,[62] heeding the critiques of Delores S. Williams[63] and Robert Allen Warrior.[64] Liberation, as important as it is, must be more fully contextualized in relation to God's love and the complex realities of this world. Second, for reasons noted in chapter 1, it is not enough to stick with an account of Black love that stays too closely within the terms of the Black/white binary.

Finally, it is not enough to say that God chooses us or that God has a special love for those oppressed. What we need—and bearing this out will be one of the central tasks of the next two chapters—is a theology of love that is grounded in a theological imagination in which God *needs* us, we are made to need one another as we need ourselves, and we are called to embrace that need and follow it to its conclusion, aided by the boundary-breaking power of the Spirit.

CHAPTER SIX

Getting to the Heart of Divine Love and Power

God *needs and desires* creation, unconditionally. This is what it means to say that God is love, when we consider God in light of the erotic power revealed through Black love.

This two-part claim—that God needs and desires creation and that this need constitutes divine love—is a challenging theological statement for a variety of reasons, some of which I will address later in this chapter. Right at the start of this chapter, though, I want to address an issue that looms large whenever we think about a Christian understanding and practice of love of the enemy in relation to antiracist work. That is, to make a meaningful argument about love of the enemy in the wake of decades of selective veneration of King's legacy, I must account for the dominant Christian theological understanding of love of the interracial enemy: *agape*, the self-sacrificial love that is often lifted up as the highest form of human love insofar as it mirrors the mode of love that is presumed to be definitive of God's nature and God's relation to creation.[1]

Bishop Michael Curry offers a powerful, succinct definition of *agape* in his theologically rich memoir, *Love Is the Way* (coauthored with Sara Grace). Curry describes *agape* as "love for the other—sacrificial love that seeks the good and well-being of others, of society, of the world."[2] Taken out of context, this definition of *agape* is highly compatible with the distortion of love discussed in chapter 2. Too easily, the preservation of white comfort and happiness becomes the key criterion by which we judge whether love demands sacrifice. Too often, *agape* is code for sacrificial love *by BIPOC folks on behalf of white folks.*

Curry works to avoid this pitfall in his discussions of love. Two key points highlight Curry's efforts to resist the distortion of love: his embrace of self-love and his attention to the political dimensions of love. Curry centers self-love in his sense of what it means to follow God's call, describing this as a call to become the "true you: someone made in the image of God, deserving of and receiving love."[3] This positive affirmation of oneself is intimately connected to love of one's neighbor as we are called to regard others and ourselves equally as created in God's image.[4] Further, the active embrace of self-love causes that self-love to "radiate" joyously, energizing us as we seek to love others.[5]

In his attention to love's political power, Curry honors the fullness of King's legacy. Refusing to individualize *agape* or put it in service of the status quo, Curry discusses love's political potential in terms of deepening connections across lines of political disagreement. He does not simply claim that becoming friends will resolve serious political differences but instead argues that we can find shared values, share the stories of how we came to embrace those values, and find ways to build a common life based on those shared values.[6] This is closely aligned to the work of community organizing, in which love takes political form through grounding political transformation in the embrace of connection. For Curry, this loving approach to politics reflects his conviction that "the path to love needs to look like love," taking the form of collaboration rather than competition.[7]

I appreciate much about Curry's discussion of love—and there's even more that I admire about his practice of love through his work as a bishop—but even the promising aspects of his theology of love lead to a fundamental theological problem. An understanding of love that places sacrifice at its heart simply falls short when evaluated in relation to an erotic understanding of Black love, in which the heart of love is one's need for others *for the sake of one's own basic well-being.* The problem of *agape* ultimately undermines both Curry's appreciation of self-love and insistence on the political implications of love in three ways.

First, while Curry acknowledges the importance of self-love as an affirmation of our creation in God's image, his understanding of God's love is wholly other-focused: "God gave. God did not take. God gave. That's agape. That's love. And love such as that is the way to the heart of God, the heart of each other."[8] This simply is not the biblical relationship that God has with creation, in any consistent sense. I address biblical support for my understanding of divine love later in the chapter, but I will lift up one prominent example here. At the heart of God's covenant with Israel—the Ten Commandments brought down from Mount Sinai by Moses—is the demand that God's people will never reject God or put any idols before their God. They are to devote themselves wholly to the God who brought them out of Egypt.[9] God's demand for worship and love is never separated from God's own care for creation and God's people, but God does not give selflessly.

Second, this emphasis on other-focused, sacrificial love sets us up to be suspicious of the erotic power through which the Spirit empowers us to engage in transformative political action of the very sort that Curry would have us pursue. If we are to build bridges with others across deep lines of political difference, it will not be because we gave and did not take.[10] That is the path to ever-greater exploitation, in which one side makes marginal compromises to appease the other in hopes that such self-giving will inspire self-giving in return. No, if we are able to build bridges, it will be because we have found in one another something that we cannot live without and communicate to one another, "If you want what you need from me, you cannot simply take from me; you have to give *and* take because I need something from you." We must ground ourselves in our need for one another, fostering that need's growth into desire. We are ill-served by an understanding of love that sets a moral standard for humanity that fundamentally contradicts the reality of erotic power. Instead, we need a theological understanding of love rooted in the deep, personal need for wholeness with which God created us and through which the Spirit emboldens us to seek connection with others.

Finally, Curry's embrace of sacrificial *agape* leads him to unnecessarily dismiss an important "negative" emotion: hate. Curry makes his case for his wholesale rejection of hate in the context of a litany of hateful social structures (e.g., mass shootings, racism, anti-Semitism, dictatorships) and ultimately draws a sharp distinction: "Love builds, hate destroys."[11] In doing so, he's hardly making a radical argument, especially in the context of progressive Christian theology. It's relatively uncontroversial to say that hate is bad. When it comes down to it, though, "love builds, hate destroys" isn't the slam-dunk argument it seems to be. Sometimes, destruction is necessary. In some cases, hatred is faithful.

Hatred—that feeling that drives us to destroy—can be contrasted with love. If love is a fundamental need for the beloved, hatred is an equally fundamental inability to coexist with the hated. Hatred is the deep need for the hated to be eradicated, and it can be an appropriate complement to love. As a *complement* to love, hatred cannot be faithfully directed toward anything that should be an object of love. That is, none of God's creatures is rightly the object of hatred, no matter how obvious a threat they present to us. We need one another and should never embrace a perceived need for one another to be erased from existence. However, how should we feel toward the systems humans have built that pit our interests against one another? How should we feel about anti-Blackness and white supremacy, about colonialism and environmental degradation, about transphobia and ableism? How should we feel about evil? About sin?

Homophobic Christian theology has done us all a great disservice by poisoning the phrase of which my LGBTQIA+ readers have likely already felt echoes in the paragraph above: "love the sinner; hate the sin." That phrase has been tainted beyond redemption by its use to wrongly portray as sinful any expression of gender or sexuality that deviates from a tight binary-gender, heteronormative framework. When we can correctly identify what is sinful, however, there is a deep truth to the idea that while we should not hate those who are complicit—even eagerly—in systems of injustice, we should fiercely desire that those systems of injustice be uprooted from each of our hearts. This is what it is to await the Kindom of God: to long for a world in which all those who currently seek one another's destruction can devote themselves to mutual care, freed from the death-dealing systems of Empire. We need one another, and we rightly hate that which keeps us apart. Rather than facilitating the marginalization of "negative" emotions as demanded by distorted love, an erotic understanding of love facilitates faithful expressions of uncomfortable, even terrifying, emotions such as hatred.

So what do we do with *agape*? Perhaps, unlike me, you can find a way to successfully navigate what I have found to be an untenable tension between erotic love and sacrificial love. If so, please share this wisdom with me as it would make my job much easier! Or perhaps you're ready to charge ahead and embrace the notion that God's love is grounded in need and that God made us to be creatures who experience the same holy need. If, however, you find yourself interested in what I'm proposing but cautious about letting go of *agape*—either because of its importance to you or to those with whom you are in community—allow me to offer a path forward by noting a contrast between Curry's theological approach to love and my own.

Like many before him and many witnessing to God's love today, Curry takes what seems to be the most extreme form of love and makes it the norm by which all love is to be judged. Specifically, he takes the self-sacrificial pursuit of another's well-being—as ostensibly exemplified by Jesus's incarnation and death on the cross—and lifts it up as definitive of faithful Christian love. And there's a powerful pair of biblical verses that seem to demand such a prioritization: "This is my commandment, that you love one another as I have loved you. No one has greater love than this, to lay down one's life for one's friends."[12]

I don't argue that giving one's life for one's friends is not a powerful mode of love. I won't just argue with Jesus and tell you to follow me in doing so. Rather, I am inviting you to look beyond Jesus's bold statement and pay attention to its broader context, both in his ministry and in his deep, intimate knowledge of divine love. You might imagine taking this kind of approach to understanding the love parents ideally have for their children. We might be tempted to fixate on the story of a parent sacrificing their life to save their child from a house fire, as though that story tells us the most important thing we need to know about parental love. However, we are likely to learn more about how to love our children by exploring the everyday, steady, deep parental love that finds only a momentary, extreme expression in dramatic self-sacrifice.

In that same spirit of deep learning, I invite you to take in the intensity of self-sacrificial love on the cross, dig down to the roots of that tree, seek to understand what nourished such an earthshakingly powerful act of love, and dare to embrace that life-giving power yourself. In doing so, I believe that what we find is not that God's love is defined most fully by self-sacrifice but rather that God's self-sacrificial love is a function of God's need for creation. That is, God needs us so powerfully that God took on flesh to be part of their creation as wholly as possible, and in that flesh accepted death as a creature rather than accept separation from their creation.

DIVINE LOVE AND THE BODY OF GOD

No idea of divine love—however compelling and consonant with Black love—can ground the day-to-day practice of Christian faith if we can't express it in terms of some metaphor or image. We need such metaphors to enrich our prayers, inspire our liturgies, and otherwise enflesh our theological language so we can relate to God as more than just an idea. So if we want to give the idea of God needing creation a chance, we need a metaphor that expresses the relation between God and the creation they need so deeply.

Specifically, we need a metaphor that connects the divine to the deepest need humans experience, grounding our theological reflections in the sacred, dark depths of Black love. We may be inclined to turn to human relationships in search of such a metaphor. Romantic lovers, parents and children, revolutionary comrades, and lifelong friends all point us toward a need for the other that goes beyond superficial attraction. However, each of these relationships is at least one step removed from that deepest need that is at the heart of Black love: the erotic drive for satisfaction. That deepest need is situated in what I will adopt as a metaphor for God's deep need for creation: our bodies. Creation is the body of God.

It is perhaps obvious that our bodies cannot possibly capture everything there is to the divine. Ecofeminist theologian Sallie McFague—whose theology, along with that of her fellow ecofeminist theologian Ivone Gebara, explores the idea that creation is God's body—describes our efforts to perceive and describe God in terms of Moses's experience of witnessing the glory of God.[13] Like Moses, at no point should we believe ourselves capable of perceiving the full reality of the divine, that which makes reality "real" in the first place. We can only hope to perceive God's back, in passing, trusting that what we have perceived is a true experience of God but only *a* true experience.[14] God is ever beyond, beside, or beneath what we might claim about the divine[15] as we offer our interpretations of that which defies supposedly objective description.[16]

"Body" is a limited metaphor for God's relation to creation, as any metaphor must be limited. It is, however, a particularly useful metaphor for two reasons. First, humans have an incredibly intimate relation to our bodies, to the point that it is unclear what it means to talk about "us" without also talking about our bodies. And through our bodies, we are inextricably connected to one another and to earth, our home and the provider of our bodily needs.[17] Ultimately, any claim we might make about God cannot be made apart from our bodies and whatever connection to the divine that they have.[18] Our connection to our bodies is theologically rich, particularly as we consider our bodies' centrality to the deep need that is at the heart of Black love.

Second, it is imperative that we learn to honor all bodies as fully as possible, and that includes nonhuman and nonliving bodies. Our planet and nearly all the creatures on it are suffering because abstract concepts of profit and progress have been prioritized over the well-being of bodies, in all their humble neediness. Christian theologies that value the spirit over against the body simply will not guide us toward relationships with the broader creation that honor that which God has called good. We require theologies that will help us to identify with all bodies,[19] recognize signs of divine glory in all bodies,[20] and perceive all bodies as "fearfully and wonderfully made."[21] This is certainly true in relation to the work of antiracism as our bodies are central to the operation of structural interracial enmity. We need to be able to understand our bodies differently so that we might interrupt the stories white supremacy and anti-Blackness tell about our bodies, telling a new, Spirit-infused story instead.[22]

Five claims ground what I mean when I say that creation is the body of God: (1) God's body is collective rather than individual; (2) God relates to God's body in a personal way; (3) God strains against and stretches, but is not finally constrained by, the limits of God's body; (4) God needs God's body; and (5) God's loving need consistently kindles divine desire for creation.

First, God's body is collective rather than individual. I am not claiming that the universe functions as the physical body of God, with arms, legs, or any other anatomical structures.[23] Perhaps more importantly, I am not suggesting in conceiving of creation as God's body that we should picture any particular kind of gendered and racialized human body.[24] Rather, God's body is the universe in its full reality. We do not need to conceptually contort creation into the mirror of a human body to recognize that all things in the universe exist in a single, infinitely complex web of interconnection. The body of God comprises not just human but also cosmic difference and diversity in a coherent, interconnected whole throughout which God is intimately present.[25] Further, God is embodied in creation without compromising the distinctiveness of the many creaturely bodies that make up the majestic diversity of creation.[26] Body is, in this way, an apt metaphor for creation's relation to God in much the same way as we describe the church as the body of Christ. God's body—as befits divinity often described in trinitarian language—is simultaneously one and many.

Second, God relates to God's body in a personal way. This does not mean that God reigns over creation as a singular, dominating will with perfect plans,[27] as comforting as such certainty can be. God does not exist in some unchanging, dispassionate isolation from the chaos of creation.[28] God does not, in other words, rule over God's body as theologians have too often imagined our minds ruling over our bodies or those identified with reason ruling over those identified with the flesh. Rather, if we might borrow a metaphor from science fiction, God's will is something more like a networked consciousness that cannot be reduced to its individual components but is ultimately inextricable from them.

God is a "center of being"[29] for God's body, relating to each part in something like the way that we relate to the parts of our body. As I wake each morning and slowly wiggle fingers that are stiff with mild arthritic inflammation, I *am* those fingers, and I am annoyed with them. I care for them as distinctive parts of my body, and through caring for them, I care for *myself.* I have a center of being that beholds my fingers, but that does not exist apart from those fingers. And we, parts of God's body, experience our relationship with God personally, even if the fullness of God exceeds that personal relation.[30]

Third, God strains against and stretches, but is not finally constrained by, the limits of God's body. God does not exempt themself from any aspect of creation, preserving their divinity through some means entirely separate from their wholehearted participation in creation. Rather, what happens to God's body happens to God. God experiences their body's pain.[31] God is present in dirt, disease, disaster, and all other creatures—misunderstood or quite rightly regarded as unwelcome—that refuse to stay out of our lives despite their capacity to bring disruption and even devastation.[32] The body of God includes aches and pains, and those aches and pains are God's. At the same time, God is not trapped by the constraints of God's body. Rather, God is in everything that is good in their body, not apart from the body but in and through it.[33] God's transcendent reality is not something that exists in some kind of divine retreat from the messy universe but is to be found in the extraordinary parts of God's body,[34] though as ever, what God deems extraordinary may be precisely that which we would overlook or disregard. God does not reject the limits of God's body but works within them to create new possibilities, to open up the otherwise possibilities discussed in chapter 3.

Fourth—and I'll take a few pages to flesh this point out—God needs God's body. This divine truth is perhaps most powerfully revealed in Jesus Christ, in whose body of flesh, blood, and bone Christians most readily recognize the fullness of God's presence. In Jesus, we see the ways in which all bodies reflect the nature of God's body. After all, in being fully human, Jesus is as fully *of* God's body as any human, any tree, or any worm.[35] God's incarnation in Jesus urges us to recognize that God does not keep creation at a metaphysical distance. God is inside their creation, making it move and breathe,[36] even moving and breathing with their body. After his death, Jesus returns to his friends in the flesh. And even in his ascension—at which point we might imagine that God has made their point and need be embodied no longer—Jesus is physically taken into heaven so that his disciples might recognize the power of the Spirit at work in their very own bodies and experience the presence of God in and among them, without their teacher's obvious physical presence.[37] The incarnation, from birth through ascension, reveals God's intention to inhabit God's body as fully as possible.

Like all of us, Jesus does not stand alone—he could not be who he is by himself—but is composed of many: his mother, his people, his misfit friends, those in need of healing or justice who made their demands of him.[38] Jesus reveals nothing on his own but is always the child of Mary, the courageous woman who said yes to God and taught her son to do the same.[39] Even as we think about Jesus, he is not one person but many. We remember those Jesus encountered as we remember Jesus himself. We remember the child Jesus in the temple teaching *the teachers,*[40] the wandering Jesus telling *the rich young man* to sell all his possessions and give his wealth to those who are poor,[41] the risen Jesus appearing *to Mary Magdalene* and asking her why she wept.[42] Even as the focus of our faith, Jesus is never himself in isolation but is also all those humans, fig trees, and heavy stones that make up his story. Jesus, in his interconnectedness, points to the full embrace of creation by God. Jesus never stood alone but was always drawn into relationship and incomprehensible apart from those networks of relationship.

God in human flesh, Jesus represents God's full embrace of need. At every point in his life, Jesus needed others. Like any child, Jesus surely needed care and supervision from the parents who worried as he wandered off to teach those teachers in the temple. Like any asylum seeker, he needed shelter in a foreign land.[43] Like all the faithful who flocked to his cousin John, Jesus needed to receive baptism from another.[44] When tempted in the wilderness to set himself apart from the rest of creation, Jesus rejected self-sufficiency and supremacy over creation.[45] Confronted by his immanent betrayal and murder, Jesus needed someone to pray with him for courage and rescue and grieved as his friends let him down.[46] As a defendant in the court of an oppressive empire, Jesus needed mercy and justice. Finding neither, like so many to this day, he was murdered by the state.[47] Even after the life left his body, his need continued as his body required proper, dignified care.[48] From birth through death and beyond, Jesus's body reveals that God takes embodiment seriously, embracing it wholly, not shying away from need as incompatible with divinity but instead embracing need as the heart of divine connection to creation.

Fifth, as mirrored in the erotic power that is God's loving presence within us, God's loving need consistently kindles divine desire for creation.[49] From the beginning, God has longed for the goodness they brought into being,[50] that which they found satisfying as the fruits of their creative labor. In his commentary on Acts, Willie James Jennings stresses that the movement of the Spirit throughout Acts reveals the pleasure God takes in joining creatures to one another and, thus, to Godself.[51] God's presence throughout creation is not a matter of reluctant obligation but of enjoyment.[52] Insofar as we find ourselves struggling to understand God's presence with us—as the Ethiopian eunuch struggled to find the truth of Isaiah's words—God chases after us so that we might learn to desire God as fully as God desires us.[53]

God's insistent desire does not seek to erase the distinctiveness of the desired, as human desire gone wrong does too often. Rather, God's desire for creation—even as it is rooted in a deep, unabating need—preserves the otherness of creation. God's desire is that pointed to in reflections on the trinity, in which three persons are involved in an eternal movement of give and take, without domination, consumption, or erasure.[54] As it is received by creation, God's love draws us all toward a world in which justice and compassion are lived out fully[55] and clearly does so without eliminating our capacity to go our own way.

God's love is miraculously reflected in the erotic power at the heart of Black love. Nonetheless, divine love itself is distinct from our response to that love. I will cover faithful human love toward the end of this chapter, but for now, I will note two key differences. First, while human love involves the steady growth of desire on the foundation of our embraced need of our beloved, God's desire is ever desire in its fullness. We might understand God's faithfulness to Israel throughout the Bible in the context of divine desire. To say that God is faithful to God's chosen people is to say that God's desire for Israel is unceasing and unabating.[56] We might understand our love, in this light, as continually pursuing the fullness of God's desire for those we are only ever learning to desire. Second, where human love rightly strives for mutuality but regularly falters in one way or another, God's love persists wholeheartedly despite our failures to embrace our need for God or follow that need toward desire. Humans may appropriately step back when our love is exploited or taken for granted, but God's love is never withdrawn.

In turning to body as a metaphor for God's loving relation to creation—and particularly in stressing the importance of God's need for creation—I realize that I have likely offered quite a theological challenge to some readers. After all, many of us have been taught that it is absolutely essential to accept that God could be just fine without us, that God is fundamentally separate from creation in God's triune self, except insofar as Jesus maintains a link to humanity, and the Spirit does their work down here in creation. God's love is to be cherished, in this framework, precisely because God *could* simply be without us. This is certainly a key claim that I was taught in the early days of my faith journey.

If you are having trouble wrapping your head around this idea that God needs God's body because you were also taught that God could be without us, allow me to suggest that you don't have to turn your reason completely inside out to follow along. Let's allow that God *could* be without us in the same way that you *could* be a consciousness without a body. And let's continue by accepting that while you could be a consciousness without a body, you are not, and while God could be without God's body, God is not. We can imagine this alternate state of reality—and great philosophers and theologians have built entire systems of thought on each of these claims of disembodiment—but in *this* reality in which we live and love, you have a body, and so does God.

God *is not* apart from us; this is the reality of things as revealed through Jesus. We should certainly acknowledge that we are small and seemingly insignificant in the broad sweep of creation,[57] small and humble parts of God's body. Yet we should also embrace the reality that *God* took on flesh *as yet another small and seemingly insignificant thing*, a baby born to an unwed mother among an occupied people. God embraced the small and seemingly insignificant as essential to the well-being of God's own body.

We might imagine that there was a time before time in which God did not need creation, in which God was a disembodied presence out in some interminable void. If there was such a time before time, then it has passed. God now has a body. God needs us and will not be without us. God carved out a home from that void for each and every creature,[58] and God will not reclaim that home like some landlord looking for a higher return on their investment.

If God makes choices in something like the way we make choices, then I invite you to embrace with your whole heart the belief that God has chosen never to be without us. God will always be more than God's body,[59] but God will not be without that body. In short, God loves us and all of creation. God needs creation even more intensely than we need our own bodies, and God desires their body in a way that highlights how we should all delight in our own bodies, overflowing with divine beauty and goodness as parts of the body of God.

DIVINE POWER IN THE HEART OF GOD'S BODY

It's one thing to claim that God's love can be understood in terms of need. Even accepting that idea, however, it still may be difficult to believe that divine need could be compatible with the degree of power we attribute to God. We are consistently presented with images that conflate power with mastery, from contemporary politics and entertainment to the Bible itself.[60] Nonetheless, we do not need to believe God is the unquestioned master of creation—controlling and in control—to believe God is truly powerful.

Belief in a powerful God does not require that we believe God is controlling in character. We need not proclaim that God reduces their creatures to possessions like a divine slaveowner. We need not accept that God dominates creation, imposing their will to properly order creaturely existence, relating to creation as men too often relate to women.[61] We need not believe that God is the victor in a universal contest of power,[62] consolidating all power in their hands lest creatures go astray. We need not, in short, believe that God fulfills the role of a cosmic patriarchal emperor, a divine Father who resembles a bit too closely fathers whose displays of patriarchal mastery tragically fail to provide the love their children need.[63]

Belief in a powerful God also does not require that we believe God is in control of the course creation takes. As discussed in chapter 3, we need not proclaim that God can guarantee everything will work out to maintain hope in otherwise possibilities. By the same token, we need not maintain a belief that God is in control of the chaos around us to believe God is powerful in a meaningful and miraculous way. Insofar as we understand creation as God's body, we do not have to picture God as some kind of divine high-performance athlete, firmly in control of a perfectly ordered body that will do precisely what God demands of it. God's body does not need to be perfectly ordered to be sacred, beautiful, good. God does not need to be a projection of our standards of mastery to be the source of all power in creation.

All forms of power among humans have their source in the erotic power of connection between us.[64] No dictator can reign without the cooperation of soldiers and collaborators among the ruled. No CEO can amass wealth without the efforts of workers. No teacher can educate without the cooperation of their students. No parent can feed a baby without their kid opening their mouth and swallowing instead of dribbling their food onto their bib. To the extent that we believe the dictator, CEO, teacher, or parent inherently has power by virtue of their role, we are deceived into confusing the harnessing of power for its source. Erotic power can be harnessed to bring life in ways that reflect God's loving presence or misused to reinforce structures of control, domination, and mastery.[65]

In considering erotic power as a manifestation of God's power at work in creation, I find it helpful to borrow feminist theologian Rita Nakashima Brock's description of this power as the power of *heart*, emphasizing the capacity of connection to bring life and healing even in the midst of suffering and trauma.[66] God's power—the heart of creation—is power that sends life-giving nourishment throughout God's body. This heart steadily and faithfully works for the good of the entire divine body that is creation. God's heart is the power to maintain an intimate connection with creation and foster the power of heart in God's beloved creatures. To describe God's power as the power of heart is to claim that God's power works through relationship rather than control.[67]

Again, it can be hard to recognize this power as sufficiently potent to be God's power because we are so often forced to affirm mastery as power. We are regularly compelled or manipulated into falling for the same trick about which prophet after prophet warned the people of Israel. The rulers of Egypt, Assyria, Babylon, and Rome—and more than a few of Israel's own kings—claimed to have power over God's people. And again and again, prophets and Jesus himself encouraged the people of Israel not to believe that these rulers' power of mastery was somehow greater than the power of their God. We might be led to believe that this means God's power is above that of a pharaoh or emperor, as though God is the biggest, baddest king of them all.

If we take seriously the God's power of heart, we can consider the possibility that God's power was not *above* the power of kings but instead the foundation on which those kings built their crooked kingdoms. The power of Pharaoh or Caesar was ultimately only the power of tribes and nations cooperating out of fear of violence. They were patriarchal parasites, leeching off the power of imperial subjects and claiming for themselves mastery over everything within their reach. They were, ultimately, entirely dependent on the power of God, and that power could undermine and topple them. The power of heart could, we might imagine, undermine and tear down white supremacy and anti-Blackness today.

God's power—the heart of God's body—both sustains divine connection with creation and empowers creatures to exercise this power of heart ourselves. God's love is the source of all life in creation, and it has steadily and faithfully sustained creation for billions of years. The grand diversity of the universe all draws on this divine power of life-giving connection without draining it. To focus in on the power of heart at work between God and humanity, God has sustained connection with us even in the face of resistance and rejection.[68] Enduring the divine need for creation and the intense desire that accompanies that need, God has sustained their connection with us as we exploit their beloved creation and bring death wherever we can reach, even executing the one in whom God took on human flesh.

God's power of heart overflows into God's creatures, empowering us to exercise that power ourselves. Tapping into erotic power as God's power igniting a power within us, we can sustain connection through trials we might expect to sever the ties that knit our communities together. We find that—when we can draw more fully on that power of heart—we are able to work through substantive differences that threaten the work of community organizing, continue to treat our children as good and beautiful despite the ways they push us away in fear of judgment, contest our loved ones' transphobic speech while offering them the opportunity to grow in compassion and understanding, or return to heal a relationship when we've had to step back temporarily to preserve our health and safety. As we exercise this power, sustaining connection through trials both everyday and extraordinary, the power of God's heart works through us to empower others. Through inspiration, healing, and encouragement, divine power creates a cascade of empowerment that flows abundantly into and throughout creation.

The power of heart is reflected in Jesus, whose ministry was marked by fostering connection, sustaining community, and empowering those around him. God did not take on human flesh in the form of a mythic hero overturning injustice through superhuman might, leaving a changed world in his wake. Rather, in Jesus we witness God entering the everyday as clearly as possible[69] and revealing the ways in which God's power was always already at work. In

Jesus, we witness an individual human body truly living *as if he is the body of God*, intimately woven into the lives of others as they are woven into his own.

Jesus lived his life as fully in sync with the flow of divine power and love as possible. He was not yet another mighty man, claiming to be even more powerful than the rest and amassing followers who could lift him above others.[70] Rather, he immersed himself in the everyday needs of his people, finding ways for them to form community in new ways, restore to community those who had been cast out, and empower one another to bring healing and even sustain that power-filled community after his death.[71] Jesus attuned his followers to the power of God's heart at work among them. As they participated in that power, Jesus's followers lifted him up in a way Brock describes as "like the whitecap on a wave," not standing alone but capturing our attention as the most clearly visible part of a wave that carries power collectively.[72]

If Jesus was a fountain of life-giving power, it was not because that power flowed from him like water flowed from the rock struck by Moses.[73] Rather, he consistently channeled the divine power of heart, never clinging to power or striving to accumulate it to exalt himself but instead empowering others as he was empowered by them. Jesus spread life-changing love in his community and did so as a child of that community who had already been shown life-changing love.[74] He proclaimed a world-changing witness to God's love and did so as one inspired by his people's traditions to be sensitive and responsive to suffering and marginalization.[75] Jesus brought healing—unblocking the flow of divine power in the community by restoring connections—and regularly did so in response to the faith and agency of those whom he healed, as with the hemorrhaging woman.[76] The power we witness in Jesus is that of a human embracing the power of heart so fully we could recognize them as God in human flesh.

The power of heart is the mode of power employed by a needy God who will not be separated from their beloved body, and it is miraculous, world-changing power. This power is miraculous in that we can believe that the flow of power throughout creation has not been short-circuited by generations of efforts to disconnect humanity from it and bind the rest of creation to humanity's will—or, rather, the will of an extreme minority of wealthy humans. The power of heart is miraculous in that it has persisted despite those death-dealing designs. It has flowed throughout the centuries as Black love, prideful and politically transformative, ever connecting honored ancestors to new generations of organizers, artists, caregivers, and educators. Even those who are most tightly caught up in the snare of separation and supposed self-sufficiency only need to embrace that grace-filled flow of power, shake off their shackles, and empower others in turn.

God's power of heart courses through the veins of creation. Despite attacks on the body of God from within that very body, divine power still flows among us. Despite the efforts of forces designed to cut us off from one another and pit us against one another, there is still Spirit-filled breath in the divine body that is creation and in the small part of that body that is humanity. For those who have committed to the work of antiracism, confronted the reality of structural interracial enmity, and recognized what it takes to sustain connection and continue to believe in the possibility of healing, the power of heart truly offers something miraculous and world changing.

HUMAN PARTICIPATION IN GOD'S LOVE AND POWER

If God's relation to creation is understood in terms of divine need and desire engaging the power of heart in God's body, there are important implications for how humans understand ourselves. Crucially, there are important implications for what we understand to be faithful love since—as discussed in chapter 2 and again in this chapter—human love is morally ambiguous. The power of connection can be misused and distorted, promoting exploitation and justifying inequity. If we take seriously the nature of divine love and power, though, we can gain important guidance for what it means to love faithfully—and, ultimately, what it means to faithfully love our enemies.

At a basic level, we need to accept that being human is not a matter of sovereignty, independence, or any other ostensibly positive quality that signals a fundamental separation from other creatures.[77] We are made in the image of a God who embraces their need for creation and will not be separated from it. We are made up of atoms loaned from celestial bodies, consumed from creatures that became our food, and destined to be passed on to other creatures through our ashes or decomposed remains. We are of God's body, never made to stand on our own. We cannot even be understood in isolation from others. Like Jesus, we are made up of the stories of others.[78] Like God—and God's body of which we are each a part—every one of us is simultaneously one and many.

The reality of our existence as part of God's body demands an understanding of human personhood that embraces the collective dimensions of our existence. We must understand that, fundamentally, we share a collective personhood. We constitute one another in every aspect of our being that has been shaped by God for connection. We cannot be fully understood when considered in isolation any more than the cells of our bodies can be fully understood when considered apart from a broader set of cells, tissues, and systems. Together with the rest of creation, we are God's body, one person in all our shared complexity.[79] We are one person, our personhood held together across time and space through the many connections that bind us, just as the many atoms and cells that make up our individual bodies are bound together through forces that yet elude our full comprehension. This unity of personhood is not free of tension and conflict, of course. However, no person is free of some degree of tension and conflict.[80] As we are made up of one another, we are partly constituted by the very systems of injustice we strive to dismantle.[81] We might consider that even Jesus wrestled with himself in the garden of Gethsemane.[82] Ultimately, we are—at least as much as we are individual persons—one person, one body of God together with all of creation.

In this light, we can understand God and humanity both as defined by love. Neither God nor humans exist apart from love, and choose in each moment whether or not to love, but are instead composed of love.[83] Like God, we are inseparable from our need for the rest of creation. We can faithfully embrace that need or fail to do so, but either way we are fundamentally interdependent, love-bound creatures. Our very bodies are love, as suggested by the creation story, in which human bodies are taken from the soil but never fully disconnected from it, taken from one another's flesh but ever needing one another.[84] Love is within us, deep at the core of our being, drawing us to other creatures so that we might find wholeness.[85]

We are made of love, and yet that love is morally ambiguous, capable of fueling exploitation. So how should we love *as faithful Christ-followers*? God inhabits the intimate state of interconnectedness that is love with unending commitment, always embracing God's need, enduring the intensity of desire for the fullness of creation and each creature in it. Humans, however, understandably fall short of divine perfection. Nonetheless, we are called to embrace the love at the heart of our being to the fullest extent possible,[86] living in sync with that divine power of connection in the way modeled by Jesus.

This, then, is what it means to love faithfully: to hold true to the flow of God's loving power by embracing our need for ourselves and one another, following that need toward desire, and holding that desire accountable to mutuality. Born as creatures of need, we are called to embrace our need for other creatures as fully as we are able, following that need to deepening connection with others. We are to choose one another in everyday ways and at crisis moments,[87] resisting as fully as possible competitive pressures to separate our needs from others'. We are to live in the recognition that *we are our neighbors*,[88] fundamentally of the same body as them, and should embrace our need for them with the same love we should have for ourselves as individuals. Our need guides us to desire as we come to better understand others and long for what we come to understand, coming to perceive them more fully as God perceives them in their full beauty and goodness. Our desire for fullness of life together with others should lead us to pursue relations of mutuality with them, in sync with that empowering flow of God's love, the current of God's Spirit breath filling God's body with life. This requires a reimagining of our world, that we might recognize erotic power—the power of God's heart at work deep within our own hearts—as real power, freeing us to participate wholeheartedly in the cascade of empowering love that is God's heart power at work in creation.

Of course, as I've covered at multiple points, love gets twisted up, turned into domination and exploitation, used to fuel violence and reinforce structural enmity.[89] Love gets distorted, creating a new, dangerous feedback loop between inequity and distorted love. But as it does, the Spirit's empowering work continues faithfully, employing God's power of heart to ground us in our need for one another, correct those distortions, and steadily foster the growth of desire and the pursuit of mutuality. As such, faithful Christian love necessarily includes the discernment of faithful love from distorted love and of the Spirit's work from Empire's.[90]

The church exists to help Christ-followers engage in this work of love-filled discipleship and discernment together, even if it falls short as often as all human institutions. Just like the humans who make up the church, though, love should ground and empower the church. Throughout his commentary on Acts, Willie James Jennings highlights how the Spirit's work of love has been building and guiding the church from the very beginning. At Pentecost, the power of the Spirit was revealed through the joining of disparate nations, as God replaced assimilation and subjugation as paths to joining with the desire to join with people in their distinctive wholeness.[91] In Saul, who would later be known as Paul, the power of heart comes to life, making a fierce persecutor of Jesus's followers into one who felt their suffering and responded by joining them, needing and desiring them to an increasing degree.[92] In Peter, we witness the Spirit working through bodily need—literal hunger—to push Peter to never again call another unholy or unclean, stretching his capacity to desire those different from himself until that desire could encompass all God's beloved children.[93] Throughout the book of Acts, the Spirit builds the church by inspiring desire that interrupted the destinies charted out by competing nations to point to a new shared destiny of joining together in God.[94]

The Spirit is still activating God's power of heart as active erotic power in the church to this day, inviting us to imagine what the church might be if we fully embraced that loving power. A church that—like Christ, whose body we are—is fully in sync with the power of heart would redefine all our relationships. Church could become the definitive intimate space for Christ-followers rather than relationships built on shared interests or shared blood. Such a church could build in us the capacity to offer our love to an ever-growing circle of people, to whoever shows up seeking signs of God's love, rather than whoever is most likely to benefit us.[95] We might more faithfully follow Jesus, who gathered disciples not by turning to those who were desirable but by going where the Spirit led him and learning to desire those people for whom he first embraced his need. Rather than cultural similarity or the possibility of imposing our culture on others, our common vulnerability and need could become our starting point as we share the gospel in a journey of mutual learning and spiritual growth.[96] Ultimately, a church deeply rooted in God's power of heart could become Christian community that follows its collective need for connection to desire and mutuality with individuals, communities, people of all faiths, and nonhuman creatures alike.

To be clear, I am not suggesting that love is the surefire way to make the church into what we want it to be or to retrieve a lost glory it once had in the United States or elsewhere. Love is not the answer to save any given congregation or denomination from the widespread decline in church attendance or religious affiliation. Rather, love is the power of the Spirit guiding the church to embrace the powerful love that filled the life of Jesus and flourish in its role as a beautiful part of the body of God.

CONCLUSION

I have sketched out a theological imagination anchored by the idea that need is at the heart of divine love. In doing so, I do not hope to have fully captured the full truth of the divine. Rather, I hope to have offered *some* truth about God and particularly hope that it is truth that will support our efforts to faithfully love our enemies in the midst of structural enmity. In the next and final chapter of this book, I will offer my best effort to follow through on this hope, finally turning to what this understanding of faithful love means for love of the enemy, specifically, and how we might understand and practice faithful love of the enemy in the context of Christian antiracist work.

At the close of this chapter, I want to tie up a biblical loose end, returning to those verses that seem to give such strong support to the privileging of *agape* in Christian antiracist work. Recall Jesus's words in John 15:12–13, "This is my commandment, that you love one another as I have loved you. No one has greater love than this, to lay down one's life for one's friends." These verses—especially when read in the awareness that Jesus would be worshipped as the one who gave his life that all of creation might be redeemed—seem to demonstrate beyond doubt the definitive importance of self-sacrifice in faithful Christian love.

Self-sacrifice can certainly be a powerful expression of Christian love, but it does not spring forth as if created out of nothing. Faithful self-sacrifice is a response to intense need in a particular context. It is an expression of a deeply rooted love in a crisis moment.[97] The power of heart in creation connects us to one another, such that we are always receiving love and pouring love out. Over the course of a lifetime, we are caught up in the rhythm of the divine heart's labor of love. And when we are confronted by need that is simply too great for that normal flow of love to meet, *if* we are sufficiently in tune with God's loving power connecting us to others—as Jesus surely was—then God's loving power might burst out in an intense act of self-sacrifice as it did when Jesus refused to abandon his ministry, his people, his family, and his friends.

There may be no greater love than this—the mightiest rush of creation's lifeblood as it floods into a space of intense need—but that great love could not come into being without the erotic power of heart that makes it possible. In the end, self-sacrifice feeds back into that flow of love, empowering those who witness it and those to come, as love continues its powerful rhythm of give and take, from generation to generation. Self-sacrifice is one part of God's body sustaining another part in a particularly intense way, going beyond what can be easily replenished. But such love is ultimately rooted in that same source as all love, carried along the same flow of love that brings life throughout creation.

As you consider the relation of self-sacrifice to erotic power, to need, desire, and mutuality, also consider what it might mean if, instead of being fixated on one extreme case—a fixation that routinely leads BIPOC folks to accept exploitative emotional labor as the cost of recruiting white folks into antiracist work—we were wholly grounded in the powerful source from which radical self-sacrifice springs forth. Consider the possibility that self-sacrifice should not be pointed to as a goal toward which we should all strive but should instead be allowed to arise naturally from our cultivation of faithful love: embraced need for one another, ever-deepening desire for one another, and commitment to mutuality with one another.

CHAPTER SEVEN

Faithful Love of the Enemy

Interracial enmity insinuates itself into loving relationships, too often breaking them apart or compromising them. These relationships do not succumb to the influence of enmity because their love is insufficient or insincere. Rather, the very intensity and earnestness of love can be co-opted by enmity to encourage us to willfully ignore the ways in which we are enemies to one another, vainly clinging to the hope that affection and enmity are mutually exclusive. While love of the enemy has long been the heart of Christian antiracist work, both enmity and love have been tragically misunderstood. My hope is that if you have read the preceding chapters of this book, you have a clearer understanding of enmity and the faithful practice of love, but I'll summarize them here in case you're reading this chapter on its own.

Interracial enmity is structural in nature, not private. That is, it is not a matter of reciprocal, escalating conflict, in which people of different races have engaged in a centuries-long cycle of violence and exploitation. Rather, to say that people of different races are enemies is to acknowledge the ways in which our interests are structurally opposed to one another in the context of competitive economic, social, and political systems. Structural interracial enmity does not go away because people of different races become friends. Structural interracial enmity simply serves as part of the context for such friendships, applying pressure on them and standing as an ongoing obstacle to those friendships' flourishing.

Churches are not free from the influence of structural interracial enmity as it has deep roots in Christianity through the thorough entanglement of colonial conquest and enslavement with Christian mission. Sincere, deeply felt love—including deeply self-sacrificial *agape* love—has coexisted with white supremacy and anti-Blackness for their entire existence, and it has not consistently worked to undermine structural interracial enmity. At its worst, love has been distorted by white supremacy, serving primarily to protect the comfort of white people at the expense of the BIPOC folks with whom they claim to desire faithful relationship.

In hopes of offering a love of the enemy that might empower antiracist work, I have proposed an alternative to the self-sacrificial *agape* love that has been central to Christian antiracist work since its articulation by Martin Luther King Jr. Where *agape* grounds itself in one extreme expression of love—the willingness to lay down one's life for one's friends—I have sought to unearth the source of love itself: the fundamental need for connection with which God created us.

Faithful Christian love consists in our embrace of that need for others, our pursuit of the growing desire for others as we embrace our need for them, and our commitment to the mutual relations with others that are necessary for us to experience relationship with them in their fullest selves. Such love reflects the love God bears toward creation and is exemplified in Jesus's love toward his nation, friends, and family. Self-sacrifice can be one extreme manifestation of this love, reflecting an embrace of another so complete that one would rather risk one's life than give up one's relationship with one's beloved. Faithful love of the enemy is another extreme manifestation of faithful love.

So just what is faithful love of the enemy, that concept toward which this entire book has been building? Faithful love of the enemy is the embrace of our need for *those against whom we have been positioned as enemies*. As a manifestation of faithful love—human participation in God's life-giving power of heart—faithful love of the enemy leads us to desire our enemies more and more fully. Faithful love of the enemy requires our commitment to relations of mutuality so that we might truly be able to encounter our enemies in their fullness, as free as possible from the constraints of enmity.

That's it. There's no surprise twist at the end of the book. Faithful love of the enemy isn't something other than faithful love in general. Rather, it's just love that follows God's power as it guides us to those with whom we are intended to have no possibility of deep relationship. Faithful love of the enemy is just love when it flies in the face of powers that would confine or constrain our love in accordance with the structures of enmity.

Faithful love of the enemy is the love we witness at work throughout the book of Acts, if we follow Willie James Jennings's reading. Throughout Acts, God urges Jesus's disciples to live within God's desire for people. The disciples are pushed to learn to desire the Samarians, whom they had been raised to view as fundamentally undesirable.[1] They are even challenged to imagine a new life for themselves, following Christ right into life shared with gentile Christ-followers in a destiny defined by God's boundary-breaking love.[2] God's power of connection drew those who had been positioned as enemies to grow beyond an exclusive love for their people into a love that could create a new people, empowered by the Spirit.[3] Where Empire sought to capture all humanity within the desire for empire—to be pursued through victory in empire's competitive order—God's love offered an alternative desire to all those to whom Jesus's disciples shared the gospel. That desire—to join the divine life and thus join one another[4]—offered the pathway toward that otherwise possibility called the Kindom of God.

This understanding of faithful love of the enemy is even compatible with Jesus's Sermon on the Mount. Structural enmity may not have been what Jesus had in mind on that day so long ago, but he was nonetheless a living expression of the very power of heart that calls us toward our enemies today. Consider again Jesus's teachings:

> 43You have heard that it was said, "You shall love your neighbor and hate your
> enemy." 44But I say to you: Love your enemies and pray for those who persecute
> you,45so that you may be children of your Father in heaven, for he makes his
> sun rise on the evil and on the good and sends rain on the righteous and on the
> unrighteous. 46For if you love those who love you, what reward do you have? Do
> not even the tax collectors do the same? 47And if you greet only your brothers
> and sisters, what more are you doing than others? Do not even the gentiles do
> the same? 48Be perfect, therefore, as your heavenly Father is perfect.[5]

Though I am reading this passage against a more prominent interpretation, no mental gymnastics are required to read this passage in light of my understanding of faithful love of the enemy.

We can break this passage down into four key points. First, in verses 43–44, Jesus exhorts his listeners to love their enemies, to pray for those who persecute them, and (by implication) to not hate their enemies. Second, in verse 45, he presents love of the enemy as a key to being children of God, who blesses all people regardless of their righteousness. Third, in verses 46–47, Jesus impresses on his listeners the importance of exceeding the moral standard set by tax collectors and gentiles, who behave as Empire dictates and only love those who love them. Any reward to be had will be gained by loving their enemies. Fourth, in verse 48, Jesus suggests that to love one's enemy is to be perfect as God is perfect.

Together, these points offer coherent, powerful guidance regarding the practice of enemy love in the context of structural interracial enmity. First, we are indeed called to embrace our need for those against whom we have been positioned as enemies and ought not regard ourselves as better off without them. This is true even of those we might perceive as persecutors, whether that is because they are truly committed to doing us harm or because we misinterpret their self-love and resistance as hatred. To be clear, faithful love of the enemy does not demand that we accept others' harmful actions because we embrace our need for them. Rather, we are called to recognize and live as if we depend on one another and that we would be better off with their fullest selves—freed from the influence of white supremacy and anti-Blackness—than if they were gone altogether.

Second, to love in this way is to be a child of God, motivated by the same divine power of heart that is God's mode of presence in creation. Through this love, God blesses and binds together all creatures, even those who actively seek to subvert, exploit, or deny loving interdependence.

Third, there truly is no reward in behaving as Empire dictates, loving only those who fit within your assigned race. To love as Empire would have us love is to allow our love to be exploited for the sake of those who position themselves above others, taking advantage of the labor and political power of others while convincing us that we are dependent on their supposed benevolence. The only reward offered by Empire is the false, cruelly optimistic[6] hope that we will benefit from our participation in a competitive, death-dealing order.

Fourth, we are called to be perfect as God is perfect. We are not to seek to live without making mistakes or to somehow be unaffected by the world around us. Rather, we are called to strive for perfect love that mirrors the perfection of God's love: love that embraces connection and need even when it is challenging. This does not mean never stepping back or resting—even God rests, as we certainly see in the life of Jesus—but it does mean refraining from accepting the lie that we just don't need *them*. We might need space from whoever it is that's hurting us. It might be the case that they will never behave in a way that makes ongoing relationship possible. Like God, though, we are called to remain open to a future in which our love is met with love, even across lines of enmity.

TESTING FAITHFUL LOVE OF THE ENEMY

To get to this understanding of faithful love of the enemy—as the embrace of our need for those against whom we have been positioned as enemies, which grows into increasing desire and is committed to relations of mutuality—I've led you through multiple chapters' worth of discussion of love. Before that, across the first two chapters of this book, I presented a list of ten requirements for any understanding of love of the enemy that would adequately respond to structural interracial enmity and resist the distortion of love by white supremacy. Before moving on to sketch out some of the implications and applications of faithful enemy love, I believe it is important to circle back to these requirements and hold myself accountable to my own critiques by using them to test my notion of faithful enemy love.

1) Faithful love of the enemy must enable us to persist in loving in the context of the irreconcilable interracial antagonism that is structural interracial enmity. This requirement gets at one of the troubling dynamics in US American Christian antiracist work that inspired me to write this book: when it becomes clear that the antagonism at the heart of race won't go away anytime soon—even among those who are engaging enthusiastically in antiracist work—feelings get hurt, well-meaning folks falter, and antiracism teams fragment. My understanding of faithful love of the enemy meets this challenge by framing love in terms of need, desire, and the pursuit of wholeness rather than the preservation of pious purity. Ongoing enmity with one another is neither a stain on the quality of our love nor a sign that our love has failed. It is simply the context in which we are called to love one another. Knowing this does not mean it won't still hurt when we fail to understand one another's feelings or when there are tensions between us that we just can't shake. It does, however, mean we can recognize that such misunderstandings and tensions are manifestations of the very structures we have come together to dismantle. Understanding love in the context of *ongoing* structural enmity enables us to persist in embracing our need for one another, even as our capacity to recognize that need and perceive one another as desirable or capable of mutual relations is challenged again and again.

2) Faithful love of the enemy must guide us in navigating the manifestation of structural interracial enmity in the consistent, inequitable racialized distribution of exploitation and violence. In its orientation toward desire for one's enemy *in their fullness*, faithful love of the enemy necessarily ties love of the enemy to attention to their circumstances. The ways in which we each struggle and thrive in our efforts to navigate structural interracial enmity are part of who we are. We are our stories of privilege and marginalization, pride and humility, unearned wealth and unrecognized merit. As we embrace our need for one another, recognizing that we are part of one another, we embrace the ways in which our stories have a claim on each other's lives. Embracing one another's stories in love—especially with a commitment to dismantle whatever gets in the way of joining together as our fullest selves—can only help us more deftly navigate the ways in which enmity orders exploitation and violence in our communities.
3) Faithful love of the enemy must undermine competition. Grounded in embracing our need for those we love, faithful love of the enemy establishes connection with one's enemies as a condition for one's own flourishing. Rather than framing enemy love as inherently a matter of sacrifice, faithful love of the enemy embraces self-interest, clarifies it, and refocuses it. Competition with one's enemies—on any level beyond that of friendly games—is fundamentally counter to the nature of God's presence in creation and the nature of our existence as creatures formed by and for love. We flourish individually and communally when we move in sync with God's heart, drawing together in a growing network of Spirit-filled empowerment. Competition simply does not serve us. Competition does only what it has done since the time of ancient Rome: competition divides us so that we might be conquered, colonized, and held captive. Our only path out of structures that pit us against one another to the short-term benefit of those wealthiest is to embrace one another in love, recognizing that our need for one another is greater than the false need to outcompete one another.
4) Faithful love of the enemy must foster the capacity of both lover and beloved to strive for flourishing, freedom, and fully acknowledged dignity. Faithful love of the enemy is grounded in the erotic power

that is at the core of our being and is a manifestation of the divine power of heart that binds all creation. This is a love that begins with self-love—the basic conviction that we deserve wholeness and satisfaction—and reaches out to embrace others in their own wholeness. To orient our antiracist work by this understanding of enemy love is to ground that work in this basic longing for mutuality and shared flourishing rather than relying on an external obligation to pursue reconciliation that routinely demands more of BIPOC folks than white folks. We undertake antiracist work because we want to be whole and recognize that we can only be whole together with our enemies.

5) Faithful love of the enemy must facilitate simultaneous response to local relationships and their national and global contexts. Antiracist work that is grounded in faithful love of the enemy can avoid the errors of either dismissing the importance of particular interracial relationships or diminishing the ongoing importance of structural interracial enmity even in those close relationships. Oriented toward desire for individuals and communities in their full particularity, faithful love of the enemy promotes an understanding of those we would love that includes the ways in which the broader world impacts them. Our antiracist work can and should meaningfully develop local relationships. If it is grounded in faithful love of the enemy, however, it will necessarily develop local relationships with careful attention to their broader contexts.
6) Faithful love of the enemy must decenter whiteness and deprioritize white folks' happiness as a criterion of love. My understanding of love of the enemy offers a clear criterion for the faithfulness of such love: its grounding in God's power of heart as it is manifested in one's life and community. This love is demonstrated not by comfort or happiness but by embracing our need for one another and the increasing development of mutuality in our relationships. Faithful love of the enemy reveals the distorted love that centers white folks' happiness as *idolatrous love*. Distorted, idolatrous love puts whiteness in the place of God as the criterion of the divine power that rests at the core of our being and binds us to the rest of creation. By keeping structural interracial enmity in focus, faithful love of the enemy helps us to reject as the work of enmity any

efforts to misappropriate God's love in service of white happiness or comfort.

7) Faithful love of the enemy must disentangle good feelings and good relations. Faithful love of the enemy focuses our efforts toward that which will bring wholeness for all those who strive to love one another in sync with God's healing love. This means striving to repair the effects of harmful relations and actively building toward relations of mutual care and flourishing. Such efforts cannot proceed solely through the preservation of "positive" feelings but will rightly involve at least some discomfort, guilt, anger, frustration, uncertainty, and disappointment. Faithful love of the enemy invites us to reject the shallow performance of tranquility for the slow development of ever-deeper relationship.
8) Faithful love of the enemy must hold together love and acknowledgment of enmity. We cannot afford to act as though ignoring the reality of enmity is a faithful practice of love. Doing so may spare people's feelings and serve as an outward affirmation of the power of love, but it is actively corrosive to love's essential work of healing and connection. Faithful love of the enemy has no need for some idealized version of a relationship, for which it would work to remove any conceptual obstacles to our continued affirmation of that illusion. Instead, faithful love of the enemy is based on our deep need for actual people in their particularity and works to remove obstacles to having those people—in their fullness—in our lives. To love someone faithfully is to embrace our need for them, whether or not enmity strives to prevent us from doing so. We can embrace our need for both those who are enemies and those who are not without needing to ignore the different challenges each kind of relationship presents.
9) Faithful love of the enemy must have a healing impact on our other emotions. Distorted love corrupts other emotions, twisting them to defend white fragility and facilitate the exploitation of BIPOC folks' emotional labor. Faithful love of the enemy, however, drives us to embrace people in their fullness. This means embracing their full range of emotions, including feelings that often cause difficulty in antiracist work: BIPOC folks' anger and white folks' shame. For BIPOC folks, our anger can certainly be misdirected or clung to as

a defensive response where communication would suffice. However, if we can make some room for anger within antiracist work, we can learn to appreciate its ability to identify what's getting in the way of being together—sometimes pointing out injustice before it is consciously recognized—and its capacity to supplement courage. For white folks, shame can sap their ability to embrace others or even serve as misguided evidence of their love.[7] If we can hold off on too quickly shutting down shame, it might reveal its capacity to identify where one falls short of that to which one is called and signal the deeply felt desire to do better. Anger and shame are two examples of emotions that can find a renewed role when influenced by faithful love. Ultimately, though, all our emotions should be lifted up for discernment of what is faithful from what is distorted, as none of our feelings is beyond the influence of God's healing power of heart.

10) Faithful love of the enemy must encourage the development of emotional and spiritual endurance. Understood in relation to the erotic power that is the source of power within each of us, we can understand white fragility as a condition that separates those who experience it from that very source of power. White fragility convinces them to cling to their perceived need for whiteness rather than embracing their need for others. By resisting the temptation to center white happiness and building power—individual and communal—through connection, faithful love of the enemy guides us all into a process of developing our capacity to embody God's power of heart and the divine capacity to sustain relationship through challenges. As we embrace our deep need for one another and therefore seek deeper relationship with one another, we necessarily take on the work of building our capacity to endure the gap between life as it is and the complete fulfillment for which we long.

ENMITY'S RESPONSE TO FAITHFUL LOVE

This understanding of love of the enemy is indeed *faithful* in that it is grounded in committed human participation in God's work in creation, as revealed in

Jesus Christ. It also promises to be *effective* in that it addresses the failures of dominant understandings of enemy love. Faithful love of the enemy neither abandons hope nor lessens the power of love but instead confronts the stark reality of structural interracial enmity with the power of connection that is at the root of all power in this world. Grounding antiracist work in the power at the core of our being invites us to give our whole selves to this work while offering a path through that work toward individual and communal wholeness.

Faithful love of the enemy can help Christians avoid creating unnecessary struggles for ourselves. However, it does not enable us to pursue antiracist work without struggle entirely. As we strive to undermine enmity itself, enmity will not cease its work of undermining our capacity to love as freely as God loves. We will continue to feel pressure from structures that have developed over centuries to drive us apart and even break each of us apart on the inside.

Jennings's reading of Acts highlights a particularly hurtful form this pressure takes: betrayal of one's people. From the very beginning, the way of following Jesus has been a path of betrayal. To follow Jesus, we turn our backs on the stories our peoples lay out for us and the destinies toward which our peoples have worked for decades or centuries.[8] Each of us has a role to play according to the people who claim us as their own, that we might contribute to the preservation, resurrection, or founding of a nation. Jesus, however, inexorably draws his followers into the story of God's love, the story in which every people's destiny is to join together with others in new, ever-changing ways.[9]

To follow Jesus is not to betray one's people in the sense that one wishes harm on them. Nonetheless, it is true betrayal. It is to disagree at a fundamental level about matters of right and wrong, about the basic interpretation of history and destiny. And despite our conviction that we seek a world that is good for all people, we will be recognized as betrayers by those whose perceptions of the world and its possibilities are yet shaped by groups locked into competition by enmity. This truth is borne out again and again as those who commit to antiracist work find themselves increasingly alienated from the very families who raised them to seek justice and peace or from churches that inspired them to long for racial reconciliation. When we start working to dismantle whatever gets in the way of our full embrace of our enemies, we discover that what we have to dismantle are the very ways of life that continue to make sense of the world for our own peoples.

When we seek to live in sync with God's power of heart, as Jesus did, we discover the truth of Jesus's warning: "If you come to me but will not leave your family, you cannot be my follower."[10] We may hope that leaving our families is temporary. We can work to continue extending an invitation for our families to join us in our embrace of those they taught us not to desire. And—as my grandfather's story and so many others demonstrate—that invitation can be accepted, opening up new possibilities of community and healing, new ways to be family. Sadly, this betrayal is not guaranteed to resolve into a renewed bond but may instead become yet another way that enmity places pressure on us to give in and accept its order as inevitable.

As we engage in antiracist work, then, we need to be ready to respond to enmity's ongoing pressure. With respect to the issue of betrayal, two courses of action stand out. First, we need to take seriously the feelings of guilt and alienation with which some engaging in antiracist work live, as well as the family bonds they work to sustain. We need to be ready to do the hard work of sustaining one another in those times where that sense of betrayal is most palpable or when those relationships break down completely. Insofar as those of us who feel no such guilt recognize our need for those who do, we need to avoid the temptation to confuse the difficulty of addressing complex family matters with a lack of commitment to the work of antiracism. Those who do indeed leave their families that they might follow Jesus are also called to hold open an invitation for their families and communities. We can always hope that these loved ones will join in betraying those ways of life that have helped us to seek prosperity by compromising with enmity but that cannot help us to unmake enmity.

Second, we need to be on guard against the resurgence of the ways we seek to leave behind. We cannot—as too many Christians engaged in antiracist work have—mistake our commitment to love for the moral purity of that love. Love is a reliable guide insofar as it is in tune with the movement of the Spirit and the flow of divine love throughout creation. However, enmity is woven into the very stories that make us who we are. No matter how fully we might feel we've left those stories behind, we remain creatures who strive to live in that state of perfect harmony with divine love but who inevitably falter. As such, those who would follow Jesus into conflict with enmity must be attentive, ready to notice those moments in which we are returning to the ways we would leave behind, in which we twist the power of love into power as control or exploitation.[11] We must work to understand our communities—both the ways in which they have been entangled in enmity and the ways in which they are already reaching out toward otherwise possibilities—so that we might recognize the difference between work shaped by faithful love and that shaped by distorted, idolatrous love.[12] Love is vulnerable by its nature, but we can certainly do our best to support it with careful attention and humble openness to correction.

CULTIVATING FAITHFUL LOVE OF THE ENEMY IN CHURCHES

As I close out this book, I want to offer some practical guidance on how we might cultivate faithful love of the enemy through churches' regular activities. Ultimately, this work—like all antiracist work in communities—is highly contextual. This is important for two reasons relevant to the guidance I offer in this section. First, the practices listed below are dependent on your knowledge of your community and the ways in which enmity is at work in it. Second, I encourage you to think of the guidance below as serving a purpose akin to that of the string you would use when making rock candy. For those who have not had a chance to make rock candy, the process is simple: you saturate water with sugar, take a string coated in sugar and dip it into the sugar solution, then wait for a couple weeks as sugar crystals form around that string. So while I am suggesting practices that can help cultivate faithful love of the enemy in churches, my suggestions are not really the point. My hope is that my suggestions will provide a bit of structure, serving as a catalyst for the formation of your own ideas about which practices might help in your community. If something below is helpful on its own, then run with it. If you come up with something more suitable to your context, though, I wholeheartedly encourage you to try it out.

Testimony

Testimony can play an important role in the worship life of a church. By *testimony*, I mean any opportunity for members of the community to share their experiences with the congregation. This could focus on particular moments in their lives or draw on a broader account of their faith journey. It can emphasize attention to God's presence in their stories or simply serve as a space for sharing stories of personal importance. Testimony is already an important part of some traditions, while for others it may be unfamiliar or even uncomfortable. Whatever the form it takes or however familiar a practice it might be, testimony encourages us to recognize our need for one another by pressing us to embrace one another's stories as an integral part of our worship life.

Testimony can be integrated into a church's worship life in a variety of ways. In fact, given the range of people's gifts, cultural backgrounds, and cognitive abilities, it is good to allow testimony to take different forms. Not everyone can tell their story effectively in the moment, or by themselves, or in a congregation's dominant language, or with words at all. I hope you'll give some thought to the form testimony might take in your community.

For my part, I'll offer two ideas I think are particularly helpful. First, those offering testimony can be invited to do so in connection with something that they are inviting the congregation to incorporate into its practices of worship or fellowship.[13] This could be a food item for a potluck or coffee hour, a practice of prayer, or a song. For newer folks in a community, it might mean getting a clearer sense of why some old traditions hold meaning for folks who've been around longer. And for those who've been around, it might mean giving some context to new practices newer folks want to introduce. Taking a step beyond receiving a story to participating in one another's sacred and sentimental practices—embodying the demand one another's stories make on us—can help make testimony into a transformative event for a community. This can reveal the ways in which our communities can not only survive such transformation but even thrive because of it.

Second, those offering testimony can be encouraged to share ways folks in the community can get to know them better. For some folks, that might just mean that they offer a straightforward invitation to talk over coffee or during a walk. For others, though, it might mean playing games together, participating in a cause they care deeply about, showing up for their kids' concert or game, or cooking together with them. Such invitations and the experiences that come from following up on them can help us develop a clearer sense of our capacity to appreciate people in their distinctiveness.

In using testimony to cultivate faithful love of the enemy, consider how you might encourage connections across lines of enmity while paying attention to the particular kind of emotional labor involved in asking folks to share their stories with their enemies or receive the stories of their enemies. Consider what kind of scaffolding or support might be needed to empower folks to share their testimonies in ways that feel true to themselves and compelling to the community. Consider how the community might offer encouragement and affirmation in response to testimonies, building up those who have courageously offered their stories to the community. And consider how the community might follow up on testimonies so that they become more than a gesture of need and desire and open real opportunities for transformative connection.

Consensus-Building

Competition is a central part of the operation of many churches. Decision-making bodies at both the congregational and denominational levels commonly deliberate using Robert's Rules of Order and make decisions through majority votes requiring various thresholds for different types of decisions. When deciding on budgets, policy changes, calling pastors, and all sorts of essential administrative matters, many churches accept competition as the most reliable way to make difficult decisions. Where there is disagreement, the side that can secure more votes wins, and we are expected to accept that this victory reflects the will of the community. We might hope that our decision-making bodies will engage in meaningful, open-minded discussions, coming to decisions that reflect the wisdom of the group. If they do so, it is despite the decision-making model they employ, not because of it. There is a high likelihood that those who disagree will be left frustrated, that the decision that's been made will be undermined by those who disagree, and that questionably legitimate decisions will be made before any formal discussion has taken place. All too often, what decides the outcome of a majority vote carried out using Robert's Rules of Order is not wisdom but participants' knowledge of procedure and willingness to secure votes before meetings are held.[14] Over time, voting blocs develop, negating the need for meaningful discussion to happen with the entire decision-making body. And, in relation to antiracist work in churches, such patterns of competition and circumvention of communal discernment can serve as a key means through which white supremacy is protected while maintaining the illusion of communal consent.

Consensus-building represents a more faithful alternative approach to decision-making. As the name implies, a consensus-building approach is designed to achieve general agreement rather than majority agreement.[15] Every effort is made to ensure that a group comes to decisions with which everyone can agree, even if they are not decisions that are ideal for any particular member of the group. This involves various strategies, such as ensuring that each member of the group is given a chance to share their insights during discussion or encouraging all members to advance proposals for consideration that they believe will satisfy as many people as possible. Through a consensus-building approach, the group is ultimately empowered to hold all members accountable to a decision that reflects the entire group's wisdom.[16]

There is much more to consensus-building than I can get into here,[17] but I will note two practices that are quick to learn. Even if you aren't ready to fully dive into a consensus-building approach to decision-making, these practices can help to produce more equitable and well-considered decisions even in a majority vote system. First, a decision-making group can adopt the fist-to-five technique. When a proposal is put before the group, whoever is facilitating the meeting pauses and asks participants to raise their hands and show a fist or anywhere from one to five fingers, indicating how they feel about that proposal. Five fingers represent complete agreement, with the proposal fully satisfying that person's desires. Other numbers of fingers represent differing degrees of disagreement or agreement, with one finger signaling that a person has serious doubts but will support the decision. A fist indicates that a person finds the proposal completely unacceptable and—if full consensus is required for approval—will veto that proposal.[18] Equipped with this information about one another's reactions, discussion can proceed accordingly. Those who indicate strong disagreement can be given a chance to share their concerns and suggest ways in which the proposal could be amended to satisfy them. Adopting this practice not only removes the temptation to rush to a quick vote without truly considering everyone's needs but also encourages us to act as though we truly need one another, even when we are asked to make a decision together with our enemies.

Second, decision-making groups can practice restraint when it comes to securing votes in advance of meetings. One of the most effective ways to minimize the impact of competing opinions in a majority vote decision-making process is to secure the necessary votes for a given proposal before the relevant meeting. I've certainly been guilty of this in relation to committees I did not trust to produce equitable decisions. And, speaking from experience, I can say that it didn't feel like I was doing anything wrong. I was just gaming the system in the name of justice. In the long run, though, the victories I secured through those means just didn't last. I could manage to get a policy on the books that was equitable on paper but that would be ignored by the folks whose concerns I had ignored in playing to win. Meetings in which we could have been working to understand one another's needs became frustrating, anxious sessions in which outcomes were predetermined and disagreements came out in unhelpful, hurtful ways. In order to build connection within our communities while we work to make equitable decisions, we can't take competitive shortcuts. Rather, we need to commit ourselves to the challenging, vulnerable work of communication and endure our uncertainty about outcomes and even others' motives. Of course, we should engage in some of the important work of relationship-building and persuasion outside of meetings. When it comes to fixing the outcome of votes, though, it is best to resist the temptation to guarantee victory and come to meetings ready to make decisions together.

I hope that this brief sketch of consensus-building is enough to allow you to start imagining a church where members aren't wrangling to beat one another's ideas but instead come together to find something that works for everyone, even if imperfectly. Such a church is one that is building its capacity for faithful love of the enemy—of those whose interests are opposed to our own—particularly if decisions are made with attention to the influence of structural interracial enmity in the community.[19] Adopting a consensus-building approach involves making a shift from making decisions through competition to recognizing that we need one another to make good decisions and follow through with meaningful action.

Further, this shift naturally encourages the deepening of desire for those with whom we work to make decisions. I imagine everyone reading this book has been involved in some kind of committee or team in which every meeting felt like a fight. Such "teamwork" is draining, making us dread the meetings, emails, and even casual conversations in which we encounter those teammates or coworkers who gradually become our antagonists. When we work together in a way that ensures each perspective is given attention and each member is satisfied with decisions, we gradually come to appreciate one another more deeply. Those who might have stood as implacable obstacles in a majority-rule system instead become those who guard against our own errors and raise ideas we couldn't have thought up. We need not fear that their ideas will overwhelm our reservations. We don't need to try to undermine their influence. We have room to learn how exactly it is that we need those with whom we wouldn't have imagined collaborating and even come to the point that we *want* to work together with them. Church committees can, believe it or not, become an important site in which we cultivate faithful love of the enemy.

CONCLUSION

Love of the enemy is truly the theological and ethical heart of Christian antiracist work. If we understand love of the enemy as a matter of need and desire—as an expression of the divinely created power at the heart of each of us—love of the enemy will go from a moralistic, energy-draining concept that we negate through efforts to act as though we have no enemies to an empowering, life-giving practice. If we have the courage to face what it means to have enemies across lines of race and are sufficiently in touch with the erotic power at the core of our being, we can do transformative, faithful antiracist work.

Faithful love of the enemy sets us up to do the hard work of antiracism. Grounded in God's loving power deep in our hearts, we can face the ways in which all of us have been deeply formed by white supremacy and anti-Blackness. We can question our family histories and our greatest sources of pride, asking to what extent they guide us in the way of God's love and to what extent they fit neatly within the grand narrative of structural interracial enmity. Embracing our need for others, we are empowered to maintain relationships despite the ongoing pressure of enmity, even recognizing the pressures in our most intimate relationships. Compelled by desire, we are freed to allow relationships to become more intimate with folks with whom we hadn't imagined genuine relationships could be possible at all. Committed to mutuality, we can follow through on reparations, from acknowledgment of harm to monetary compensation to long-term structural change. Needful, desirous love can inspire white folks to recognize reparations as good for themselves and allow BIPOC folks to recognize that it is both faithful and loving to demand a path toward the dismantling of the enmity that keeps pulling people apart.

Faithful love of the enemy demands that we rework every aspect of our lives, just as they have been shaped so thoroughly by enmity. We must reimagine friendship, no longer clinging only to those with whom we share interests or cultural commonalities but even seeking out the opportunity to grow and change through surprising friendships. We must critically engage the ways in which our sexual desires and ideas of romance have been disciplined by enmity, vigilantly guarding against those pressures that shut down attractions as soon as they start to form. I don't imagine that every person will find every other person attractive, but when there is a spark, we must not allow the influence of enmity to short-circuit the power of connection with lies or manipulations like "It could never work" or "My family wouldn't understand." We must allow our understandings of work and citizenship to be transformed such that our participation in our nation's economic and political systems is accountable to love rather than to the competitive rules of these systems. We must allow our sense of what it means to be a responsible parent or a respectful child to be separated from the work of racial formation that is so often part of those relationships. All of our relationships and roles have been influenced by race and must be transformed by our participation in God's work of love.

Faithful love of the enemy positions us against the world. We are called to build relationships where the structures that organize society actively oppose such relationships. We are encouraged to find precious value in places and people we're told are worthless or dangerous. We are invited to seek belonging in places we are told that we don't belong, not by assimilating to those places but by changing them and being changed through the complex work of loving community. We are urged to work against what we are told again and again is the sure path to safety and security—that is, performing whiteness as fully as possible—even when seeking a more faithful path means betraying our people's cherished hopes and histories.

Faithful love of the enemy sets us up for hard work, demands that we rework every aspect of our lives, and positions us against the world even as we work to bring healing and liberation. In short, faithful love of the enemy is an expression of what following Jesus has always been in a world ruled by Empire. Following Jesus, we follow the pull of love toward community with those from whom enmity would keep us apart. Following Jesus, we follow the call of our own hearts toward wholeness when so much in this world is designed to break us apart. Following Jesus, we follow God's call to be what God made us to be: creatures who need, desire, and care for one another.

Notes

INTRODUCTION

1 Specifically, students in the master of divinity program.

2 Throughout this book, I will use the terms *antiracism* and *antiracist work* to refer to a broad range of work aimed toward the dismantling of white supremacy, including that which may be referred to as *racial reconciliation work*. There are plenty of distinctions that can be drawn between the categories of antiracist and racial reconciliation work, but drawing such distinctions is not the purpose of this book. Rather, insofar as *antiracism* signals a more radical commitment to the dismantling of white supremacy that is nonetheless integral to any pursuit of racial reconciliation, I choose to normalize that term in this book and explore the possibilities of love in relation to that more radical concept.

3 While the racialized arrangement of exploitation and violence that is white supremacy takes different configurations in different settings—and I therefore encourage readers to spend at least some time learning about the history and current reality of white supremacy where they live—it will nonetheless be helpful to take a more in-depth look at a particular location.

4 In "A Tale of Three Cities," the report focusing on white, Black, and Latine Chicagoans, the limitations of quantitative data are discussed. Race cannot be entirely reduced to quantitatively measurable phenomena such as incomes, population counts in different neighborhoods, and mortgage rates. These reports do not offer a complete picture of the lived experience of race in Chicago—or, for that matter, in the United States more broadly—but they serve well to illustrate the structural impact of white supremacy and anti-Blackness, thus grounding this introductory chapter. I should note that these reports themselves, limited as they may be, offer far more data and analysis than I summarize here. Kasey Henricks et al., "A Tale of Three Cities: The State of Racial Justice in Chicago Report" (Chicago: Institute for Research on Race and Public Policy, University of Illinois Chicago, 2017), 20, https://stateofracialjusticechicago.com/a-tale-of-three-cities/.

5 In Chicago, this segregation tends to be neighborhood by neighborhood. Black-white segregation is particularly deeply entrenched as it remains significant regardless of household income, whereas other racial groups experience less segregation as the household income rises. Henricks et al., "A Tale of Three Cities," 2.

6 Henricks et al., "A Tale of Three Cities," 2–3; William Scarborough, Amanda E. Lewis, and Iván Arenas, "A Tale of Diversity, Disparity, and Discrimination: The State of Racial Justice for Asian American Chicagoans" (Chicago: Institute for Research on Race and

Public Policy, University of Illinois Chicago, 2018), 3, https://stateofracialjusticechicago.com/a-tale-of-diversity-disparity-and-discrimination-the-state-of-racial-justice-for-asian-american-chicagoans/; William Scarborough et al., "Adversity and Resiliency for Chicago's First: The State of Racial Justice for American Indian Chicagoans Report" (Chicago: Institute for Research on Race and Public Policy, University of Illinois Chicago, 2019), 3, https://stateofracialjusticechicago.com/adversity-and-resiliency-for-chicagos-first-the-state-of-racial-justice-for-american-indian-chicagoans/.

7 Henricks et al., "A Tale of Three Cities," 4–5; Scarborough, Lewis, and Arenas, "A Tale of Diversity, Disparity, and Discrimination," 4; Scarborough et al., "Adversity and Resiliency for Chicago's First," 4.

8 Disparities in funding are between Chicago and suburban districts (to be clear, not all Chicago suburbs are affluent or majority white), as well as between schools within the deeply segregated city of Chicago. Henricks et al., "A Tale of Three Cities," 5–7; Scarborough, Lewis, and Arenas, "A Tale of Diversity, Disparity, and Discrimination," 3; Scarborough et al., "Adversity and Resiliency for Chicago's First," 3.

9 Incarceration rates—particularly among Black Illinois residents, who are nine times more likely to be incarcerated than white Illinois residents—have increased dramatically during a forty-year period in which crime has decreased. Henricks et al., "A Tale of Three Cities," 7.

10 Henricks et al., "A Tale of Three Cities," 7–9; Scarborough et al., "Adversity and Resiliency for Chicago's First," 4.

11 Henricks et al., "A Tale of Three Cities," 9–11; Scarborough, Lewis, and Arenas, "A Tale of Diversity, Disparity, and Discrimination," 65–72; Scarborough et al., "Adversity and Resiliency for Chicago's First," 63–66.

12 A particularly striking example of environmental racism in Chicago is the existence of the Calumet Industrial Corridor, a stretch of land in Chicago along the Calumet River that is zoned for heavy industry usage, including by several businesses that release a high amount of toxic pollution. This population of this industrial corridor—nearly 60 percent Latine and 25 percent Black—disproportionately suffers adverse health outcomes compared to the rest of Chicago. "Calumet Connect Databook," (Chicago, IL: Alliance for the Great Lakes, 2021), i–ii, https://greatlakes.org/wp-content/uploads/2021/02/Final_Calumet_Connect_Databook_2.0_January_2021.pdf.

13 This claim takes into account the fact that not all white people benefit equally from white supremacy, especially given its mutually reinforcing entanglement in global capitalism, a system of economic injustice that favors only the wealthiest.

14 I use the term *Empire* in the sense in which it is often used in current theological scholarship, drawing on the work of Michael Hardt and Antonio Negri. Hardt and Negri describe Empire as "the sovereign power that governs the world," regulating the global economic market and associated circuits of cultural exchange. Empire transcends national boundaries and national claims of sovereignty, coordinating and integrating populations and their activities in ways that sustain and propagate global capitalism. The evils of white supremacy discussed in this chapter do not simply reflect the outsized influence of US economic, cultural, and military power on much of the world but rather the integration of US American power into realities of Empire that have outgrown their European and US American origins. Michael Hardt and Antonio Negri, *Empire* (Cambridge, MA: Harvard University Press, 2000), xii–xvi.

15 Allow me to make three quick notes regarding these books and my use of them. First, each of these books offers a great deal more than the points I distill from them in this section. I encourage any readers who find my arguments interesting or compelling to read Harvey's and Walker-Barnes's work. In an important sense, this book is in conversation with these two texts and will be best understood in the context of that conversation. Second, while I use the term *antiracism* to cover all relevant work, Harvey and Walker-Barnes more commonly use the term *racial reconciliation* to describe the work they examine. The substance of their critiques applies to work in churches that is called by either name, so my hope is that this will not cause any particular confusion for readers. Third, the two write from different social locations with different purposes. Where Harvey writes as a white Christian engaged in self-critique of the antiracist work of white Christians, Walker-Barnes writes as an African American (Black) woman employing womanist theology to critique and reimagine antiracist work more broadly. Jennifer Harvey, *Dear White Christians: For Those Still Longing for Reconciliation*, 2nd ed. (Grand Rapids, MI: Eerdmans, 2020), 1–2, https://ebookcentral.proquest.com/lib/jkmlibrary/detail.action?docID=6260724; Chanequa Walker-Barnes, *I Bring the Voices of My People: A Womanist Vision for Racial Reconciliation* (Grand Rapids, MI: Eerdmans, 2019), 1.

16 Walker-Barnes, *I Bring the Voices of My People*, 23.

17 Walker-Barnes, *I Bring the Voices of My People*, 43.

18 Harvey's critique of what she calls the "reconciliation paradigm" is central to her argument. Harvey, *Dear White Christians*, 19–20.

19 Harvey describes this as a "universalist ethic." Harvey, *Dear White Christians*, 55–56, 158.

20 Harvey, *Dear White Christians*, 66.

21 Walker-Barnes, *I Bring the Voices of My People*, 23.

22 Harvey, *Dear White Christians*, 76, 92.

23 Walker-Barnes, *I Bring the Voices of My People*, 2, 10.

24 Walker-Barnes, *I Bring the Voices of My People*, 39–41.

25 Harvey, *Dear White Christians*, 152–154.

26 Walker-Barnes, *I Bring the Voices of My People*, 62.

27 Walker-Barnes, *I Bring the Voices of My People*, 204–205.

28 Harvey, *Dear White Christians*, 162–164.

29 Harvey, *Dear White Christians*, 57.

30 Harvey, *Dear White Christians*, 162–165.

31 Walker-Barnes, *I Bring the Voices of My People*, 175.

32 Harvey, *Dear White Christians*, 137, 152.

33 Walker-Barnes, *I Bring the Voices of My People*, 65.

34 Walker-Barnes, *I Bring the Voices of My People*, 113–115.

35 To be clear, Walker-Barnes—a clinical psychologist, as well as a theologian—substantively addresses issues of emotion. She highlights the need for reconciliation to address psychological and relational impact, offers a substantive acknowledgment of the affective challenges presented by antiracist work, and provides a particularly powerful analysis of whiteness as a form of moral injury. However, in embracing the claim that "racism is not about feelings" in response to Christian antiracist work that focuses on interpersonal relationships, Walker-Barnes overcorrects. She argues, for example, that "White supremacy is a systematic way of ordering societal systems, ideologies,

and relationships so that political, economic, cultural, and social dominance accrues to Whites. It exists independent of any individual person's feelings toward people of other races." She is surely correct in her emphasis on power in understanding white supremacy. However, in lifting up power, she dismisses the importance of feelings to the exercise and organization of power. In contrast to Walker-Barnes, I argue in chapter 2 that white supremacy is not *independent* of individuals' feelings but instead in a relationship of mutual reinforcement with individuals' feelings. If we want to engage in effective antiracist work, US Christians will need to take individuals' feelings seriously even as we resist the temptation to make antiracist work *only* about feelings. This means working with a clear analysis of the role of emotion in relation to both white supremacy and antiracist work. Walker-Barnes, *I Bring the Voices of My People*, 43, 125–131, 204–207.

36 Melissa Florer-Bixler, *How to Have an Enemy: Righteous Anger and the Work of Peace* (Harrisonburg, VA: Herald Press, 2021), 41.

37 I owe this connection to my colleague in New Testament studies Karri Alldredge. She highlighted Jesus's experience of betrayal in relation to those times that LGBTQIA+ folks find themselves betrayed by their loved ones. Karri Alldredge, "I Am the Speaking of My Name," Sermon presented at the Queer Intersectionality Symposium, Lutheran School of Theology at Chicago, April 24, 2024.

CHAPTER ONE: STRUCTURAL INTERRACIAL ENMITY

1 Harvey critiques this prioritization of togetherness over justice throughout the first half of *Dear White Christians*. Jennifer Harvey, *Dear White Christians: For Those Still Longing for Reconciliation*, 2nd ed. (Grand Rapids, MI: Eerdmans, 2020), 7.

2 Melissa Florer-Bixler addresses this misguided piety by framing enmity as a function of the use of power to harm or dominate others. To have enemies is to exist within such structures of power. One can act faithfully in the midst of enmity, however, using one's power against these very structures of enmity. Melissa Florer-Bixler, *How to Have an Enemy: Righteous Anger and the Work of Peace* (Harrisonburg, VA: Herald Press, 2021), 28–29, 40–43.

3 Martin Luther King Jr., "Loving Your Enemies," Sermon, Dexter Avenue Baptist Church, Montgomery, AL, November 17, 1957, https://kinginstitute.stanford.edu/king-papers/documents/loving-your-enemies-sermon-delivered-dexter-avenue-baptist-church.

4 To be fair to King's creative and courageous work as a theologian, this connection likely only seems natural because of his transformative influence.

5 To be clear, in "Loving Your Enemies," King works specifically from Matthew 5:43–45.

6 Matthew 5:43–48 (NRSVUE). We could also turn to Luke 6:27–36, the passage included in the Sermon on the Plain in which Jesus addresses loving one's enemies in similar ways.

7 Hans Dieter Betz, *The Sermon on the Mount: A Commentary on the Sermon on the Mount* (Minneapolis: Augsburg Fortress, 1995), 301–304.

8 Klaus-Peter Adam, *Hate and Enmity in Biblical Law* (New York: T&T Clark, 2022), 20.

9 Adam, *Hate and Enmity in Biblical Law*, 5–6.

10 Adam, *Hate and Enmity in Biblical Law*, 20.

11 Leviticus 19:11–18 (NRSVUE).
12 Adam, *Hate and Enmity in Biblical Law*, 213.
13 Adam, *Hate and Enmity in Biblical Law*, 199.
14 Adam, *Hate and Enmity in Biblical Law*, 225–229.
15 Adam, *Hate and Enmity in Biblical Law*, 235 [emphasis added].
16 Adam, *Hate and Enmity in Biblical Law*, 222.
17 Adam, *Hate and Enmity in Biblical Law*, 237–239.
18 Betz, *The Sermon on the Mount*, 301–313.
19 Adam, *Hate and Enmity in Biblical Law*, 200–202.
20 Betz, *The Sermon on the Mount*, 323–325.
21 This is to say nothing of the basic issues of cultural difference that arise in applying ethical principles from the first-century Palestinian context to the twenty-first-century US American context.
22 Adam, *Hate and Enmity in Biblical Law*, 20.
23 Chanequa Walker-Barnes, *I Bring the Voices of My People: A Womanist Vision for Racial Reconciliation* (Grand Rapids, MI: Eerdmans, 2019), 36.
24 Adam, *Hate and Enmity in Biblical Law*, 20.
25 Harvey, *Dear White Christians*, 55–56.
26 King, "Loving Your Enemies."
27 I use this term to distinguish from the wide range of people who name themselves "Americans" of various kinds.
28 In visualizing race in this way, I am modifying a diagram Willie James Jennings used back in my graduate school days.
29 Welcome back to the endnotes, where I put discussions and qualifications I suspect only academics will care about. I want to note here that I don't follow Wilderson to the furthest conclusions of his Afropessimism about the state of the world as it is, largely because of my faith commitments regarding the redemptive possibilities of life and love. Wilderson would surely critique my work and my use of his work if he read this book. That being said, I resist the wholesale rejection of Afropessimism that I regularly encounter in academic conversations in the fields of Christian theology and ethics. This rejection is often grounded in the charge that Afropessimism is—as its name does seem to imply—fundamentally hopeless. Ultimately, though, Afropessimism is an analysis of what's trapping us where we are, not a projection of what might be possible. As a scholar, Wilderson—to my awareness—is not particularly interested in making claims about what might be possible if we were to break free and overturn this world. Rather, he vigorously insists that such complete overturning is necessary for us to find some kind of life free of anti-Blackness. This will be discussed further in chapter 3.
30 Frank B. Wilderson III, *Red, White, and Black: Cinema and the Structure of US Antagonisms* (Durham, NC: Duke University Press, 2010), 25.
31 Harvey, *Dear White Christians*, 56–57.
32 Frank B. Wilderson III, *Afropessimism* (New York: Liveright, 2020), 102.
33 Wilderson, *Afropessimism*, 229; *Red, White, and Black*, 31.
34 Wilderson, *Afropessimism*, 192, 199.
35 Neal A. Lester, "The Disturbing 'Monkey Business' of US Black-White Race Relations," Learning for Justice, February 24, 2017, https://www.learningforjustice.org/magazine/the-disturbing-monkey-business-of-us-blackwhite-race-relations; Josh Sanburn, "All

the Ways Darren Wilson Described Being Afraid of Michael Brown," *Time*, November 25, 2014, https://time.com/3605346/darren-wilson-michael-brown-demon/.

36 Isabel Wilkerson, *Caste: The Origins of Our Discontents* (New York: Random House, 2020), 48.

37 Wilderson, *Red, White, and Black*, 28–31.

38 In particular, stories of immigration from European countries to the United States tend to involve assimilation into whiteness and growing reliance on whiteness for safety and prosperity. Wilkerson, *Caste*, 49–53.

39 Willie James Jennings, *The Christian Imagination: Theology and the Origins of Race* (New Haven, CT: Yale University Press, 2010), 32–34.

40 Willie James Jennings, "Can White People Be Saved?," in *Can "White" People Be Saved?: Triangulating Race, Theology, and Mission*, ed. Love L. Sechrest, Johnny Ramírez-Johnson, and Amos Yong (Downers Grove, IL: IVP Academic, 2018), 30–35.

41 The assignment of Blackness to reprobation was reinforced by characterizations of Africans as fundamentally spiritually immature. Jennings, *The Christian Imagination*, 34–37; Jennings, "Can White People Be Saved?," 30–35.

42 Kelly Brown Douglas, *Resurrection Hope: A Future Where Black Lives Matter* (Maryknoll, NY: Orbis Books, 2021), 14–20.

43 As Mikulich discusses, these papal bulls were not uncontested. There were European voices that resisted white supremacy, even in its early construction. Alex Mikulich, *Unlearning White Supremacy: A Spirituality of Racial Liberation* (Maryknoll, NY: Orbis Books, 2022), 61–78.

44 Jennings, *The Christian Imagination*, 34–37.

45 Jennings, "Can White People Be Saved?," 35–40.

46 Choi Hee An, *A Postcolonial Relationship* (Albany: SUNY Press, 2022), 34–55.

47 George Lipsitz, *The Possessive Investment in Whiteness: How White People Profit from Identity Politics*, 20th anniversary ed. (Philadelphia: Temple University Press, 2018), viii.

48 Of course, our performance does shape who we are inside—take as an analogy the stories that surface about method actors who take their performance too far and struggle to separate themselves from their characters—but that's something I discuss in chapter 2. Wilkerson, *Caste*, 40.

49 Ki Joo Choi, *Disciplined by Race: Theological Ethics and the Problem of Asian American Identity* (Eugene, OR: Cascade Books, 2019), 28.

50 Wilderson lays out this distinction between irreconcilable antagonism and resolvable conflict in the context of a discussion of race and film. Wilderson, *Red, White, and Black*, 5.

51 In the context of a vignette from his work as a professor, Wilderson describes this contrast between whiteness and Blackness as a matter of capacity and incapacity. Importantly, he emphasizes that the gap in capacity between romantic partners represents a powerful source of tension in interracial relationships. Wilderson, *Afropessimism*, 332.

52 Galatians 3:28 (NRSVUE).

53 Kahl does not herself use language of "structural enmity" at any point in her book. Nonetheless, I hope that my argument in the coming pages will demonstrate the compatibility between her reading of Paul and my notion of structural enmity. I should note, further, that while Kahl makes insightful connections between New Testament texts and contemporary issues such as climate justice and gender inequity, she does not, to my knowledge, address racial inequity.

54 Brigitte Kahl, *Galatians Re-Imagined: Reading with the Eyes of the Vanquished* (Minneapolis: Fortress Press, 2010), 17–19.
55 Kahl, *Galatians Re-Imagined*, 23.
56 Kahl, *Galatians Re-Imagined*, 92–106.
57 Kahl, *Galatians Re-Imagined*, 138–144.
58 Kahl, *Galatians Re-Imagined*, 49–51.
59 Kahl, *Galatians Re-Imagined*, 33.
60 Kahl alludes to the fact that *euangelion*—the Greek word often translated into English as *gospel* or *good news*—was a term originally used to refer to imperial announcements and appropriated to refer to the message at the heart of Christian faith. Kahl, *Galatians Re-Imagined*, 256.
61 Kahl, *Galatians Re-Imagined*, 190–191.
62 Neville Morley, *The Roman Empire: Roots of Imperialism* (London: Pluto Press, 2010), 95–101.
63 Morley, *The Roman Empire*, 76–77.
64 Morley, *The Roman Empire*, 90.
65 Jennifer A. Glancy, *Slavery in Early Christianity* (Minneapolis: Fortress Press, 2002), 26–27.
66 Glancy, *Slavery in Early Christianity*, 74–77.
67 Davina C. Lopez, *Apostle to the Conquered: Reimagining Paul's Mission* (Minneapolis: Fortress Press, 2010), 29–35, 108–110.
68 Martin Hengel, *Crucifixion in the Ancient World and the Folly of the Cross*, trans. John Bowden (Philadelphia: Fortress Press, 1977), 86–88.
69 Kahl, *Galatians Re-Imagined*, 158.
70 Kahl, *Galatians Re-Imagined*, 171.
71 Kahl, *Galatians Re-Imagined*, 156–159.
72 Kahl, *Galatians Re-Imagined*, 24.
73 Kahl, *Galatians Re-Imagined*, 207.
74 Readers who have contemplated the role of "works" in Paul's letter to the Galatians may be interested to know that Kahl argues that Paul criticizes those "works" of public beneficence intended to emulate Caesar—thereby justifying oneself before the competitive law of Rome—and not "works" of faithfulness or justice outlined by Jewish Torah. Kahl, *Galatians Re-Imagined*, 196–199, 207.
75 Kahl, *Galatians Re-Imagined*, 170–179.
76 Kahl, *Galatians Re-Imagined*, 207.
77 The Second Temple of Jerusalem—dramatically destroyed by Rome in 70 CE—still stood in Paul's time. Kahl, *Galatians Re-Imagined*, 212–218.
78 Kahl, *Galatians Re-Imagined*, 228–231.
79 Galatians 5:14 and 6:2 (NRSVUE).
80 Kahl, *Galatians Re-Imagined*, 252.
81 Kahl, *Galatians Re-Imagined*, 289.

CHAPTER TWO: LOVE DISTORTED BY WHITE SUPREMACY

1 While my acknowledgments record my appreciation of those who have helped me in my work, I need to make it clear that my work with Amy R. Barbour has definitively shaped

my understanding of Sara Ahmed's work, specifically. While plenty of people have offered helpful insights, pointed me toward useful texts and other resources, or even shaped my reading through their teaching, Amy's influence on my work on Ahmed is more deeply formative. We have presented and/or published several coauthored papers that engage with Ahmed's work, and because of our ongoing work together, I cannot claim that the way I read Ahmed is extricable from my work with Amy.

2 Sara Ahmed, *The Cultural Politics of Emotion* (Durham, NC: Duke University Press, 2004), 44–45.

3 Ahmed makes it clear that emotions themselves do not pass directly between people. Rather, only the objects to which emotions "stick" are passed around. The emotions that are felt are not experienced as somehow passed along with the object but instead attributed to the object itself, as if it inspires emotions simply by its presence. Ahmed, *The Cultural Politics of Emotion*, 10–11.

4 It is important to note, for example, that not all objects are equally "sticky." Some objects are invested with a greater degree of significance than others as they are passed through a community or society. Ahmed, *The Cultural Politics of Emotion*, 8.

5 Cleve R. Wootson Jr. and Derek Hawkins, "The Charlotte Police Shooting That Hasn't Gone Away," *Washington Post*, September 21, 2016, https://www.washingtonpost.com/news/post-nation/wp/2016/09/21/the-charlotte-police-shooting-that-hasnt-gone-away/.

6 For a powerful exploration of the nature and impact of such stereotyped narratives and images, with an emphasis on narratives and images of Black women in the United States, see Emilie M. Townes, *Womanist Ethics and the Cultural Production of Evil* (New York: Palgrave Macmillan, 2006).

7 While Ahmed does not discuss churches or other religious communities very often, I will proceed with the understanding that the kinds of communal processes she describes apply to churches and other religious communities insofar as they are communities that function through the activity of institutions and processes similar to those of other communities.

8 Ahmed, *The Cultural Politics of Emotion*, 8–10.

9 Ahmed, *The Cultural Politics of Emotion*, 24–26.

10 I describe this as a "relative" absence because plenty of people are rarely pain-free but still find that their attention to that pain fades absent more intense, acute pains. Ahmed, *The Cultural Politics of Emotion*, 27.

11 I do not use the term *story* to imply that such communal pain is a matter of political rhetoric used to define the boundaries of a community. Rather, as Ahmed points out, that pain is "felt on the skin of the individuals who make up that community," felt in the impact of that communal injury on the lives and emotions of those individuals. Such pain, as it is communicated for the sake of being recognized as communal pain, takes the form of story. Ahmed, *The Cultural Politics of Emotion*, 34.

12 Ahmed, *The Cultural Politics of Emotion*, 32–33.

13 While we experience the desire to remain close to those things that we associate with happiness, this association is no guarantee that we will be happy. Happiness is a matter of expectation, a promise that one will feel happy in the presence of a given object. As with any promise or expectation, however, it can lead to disappointment. Sending kids to a "good school" does not necessarily result in a happier family, whether or not it facilitates higher academic achievement and educational attainment. The

promise of happiness often involves some sense that if the fulfillment of the promise is deferred—whether in being patient for one's own happiness or in sacrificing one's own happiness to secure another's—its fulfillment will be even greater than originally anticipated. Sara Ahmed, *The Promise of Happiness* (Durham, NC: Duke University Press, 2010), 24–25, 28–29, 32–33.

14 This social promise is particularly compelling when happiness is presented as being in crisis, with social ideals and norms cast as the key to that crisis. Insofar as the members of a community have failed—or appeared to fail—to conform to those norms and ideals, that failure is portrayed as a threat to happiness. The assumption, of course, is that the ideals themselves are not inadequate to the task of pointing the way to happiness. I should note that this line of reasoning is particularly obvious in political discourses that focus on the "traditional family" and the association of same-sex marriage, abortion, and any number of other practices with familial decline and society-wide unhappiness. Ahmed, *The Promise of Happiness*, 7, 11.

15 To be clear, these myths do not correspond to reality. Both reliance on government assistance and undocumented life in the United States are fraught with surveillance, difficulty navigating social services to meet basic needs, and cultural demonization that hardly correspond to a stereotyped life of ease. Ahmed, *The Promise of Happiness*, 13.

16 Ahmed, *The Promise of Happiness*, 34–37.

17 Ahmed, *The Promise of Happiness*, 38, 41.

18 This "happiness duty" is particularly clear in the family, a central node in the formation of our desires for happiness and itself a particularly significant happy object. Ahmed argues that "the family becomes a happy object through the work that must be done to keep it together," which includes the work involved both in knowing what makes others in the family appear happy and in appearing happy when you are presented with what other family members "know" makes you happy, whether or not it actually makes you feel good. Sara Ahmed, *Living a Feminist Life* (Durham, NC: Duke University Press, 2017), 58; Ahmed, *The Promise of Happiness*, 45–47.

19 Jennifer Harvey, *Dear White Christians: For Those Still Longing for Reconciliation*, 2nd ed. (Grand Rapids, MI: Eerdmans, 2020), 69–73.

20 Ahmed, *The Promise of Happiness*, 203.

21 Ahmed, *The Promise of Happiness*22.

22 Ahmed, *The Cultural Politics of Emotion*, 135.

23 Gregory T. Carter offers a compelling argument that whiteness and citizenship have been mutually constitutive throughout US American history. "Whiteness-as-citizenship" is key to determining who belongs in this country and who does not, such that this country truly is fundamentally white. Gregory T. Carter, "Race and Citizenship," in *The Oxford Handbook of American Immigration and Ethnicity*, ed. Ronald H. Bayor (New York: Oxford University Press, 2013), 166–182.

24 Ahmed's work primarily focuses on UK society but highlights themes that readily apply to the US context. Ahmed, *The Cultural Politics of Emotion*, 129.

25 I will offer two quick qualifications here. First, Harvey focuses on antiracist work involving Black and white Christians specifically, but this insight applies to interracial work beyond that specific dynamic. Second, while I make a connection between the work of Jennifer Harvey and Sara Ahmed, Harvey neither directly addresses Ahmed's work nor uses the term "distorted love." Harvey, *Dear White Christians*, 66–69.

26 Harvey, *Dear White Christians*, 55–58.
27 It is important to be clear that Ahmed does not describe this kind of distorted love as a distorted love but simply as love. Ahmed offers a critique of love, as such, discussing how love works to entrench relations of exploitation and violence. In my view, such operations of love are signs of the distortion of love, to which I will juxtapose what I find to be a notion of love that works against such unjust relations. While I find Ahmed's insights to be quite compatible with my account of love of the enemy, I do not wish to misrepresent her by suggesting that she draws the same conclusions from her critiques that I do. It may be possible to account for this difference by pointing out that my discipline is Christian theology, while Ahmed's work is in the disciplines of literature and feminist theory. However, there are likely significant differences between our thoughts that are not reducible to disciplinary distinctions. Ahmed, *The Cultural Politics of Emotion*, 141, 193, 195.
28 For a discussion of this hope, see chapter 3.
29 Ahmed, *The Cultural Politics of Emotion*, 72–74.
30 Ahmed, *The Cultural Politics of Emotion*, 63.
31 To the extent that those who are feared do not cause harm to the one who fears, fear is not relieved but instead transmuted into anxiety. Even if this Black or brown person did not cause harm, they could have, and the next one might. Under the influence of fear, working through anxiety is not experienced as the pursuit of love through understanding but rather as the betrayal of love through lack of vigilance. Ahmed, *The Cultural Politics of Emotion*, 66–68.
32 Ahmed, *The Cultural Politics of Emotion*, 106–109, 112–113.
33 Ahmed, *The Cultural Politics of Emotion*, 119.
34 Lauren Berlant, *Cruel Optimism* (Durham, NC: Duke University Press, 2011), 1–2 (italics in original).
35 Berlant, *Cruel Optimism*, 1–2.
36 This section has grown out of an article I published in *Toronto Journal of Theology* in 2017 titled "For the Love of (Black) Christ: Embracing James Cone's Affective Critique of White Fragility." It does not quote or reproduce the arguments made in that article, but it is related closely enough that it seems appropriate to note the connection.
37 In drawing on Povinelli in this way, I once again benefit from work I have done together with Amy R. Barbour.
38 Late liberalism refers to the ways in which liberal (not as the foil to conservative US politics but in the sense of securing freedom from restrictive regulation for economic agents) governments and para-governmental institutions have responded to the "crises" of "anticolonial, new social movements, and new Islamic movements." Elizabeth A. Povinelli, *Economies of Abandonment: Social Belonging and Endurance in Late Liberalism* (Durham, NC: Duke University Press, 2011), 25.
39 Povinelli, *Economies of Abandonment*, 118.
40 Povinelli, *Economies of Abandonment*, 118–121.
41 Frank B. Wilderson III, *Red, White, and Black: Cinema and the Structure of U.S. Antagonisms* (Durham, NC: Duke University Press, 2010), 17–18, 38.
42 Almost all white people have learned to do this in response to Black resistance.
43 In chapter 6 of *The Religion of Whiteness*, Michael O. Emerson and Glenn E. Bracey II note some examples of Christian religious professionals whose careers were harmed or ended because their antiracist efforts were not welcomed by their

churches. Even such cases are different from Povinelli's examples, in which an entire community is cut off from societal support. Michael O. Emerson and Glenn E. Bracey II, *The Religion of Whiteness: How Racism Distorts Christian Faith* (Oxford: Oxford University Press, 2024), chap. 6, https://doi.org/10.1093/oso/9780197746288.001.0001.

44 They may, of course, find themselves involved in forms of political resistance that could pose a risk of imprisonment, but I am making a point that applies even to those white people who are not ready for such action.

45 As a quick internet search of her name will reveal, DiAngelo and her work have been critiqued widely for issues ranging from concerns that her books lead white people to center themselves and their feelings in antiracist work to personal critiques of her interpersonal skills. I do not feel the need to get into these critiques extensively as my use of DiAngelo here is relatively modest. I will note, however, that any scholar's insights—including my own—are best taken in relation to others' and readers' own experiences. DiAngelo certainly does not provide the singular key to dismantling white supremacy. Her notion of white fragility does, however, provide a helpful framework for understanding how white people can simultaneously believe themselves to be antiracist and reject the actual work of antiracism.

46 Robin DiAngelo, "White Fragility," *International Journal of Critical Pedagogy* 3, no. 3 (2011): 54.

47 DiAngelo, "White Fragility," 54–55.

48 DiAngelo, "White Fragility," 60–61.

49 Robin DiAngelo, *White Fragility: Why It's So Hard for White People to Talk about Racism* (Boston: Beacon Press, 2018), 103–104.

50 DiAngelo, "White Fragility," 61.

51 DiAngelo, *White Fragility*, 119.

52 Austin Channing Brown, *I'm Still Here: Black Dignity in a World Made for Whiteness* (New York: Convergent, 2018), 102–103.

53 DiAngelo, "White Fragility," 62.

54 An amusing personal example: Despite having no experience in teaching courses in ministry studies of any sort, I have been asked by a white colleague if I could teach courses in urban ministry. This colleague expresses a clear commitment to antiracism and is quite familiar with my areas of interest and expertise but fell into the trap of believing that because I am a Black theologian, I had any competence in teaching urban ministry. DiAngelo, "White Fragility," 55.

55 It should be noted that BIPOC folks also regularly internalize this racial coding of white spaces as inherently better and safer. DiAngelo, "White Fragility," 58–59.

56 DiAngelo, "White Fragility," 59.

57 DiAngelo, "White Fragility," 59.

58 We might want to believe that Christian faith would make this problem less severe among white Christians. However, Michael O. Emerson and Glenn E. Bracey II have found that the issues DiAngelo describes as white fragility are more prominent among white Christians than other white US Americans. In exploring what they call "the Religion of Whiteness," Emerson and Bracey outline a range of "boundary enforcers," responses to race-related stress that reinforce the centrality and supremacy of whiteness within Christian communities. These boundary enforcers not only include behaviors described by DiAngelo but also gesture toward the broader range of

"deflections and offensive moves" available to white Christians. Emboldened by their faith and empowered by their churches' practices, white Christians employ boundary enforcers such as insisting that race is a problem for God to address, demanding that those who mention race in a church context should "stick to the gospel," and selectively citing Scripture in ways that vilify antiracist work. Emerson and Bracey conducted national surveys, focus groups, and individual interviews over the course of their study. I encourage those interested in such an examination of whiteness to explore their conclusions in *The Religion of Whiteness*. Emerson and Bracey, *The Religion of Whiteness*, chap. 6.

59 Chanequa Walker-Barnes describes whiteness in terms of "moral injury," referring to the well-documented condition many veterans of combat face as they struggle to return to "normal" life after being put in situations in which they acted in ways that contradict their moral beliefs (e.g., killing another human when they believe that killing is wrong). Walker-Barnes argues that a similar condition is applicable in relation to the collective effect of white supremacy on white people's souls. Chanequa Walker-Barnes, *I Bring the Voices of My PeopleA Womanist Vision for Racial Reconciliation* (Grand Rapids, MI: Eerdmans, 2019), 125–131.

60 DiAngelo, "White Fragility," 64.

CHAPTER THREE: HOPE(S) IN THE MIDST OF ENMITY

1 Matthew 16:24–25 (NRSVUE).

2 I became aware of this quote—already well-known to plenty of others—through its reference in Bryan N. Massingale's presidential address at the 2023 Society of Christian Ethics annual meeting held in Chicago, Illinois, on January 6, 2023.

3 Joseph R. Winters, *Hope Draped in Black: Race, Melancholy, and the Agony of Progress* (Durham, NC: Duke University Press, 2016), 6.

4 As noted in chapter 1, Wilderson is not the only thinker associated with Afropessimism, though he is certainly a central figure. His work is, however, particularly well-suited to illuminating the nature of structural interracial enmity.

5 Kelly Brown Douglas, *Resurrection Hope: A Future Where Black Lives Matter* (Maryknoll, NY: Orbis Books, 2021), 179–180.

6 Fred Moten, "Blackness and Nothingness (Mysticism in the Flesh)," *South Atlantic Quarterly* 112, no. 4 (Fall 2013): 741–742.

7 Moten, "Blackness and Nothingness," 774.

8 Yes, I've been a nerd at least since high school.

9 Moten, "Blackness and Nothingness," 738.

10 Moten, "Blackness and Nothingness," 774.

11 To be precise, Moten writes of "the subject," which I interpret as the capacity to understand and successfully present oneself as a bearer of agency and meaning in one's own right. Moten, "Blackness and Nothingness," 756.

12 Moten, "Blackness and Nothingness," 739.

13 Fred Moten, "The Case of Blackness," *Criticism* 50, no. 2 (Spring 2008): 181.

14 Wilderson might describe this agency and meaning in terms of "capacity."

15 Fred Moten, "Black Op," *PMLA* 123, no. 5 (October 2008): 1745.

16 Moten, "Black Op," 1744–1745.

17 Moten, "Blackness and Nothingness," 756.
18 Moten draws this phrase from Wilderson's *Red, White, and Black*. Moten is clear about the fact that he makes much more of this phrase than Wilderson does and is not representing Wilderson's thought in elaborating on that phrase. Moten, "Blackness and Nothingness," 743.
19 Moten, "Blackness and Nothingness," 744.
20 Moten, "Blackness and Nothingness," 750–752.
21 Frank B. Wilderson III, "Wallowing in the Contradictions," interview by Percy Howard, July 9, 2010, https://percy3.wordpress.com/2010/07/09/frank-b-wilderson-%E2%80%9Cwallowing-in-the-contradictions%E2%80%9D-part-1/.
22 To my knowledge, neither Wilderson nor Moten has any investment in such theological terms.
23 Crawley's discussion of otherwise possibilities echoes Povinelli's notion of alternative social projects. We might understand alternative social projects as attempts to manifest otherwise possibilities in community.
24 Ashon T. Crawley, *Blackpentecostal Breath: The Aesthetics of Possibility* (New York: Fordham University Press, 2017), 2–3.
25 Winters, *Hope Draped in Black*, 6, 88.
26 Winters, *Hope Draped in Black*, 21.
27 Winters, *Hope Draped in Black*, 244.
28 Winters, *Hope Draped in Black*, 201.
29 In giving this account of hope rooted in melancholic memory, Winters draws on the work of Walter Benjamin and Anne Anlin Cheng. Winters, Winters, *Hope Draped in Black*, 16.
30 Douglas, *Resurrection Hope*, 54–55.
31 Douglas, *Resurrection Hope*, 148–149.
32 Douglas, *Resurrection Hope*, 183.
33 Douglas, *Resurrection Hope*, 201.
34 Douglas, *Resurrection Hope*, 201.
35 Douglas, *Resurrection Hope*, 186–188.
36 Douglas, *Resurrection Hope*, 192–199.
37 Keri Day, *Religious Resistance to Neoliberalism: Womanist and Black Feminist Perspectives* (New York: Palgrave Macmillan, 2016), 40.
38 Day, *Religious Resistance to Neoliberalism*, 40, 44.
39 Day, *Religious Resistance to Neoliberalism*, 19.
40 Day, *Religious Resistance to Neoliberalism*, 132.
41 Day, *Religious Resistance to Neoliberalism*, 135–136.
42 Day, *Religious Resistance to Neoliberalism*, 131–133.
43 Day, *Religious Resistance to Neoliberalism*, 162–163.
44 Thomas R. Gaulke, *An Unpromising Hope: Finding Hope Outside of Promise for an Agnostic Church and for Those of Us Who Find It Hard to Believe* (Eugene, OR: Pickwick Publications, 2021), xvi.
45 As a Lutheran (ELCA) scholar-pastor, Gaulke is substantially responding to the influence of Jurgen Moltmann's work on Lutheran theologies. His insights, however, are of much broader relevance. Gaulke, *An Unpromising Hope*, xiii.
46 Gaulke, *An Unpromising Hope*, xiv.
47 Gaulke, *An Unpromising Hope*, xvi.

CHAPTER FOUR: BLACK LOVE AS POLITICALLY TRANSFORMATIVE EMOTION

1 I discuss Winters's critique of progress-dependent optimism in chapter 3.

2 Fred Moten, Ashon T. Crawley, and Kelly Brown Douglas's insights into the connection among Blackness, hope, and possibilities for transformation are discussed in chapter 3.

3 Day uses metaphors of vision to invoke political possibility in *Religious Resistance to Neoliberalism*. In the interest of resisting the ableism that creeps so easily into Christian theological language, I have broadened these metaphors to reference imagination and perception unless directly quoting Day.

4 Day's notion of affective politics echoes the work of Sara Ahmed, which I discuss in chapter 2. It is worth noting that Ahmed herself draws on Black feminist sources, most notably the work of Audre Lorde. Keri Day, *Religious Resistance to Neoliberalism: Womanist and Black Feminist Perspectives* (New York: Palgrave Macmillan, 2016), 110.

5 It is important to note here that Day writes primarily of the hegemonic structures of neoliberalism, while I am applying her work to corresponding structures of interracial enmity. I am confident that these are not, in fact, different structures but instead the same monstrous beings viewed through different lenses. The objectifying relationships of which Day writes, for example, are shaped by the antagonistic, competitive relations of white supremacy and anti-Blackness, as Day is aware. Still, Day does not herself write explicitly of interracial enmity in my sense or in direct conversation with the sources I draw on in chapter 1. Further, I do not want to dismiss the importance of foregrounding an economic analysis in the manner that Day does. Day and I simply have different areas of focus in our respective books, and so I will highlight the ways in which Day's thought can lend itself to resistance to white supremacy and anti-Blackness, in the belief that such resistance is not incompatible with Day's focus on neoliberalism. Day, *Religious Resistance to Neoliberalism*, 111.

6 Day, *Religious Resistance to Neoliberalism*, 50–51.

7 George Lipsitz, *The Possessive Investment in Whiteness: How White People Profit from Identity Politics*, 20th Anniversary ed. (Philadelphia: Temple University Press, 2018), vii–viii.

8 Day, *Religious Resistance to Neoliberalism*, 54.

9 Lorde discusses this tendency to marginalize and stigmatize the erotic in her essay "The Uses of the Erotic." Audre Lorde, *Sister Outsider* (1984; repr., Berkeley: Crossing Press, 2007), 53–54, 57–59.

10 Day, *Religious Resistance to Neoliberalism*, 82.

11 Day, *Religious Resistance to Neoliberalism*, 78, 98.

12 Day, *Religious Resistance to Neoliberalism*, 98.

13 Day, *Religious Resistance to Neoliberalism*, 103–104.

14 David Gaspar, "What the Rest of America Can Learn from Illinois on Criminal Justice Reform," *Time*, September 19, 2023, https://time.com/6315615/illinois-ends-cash-bail-essay/.

15 Day, *Religious Resistance to Neoliberalism*, 156.

16 Hopefully, at this point, my earlier suggestion that visual metaphors are not essential to Day's argument holds true. Day, *Religious Resistance to Neoliberalism*, 72.

17 Day, *Religious Resistance to Neoliberalism*, 71.

18 Day, *Religious Resistance to Neoliberalism*, 109.

19 Recall my discussion of Povinelli and exhaustion in chapter 2. Elizabeth A. Povinelli, *Economies of Abandonment: Social Belonging and Endurance in Late Liberalism* (Durham, NC: Duke University Press, 2011), 118.

20 James Baldwin, "Notes of a Native Son," in *Collected Essays*, ed. Toni Morrison (1955; repr., New York: Literary Classics of the United States, 1998), 65.

21 In this essay, Baldwin is particularly concerned with tensions between Black residents of Harlem and Jewish business owners. He is clear, however, that these tensions are, in reality, due to those business owners' whiteness and not their Jewishness, whether conceived of as religion or ethnicity. James Baldwin, "The Harlem Ghetto," in *Collected Essays*, ed. Toni Morrison (1955; repr., New York: Literary Classics of the United States, 1998), 50–53.

22 Jamiles Lartey and Wilbert L. Cooper, "Tyre Nichols' Death: How Black Officers Alone Can't Stop Brutal Policing," *The Marshall Project*, January 28, 2023, https://www.themarshallproject.org/2023/01/28/tyre-nichols-memphis-black-police-brutality.

23 In Sara Ahmed's terms, as discussed in chapter 2, we might think of these images and feelings as "stuck" to Black skin.

24 James Baldwin, "Every Good-Bye Ain't Gone," in *Collected Essays*, ed. Toni Morrison (1977; repr., New York: Literary Classics of the United States, 1998), 774–775.

25 Baldwin's words here bring to mind W. E. B. DuBois's discussion of double consciousness in *The Souls of Black Folk*. James Baldwin, "The Black Boy Looks at the White Boy," in *Collected Essays*, ed. Toni Morrison (1961; repr., New York: Literary Classics of the United States, 1998), 270–271.

26 "Black Children Are Six Times More Likely to Be Shot to Death by Police," Equal Justice Initiative, December 2, 2020, https://eji.org/news/black-children-are-six-times-more-likely-to-be-shot-to-death-by-police/.

27 Don Babwin and Michael Tarm, "Officer Convicted of Murder in Slaying of Laquan McDonald," AP News, October 5, 2018, https://apnews.com/article/shootings-jason-van-dyke-us-news-ap-top-news-chicago-862ebaf6890d44de80c0ae74cac3949e.

28 James Baldwin, "Down at the Cross: Letter from a Region in My Mind," in *Collected Essays*, ed. Toni Morrison (1963; repr., New York: Literary Classics of the United States, 1998), 302.

29 Baldwin, "Notes of a Native Son," 78.

30 James Baldwin, "My Dungeon Shook: Letter to My Nephew on the One Hundredth Anniversary of the Emancipation," in *Collected Essays*, ed. Toni Morrison (1963; repr., New York: Literary Classics of the United States, 1998), 292–293.

31 James Baldwin, "A Report from Occupied Territory," in *Collected Essays*, ed. Toni Morrison (1966; repr., New York: Literary Classics of the United States, 1998), 734.

32 James Baldwin, "Where the Grapes of Wrath Are Stored," in *Collected Essays*, ed. Toni Morrison (1976; repr., New York: Literary Classics of the United States, 1998), 566–567.

33 What may be even more insidious is the calculation I find myself performing, given my kids' different skin tones. My younger child is significantly lighter-skinned than my older child and me, making me wonder to what extent these lessons apply to one of them and not the other. This, in turn, leads to the heartbreaking question of how well my younger child will be able to understand their older sibling and myself.

No one fully understands another's experience, of course, but the ability of race to insinuate itself into such precious relationships disturbs me.

34 As with his comments on parenting, Baldwin gestures toward what is now discussed in terms of intergenerational trauma. Also like his insights into parenting, what he describes here cannot be reduced entirely to the psychospiritual realm of trauma. Baldwin, "Notes of a Native Son," 70.
35 James Baldwin, "Stranger in the Village," in *Collected Essays*, ed. Toni Morrison (1963; repr., New York: Literary Classics of the United States, 1998), 121–122.
36 Baldwin, "Every Good-Bye Ain't Gone," 775 (italics in original).
37 While this language might seem to arise naturally from Baldwin's work, I actually owe it to Amy R. Barbour and one of our many conversations during our time together at Union Theological Seminary in the City of New York.
38 Baldwin, "Notes of a Native Son," 84.
39 Baldwin, "Notes of a Native Son," 83–84.
40 Baldwin, "Notes of a Native Son," 82–83.
41 Pavlić notes Baldwin's awareness of the harmful effects of whiteness on white people. This is indeed an important theme in Baldwin's work but is of less relevance to this chapter on Black love than it is to Pavlić's argument. Ed Pavlić, *Who Can Afford to Improvise? James Baldwin and Black Music, the Lyric and the Listeners* (New York: Fordham University Press, 2016), 25–26.
42 Pavlić, *Who Can Afford to Improvise?*, 29.
43 Pavlić, *Who Can Afford to Improvise?*, 47–52.
44 Pavlić, *Who Can Afford to Improvise?*, 55.
45 Pavlić, *Who Can Afford to Improvise?*, 88.
46 James Baldwin, "Nothing Personal," in *Collected Essays*, ed. Toni Morrison. (1964, repr., New York: Literary Classics of the United States, 1998), 700–701.

CHAPTER FIVE: JAMES CONE, THEOLOGIAN OF LOVE

1 Cone wrote two memoirs: *My Soul Looks Back* (1982) and *Said I Wasn't Gonna Tell Nobody* (2018, published posthumously). He also comments on the relation of his theology to his life experiences throughout most of his major works, most notably *God of the Oppressed* (1975) and *The Cross and the Lynching Tree* (2011).
2 James H. Cone, *A Black Theology of Liberation*, 20th anniversary ed. (Maryknoll, NY: Orbis Books, 1990), 1–3.
3 James H. Cone, *Black Theology and Black Power*, 1989 ed. (1969; repr., Maryknoll, NY: Orbis Books, 1997), 36.
4 Cone does not reduce Blackness to suffering but writes extensively of the joy in Black communities and Black churches. He does, however, regard Black suffering a key cause for deep theological questioning. Cone, *A Black Theology of Liberation*, 63.
5 Cone's participation in the Ecumenical Association of Third World Theologians (EATWOT)—as documented in chapter 4 of *My Soul Looks Back*—represents his clearest rejection of the idea that God could be understood through Black experience alone.
6 Cone, *A Black Theology of Liberation*, 78.
7 James H. Cone, *God of the Oppressed*, rev. ed. (1975; repr., Maryknoll, NY: Orbis Books, 1997), 123–124.

8 Cone, *A Black Theology of Liberation*, 114–20.
9 James H. Cone, *Martin & Malcolm & America: A Dream or a Nightmare* (Maryknoll, NY: Orbis Books, 1991), x.
10 Martin Luther King Jr., "Paul's Letter to American Christians," in *Strength to Love* (1963; repr., Philadelphia: Fortress Press, 2010), 152.
11 Martin Luther King Jr., "The Answer to a Perplexing Question," in *Strength to Love* (1963; repr., Philadelphia: Fortress Press, 2010), 140.
12 Martin Luther King Jr., "Nonviolence and Racial Justice," in *A Testament of Hope: The Essential Writings and Speeches of Martin Luther King, Jr.*, ed. James M. Washington (1957; repr., San Francisco, CA: HarperSanFrancisco, 1986), 8.
13 Martin Luther King Jr., "An Experiment in Love," in *A Testament of Hope: The Essential Writings and Speeches of Martin Luther King, Jr.*, ed. James M. Washington (1958; repr., San Francisco, CA: HarperSanFrancisco, 1986), 19–20.
14 This claim echoes Delores S. Williams's arguments in *Sisters in the Wilderness* regarding Black women's subjection to surrogacy roles.
15 Day's account of the erotic was discussed in chapter 4.
16 I provide a fuller account of Harvey's critique of the reconciliation paradigm in this book's Introduction. Jennifer Harvey, *Dear White Christians: For Those Still Longing for Reconciliation*, 2nd ed. (Grand Rapids, MI: Eerdmans, 2020), 18–20.
17 Harvey, *Dear White Christians*, 80.
18 Harvey, *Dear White Christians*, 37.
19 For instance, Gary Dorrien's *Breaking White Supremacy* situates King solidly in a Black Social Gospel tradition, highlights the prophetic and pragmatic dimensions of his ministry, and properly accounts for the misinterpretation of King that has tarnished his legacy.
20 Martin Luther King Jr., "Loving Your Enemies," in *Strength to Love* (1963; repr., Philadelphia: Fortress Press, 2010), 48.
21 While "Negro" is an entirely unacceptable term today, for King, it reflected self-respect over alternative terms of the time. As such, I leave that term as is rather than replacing it as I do with King's gendered language, an artifact of his time that does not similarly communicate committed conviction. Martin Luther King Jr., "Pilgrimage to Nonviolence," in *A Testament of Hope: The Essential Writings and Speeches of Martin Luther King, Jr.*, ed. James M. Washington (1958; repr., San Francisco: HarperSanFrancisco, 1986), 39.
22 I discuss Baldwin's prideful understanding of love in chapter 4.
23 SCLC stands for Southern Christian Leadership Conference, the civil rights group with which King is most prominently associated.
24 King, "Nonviolence and Racial Justice," 5–6.
25 Martin Luther King Jr., "An Address before the National Press Club," in *A Testament of Hope: The Essential Writings and Speeches of Martin Luther King, Jr.*, ed. James M. Washington (1962; repr., San Francisco: HarperSanFrancisco, 1986), 101.
26 King, "Loving Your Enemies," 44.
27 Martin Luther King Jr., "Showdown for Nonviolence," in *A Testament of Hope: The Essential Writings and Speeches of Martin Luther King, Jr.*, ed. James M. Washington (1968; repr., San Francisco: HarperSanFrancisco, 1986), 67.
28 King, "An Address before the National Press Club," 103.
29 Martin Luther King Jr.,, "Black Power Defined," in *A Testament of Hope: The Essential Writings and Speeches of Martin Luther King, Jr.*, ed. James M. Washington (1967; repr., San Francisco: HarperSanFrancisco, 1986), 307–308.

30 James Baldwin, "The Dangerous Road before Martin Luther King," in *Collected Essays*, ed. Toni Morrison (1961; repr., New York: Literary Classics of the United States, 1998), 643–644.
31 Cone, *A Black Theology of Liberation*, 70.
32 Cone, *Black Theology and Black Power*, 52–54.
33 J. Deotis Roberts, *Liberation and Reconciliation: A Black Theology*, 2nd ed. (1971; repr., Louisville, KY: Westminster John Knox Press, 2005), xii.
34 Roberts, *Liberation and Reconciliation*, 5.
35 Cone, *God of the Oppressed*, 220.
36 Cone, *God of the Oppressed*, 222–223.
37 Chanequa Walker-Barnes, *I Bring the Voices of My People: A Womanist Vision for Racial Reconciliation* (Grand Rapids, MI: Eerdmans, 2019), 125–128.
38 Cone, *Martin & Malcolm & America*, 292–293.
39 James H. Cone, *For My People: Black Theology and the Black Church* (Maryknoll, NY: Orbis Books, 1984), 195.
40 Cone, *Black Theology and Black Power*, 18.
41 Cone, *Black Theology and Black Power*, 53–54.
42 Cone, *A Black Theology of Liberation*, 72–73.
43 Cone, *A Black Theology of Liberation*, 70.
44 "Reverse racism" refers to the idea that antiracist efforts amount to racism against white people. Being accused of this myself during a work meeting was a particularly disorienting experience, in which it became clear that my accuser and I have entirely contradictory experiences of the world.
45 Cone, *Black Theology and Black Power*, 14.
46 Cone, *Black Theology and Black Power*, 4.
47 Here, Cone references the "poor" rather than Black people. However, for Cone, these categories are intimately tied. Poor people in all societies are those among whom God will be found, while poor people in the United States are represented most meaningfully for Cone by Black people. James H. Cone, *My Soul Looks Back* (1982; repr., Maryknoll, NY: Orbis Books, 1986), 13.
48 Cone, *A Black Theology of Liberation*, 11.
49 Cone, *A Black Theology of Liberation*, 107.
50 Cone, *Black Theology and Black Power*, 138–143.
51 Cone, *A Black Theology of Liberation*, 65.
52 James H. Cone, *The Cross and the Lynching Tree* (Maryknoll, NY: Orbis Books, 2011), 156.
53 Cone, *God of the Oppressed*, 209.
54 Cone, *God of the Oppressed*, 218–219.
55 Cone, *God of the Oppressed*, 224.
56 Cone, *God of the Oppressed*, 213.
57 Cone, *God of the Oppressed*, 219.
58 Cone, *God of the Oppressed*, 221.
59 Cone, *God of the Oppressed*, 217.
60 Cone, *God of the Oppressed*, 222.
61 Cone, *God of the Oppressed*, 207.
62 James H. Cone, *Said I Wasn't Gonna Tell Nobody* (Maryknoll, NY: Orbis Books, 2018), 120–121.

63 Delores S. Williams, *Sisters in the Wilderness: The Challenge of Womanist God-Talk* (Maryknoll, NY: Orbis Books, 1993), 144.

64 While Cone only cites Williams's critique in *Said I Wasn't Gonna Tell Nobody*, he alludes to that offered by Warrior and assigned Warrior's influential essay "Canaanites, Cowboys, and Indians" in his introductory course in systematic theology. Warrior's critique focuses on the exodus narrative and emphasizes that while God delivers the people of Israel from bondage at the beginning of their journey, God then demands and empowers their violent conquest of the Indigenous peoples of Canaan. Robert Allen Warrior, "Canaanites, Cowboys, and Indians: Deliverance, Conquest, and Liberation Theology Today," in *Native and Christian: Indigenous Voices on Religious Identity in the United States and Canada*, ed. James Treat (1989; repr., New York: Routledge, 1996), 95–98.

CHAPTER SIX: GETTING TO THE HEART OF DIVINE LOVE AND POWER

1 This was perhaps most famously the theological position of Martin Luther King Jr., as discussed in chapter 5.

2 Curry was presiding bishop of the Episcopal Church from 2015 to 2024. Michael Curry and Sara Grace, *Love Is the Way: Holding on to Hope in Troubling Times* (New York: Avery, 2020), 14.

3 Curry and Grace, *Love Is the Way*, 95.

4 Curry and Grace, *Love Is the Way*, 96.

5 Curry and Grace, *Love Is the Way*, 117.

6 Curry and Grace, *Love Is the Way*, 235.

7 Curry and Grace, *Love Is the Way*, 236.

8 Curry and Grace, *Love Is the Way*, 16.

9 Exodus 20:1–6.

10 Sallie McFague, whose work figures prominently in the rest of this chapter, stresses that true love engages all those caught up in it in a dance of give and take. Sallie McFague, *Blessed Are the Consumers: Climate Change and the Practice of Restraint* (Minneapolis: Fortress Press, 2013), 196.

11 Curry and Grace, *Love Is the Way*, 89.

12 John 15:12–13 (NRSVUE).

13 Exodus 33:18–23.

14 Sallie McFague, *The Body of God: An Ecological Theology* (Minneapolis: Fortress Press, 1993), 131.

15 McFague, *The Body of God*, 192.

16 McFague, *Blessed Are the Consumers*, 175.

17 McFague, *The Body of God*, 111.

18 Brian Bantum, *The Death of Race: Building a New Christianity in a Racial World* (Minneapolis: Fortress Press, 2016), 33.

19 McFague, *The Body of God*, 109.

20 McFague, *The Body of God*, 131.

21 Psalm 139:14 (NSRVUE).

22 Bantum, *The Death of Race*, 26–27.

23 Fellow Marvel comics fans might be picturing the way in which the cosmic being Eternity is generally depicted, as a humanoid entity with all the galaxies of the universe

swirling in its form. Others might do a quick internet search to see something that's precisely what I'm *not* saying about creation as God's body.

24 Imagining God as a Black woman, for example, makes a powerful and important theological statement, particularly in how it emphasizes divine identification with those marginalized and encourages us to perceive the divine among those who've been told they are anything but godly.

25 McFague, *The Body of God*, 37–47.

26 McFague, *The Body of God*, 155, 199.

27 Ivone Gebara, *Longing for Running Water: Ecofeminism and Liberation* (Minneapolis: Fortress Press, 1999), 113.

28 McFague, *The Body of God*, 136.

29 McFague, *The Body of God*, 139–140.

30 Gebara, *Longing for Running Water*, 105.

31 McFague, *The Body of God*, 176.

32 Gebara, *Longing for Running Water*, 107.

33 McFague, *Blessed Are the Consumers*, 189.

34 McFague, *The Body of God*, 154.

35 Gebara, *Longing for Running Water*, 184.

36 McFague, *Blessed Are the Consumers*, 189.

37 Willie James Jennings, *Acts* (Louisville, KY: Westminster John Knox Press, 2017), 15, 19.

38 Bantum, *The Death of Race*, 110.

39 Bantum, *The Death of Race*, 123–124.

40 Luke 2:41–50.

41 Matthew 19:16–30.

42 John 20:11–18.

43 Matthew 2:13–23.

44 Matthew 3:13–17.

45 Matthew 4:1–11.

46 Matthew 26:36–46.

47 Matthew 27:11–54.

48 Matthew 27:57–61.

49 As always, I am grateful for the mentorship of Willie James Jennings, who encouraged me to press beyond divine need to consider divine desire as well.

50 Cynthia Moe-Lobeda, *Resisting Structural Evil: Love as Ecological-Economic Vocation* (Minneapolis: Fortress Press, 2013), 55.

51 Jennings, *Acts*, 10–11.

52 Bantum, *The Death of Race*, 125.

53 The story of the Ethiopean eunuch appears in Acts 8:26–40. Jennings, *Acts*, 82–86.

54 McFague, *Blessed Are the Consumers*, 196.

55 Moe-Lobeda, *Resisting Structural Evil*, 6.

56 Jennings, *Acts*, 245.

57 McFague, *The Body of God*, 207.

58 McFague, *Blessed Are the Consumers*, 202.

59 McFague, *The Body of God*, 131.

60 As discussed in chapter 4, Keri Day demonstrates that the unjust economic structures in which we live work to reduce all our relationships to struggles for control. Keri

Day, *Religious Resistance to Neoliberalism: Womanist and Black Feminist Perspectives* (New York: Palgrave Macmillan, 2016), 50–51.

61 Gebara, *Longing for Running Water*, 16.

62 McFague, *Blessed Are the Consumers*, 157–160.

63 To be clear, there are certainly themes in Scripture that support the idea of a controlling, jealous, even abusive God. There is also, however, a long-established tradition of feminist biblical scholarship that examines the influence of patriarchal cultural norms on Scripture. Rita Nakashima Brock, *Journeys by Heart: A Christology of Erotic Power* (Eugene, OR: Wipf & Stock, 1988), 4–5, 50–57.

64 Reading Rita Nakashima Brock's *Journeys by Heart* for the first time was my own introduction to the concept of erotic power. Brock, *Journeys by Heart*, 26.

65 Brock, *Journeys by Heart*, 41.

66 Brock, *Journeys by Heart*, 45–46.

67 McFague, *The Body of God*, 145.

68 Jennings, *Acts*, 71.

69 Bantum, *The Death of Race*, 80.

70 Gebara, *Longing for Running Water*, 180–181.

71 Brock, *Journeys by Heart*, 98.

72 Brock, *Journeys by Heart*, 52–53, 105–106.

73 Numbers 20:10–13.

74 Brock, *Journeys by Heart*, 66.

75 Gebara, *Longing for Running Water*, 183.

76 Brock, *Journeys by Heart*, 82–84.

77 Bantum, *The Death of Race*, 37.

78 Bantum, *The Death of Race*, 99–100.

79 Gebara, *Longing for Running Water*, 82–84.

80 Gebara, *Longing for Running Water*, 92.

81 I owe this important insight to a peer reviewer. As we work to love one another and even to love ourselves, we do so as people who have been shaped and continue to be shaped by white supremacy and anti-Blackness. While the identity-obscuring nature of the peer-review process prevents me from knowing who that reviewer was, I nonetheless want to thank them openly.

82 Matthew 26:36–46.

83 McFague, *Blessed Are the Consumers*, 193.

84 Bantum, *The Death of Race*, 26.

85 Gebara, *Longing for Running Water*, 130.

86 Perhaps other creatures are called to such a conscious embrace as well. I only really know that most humans seem capable of this kind of self-reflexivity, though, so I'll leave dolphin theology to the dolphins.

87 Bantum, *The Death of Race*, 50.

88 McFague, *Blessed Are the Consumers*, 115.

89 Once again, this is discussed most extensively in chapter 2.

90 Insofar as we might indeed claim to "love the sinner and hate the sin" when it comes to white supremacy and anti-Blackness, such love and hatred must include both an awareness that the sinner is not neatly separable from the sinful systems that so thoroughly shape their society and a commitment to strive for as great a degree of freedom from those systems as possible.

91 Jennings, *Acts*, 28–29.
92 Jennings, *Acts*, 92.
93 Jennings, *Acts*, 106, 110–111.
94 Jennings, *Acts*, 12.
95 Jennings, *Acts*, 59, 61.
96 Jennings, *Acts*, 240.
97 Of course, as recent decades have demonstrated, crisis moments can span years.

CHAPTER SEVEN: FAITHFUL LOVE OF THE ENEMY

1 Willie James Jennings, *Acts* (Louisville, KY: Westminster John Knox Press, 2017), 76–81.
2 Jennings, *Acts*, 8.
3 Jennings, *Acts*, 148.
4 Jennings, *Acts*, 246.
5 Matthew 5:43–48 (NRSVUE).
6 I discussed Lauren Berlant's concept of cruel optimism in chapter 2.
7 As discussed in chapter 2, with reference to the work of Sara Ahmed. Sara Ahmed, *The Cultural Politics of Emotion* (Durham, NC: Duke University Press, 2004), 106–107.
8 Jennings, *Acts*, 9.
9 Jennings, *Acts*, 97.
10 Luke 14:26 (NRSVUE).
11 Jennings, *Acts*, 194.
12 As Jennings does throughout his commentary on Acts, he focuses on competing modes of desire: that of the Spirit and those of Empire and diaspora. My sense is that our understandings are compatible while not identical. Jennings, *Acts*, 250.
13 I owe this idea to Franklin Golden, pastor of Durham Presbyterian Church in Durham, North Carolina, where my family were members during my grad school years at Duke University. During our time in that church, Franklin led the church in a sermon series entitled "This Is My Story, This Is My Song." Church members were invited to choose a song of particular importance to them. The church band learned the song and performed it, the person who chose the song shared a bit about why it was important to them, Franklin preached a brief sermon connecting the song to a relevant passage of Scripture, and the congregation added that song to our songbook going forward.
14 Lawrence E. Susskind and Jeffrey L. Cruikshank, *Breaking Robert's Rules: The New Way to Run Your Meeting, Build Consensus, and Get Results* (New York: Oxford University Press, 2006), 11–14.
15 Susskind and Cruikshank, *Breaking Robert's Rules*, 18.
16 Susskind and Cruikshank, *Breaking Robert's Rules*, 26–32.
17 For further insights and instruction—as well as responses to common concerns such as the possibility that consensus-building will take too long to be useful—I encourage readers to read Lawrence E. Susskind and Jeffrey L. Cruikshank's *Breaking Robert's Rules*, which I cite throughout this section.
18 This technique can be employed through other means, of course. For example, participants can type a number from 0 to 5 in the chat box of a video call or signal their level of agreement via an online survey in advance of a meeting.

19 For example, specific attention to structural interracial enmity as it is at work in the community could influence who is included in decision-making (e.g., ensuring a significant proportion of BIPOC members on decision-making bodies, addressing considerations around barriers to participation such as meeting times or child care) or take the form of a decision-making process that highlights analysis of interracial enmity (e.g., prioritizing education around structural inequity for decision makers, building connections with community partners who can provide information much as we might when considering options for financing or construction).

Bibliography

Adam, Klaus-Peter. *Hate and Enmity in Biblical Law*. New York: T&T Clark, 2022. https://ebookcentral.proquest.com/lib/jkmlibrary/detail.action?docID=7013331.

Ahmed, Sara. *The Cultural Politics of Emotion*. Durham, NC: Duke University Press, 2004.

———. *Living a Feminist Life*. Durham, NC: Duke University Press, 2017.

———. *The Promise of Happiness*. Durham, NC: Duke University Press, 2010.

Alldredge, Karri. "I Am the Speaking of My Name." Sermon presented at the Queer Intersectionality Symposium, Lutheran School of Theology at Chicago, April 24, 2024.

Babwin, Don, and Michael Tarm. "Officer Convicted of Murder in Slaying of Laquan McDonald." AP News, October 5, 2018. https://apnews.com/article/shootings-jason-van-dyke-us-news-ap-top-news-chicago-862ebaf6890d44de80c0ae74cac3949e.

Baldwin, James. "The Black Boy Looks at the White Boy." In *Collected Essays*, edited by Toni Morrison, 269–285. 1961. Reprint, New York: Literary Classics of the United States, 1998.

———. "The Dangerous Road before Martin Luther King." In *Collected Essays*, edited by Toni Morrison, 638–658. 1961. Reprint, New York: Literary Classics of the United States, 1998.

———. "Down at the Cross: Letter from a Region in My Mind." In *Collected Essays*, edited by Toni Morrison, 296–347. 1963. Reprint, New York: Literary Classics of the United States, 1998.

———. "Every Good-Bye Ain't Gone." In *Collected Essays*, edited by Toni Morrison, 773–779. 1977. Reprint, New York: Literary Classics of the United States, 1998.

———. "The Harlem Ghetto." In *Collected Essays*, edited by Toni Morrison, 42–53. 1955. Reprint, New York: Literary Classics of the United States, 1998.

———. "My Dungeon Shook: Letter to My Nephew on the One Hundredth Anniversary of the Emancipation." In *Collected Essays*, edited by Toni Morrison, 291–295. 1963. Reprint, New York: Literary Classics of the United States, 1998.

———. "Notes of a Native Son." In *Collected Essays*, edited by Toni Morrison, 63–84. 1955. Reprint, New York: Literary Classics of the United States, 1998.

———. "Nothing Personal." In *Collected Essays*, edited by Toni Morrison, 692–706. 1964. Reprint, New York: Literary Classics of the United States, 1998.

———. "A Report from Occupied Territory." In *Collected Essays*, edited by Toni Morrison, 728–738. 1966. Reprint, New York: Literary Classics of the United States, 1998.

———. "Stranger in the Village." In *Collected Essays*, edited by Toni Morrison, 117–129. 1966. Reprint, New York: Literary Classics of the United States, 1998.

———. "Where the Grapes of Wrath Are Stored." In *Collected Essays*, edited by Toni Morrison, 550–572. 1976. Reprint, New York: Literary Classics of the United States, 1998.

Bantum, Brian. *The Death of Race: Building a New Christianity in a Racial World*. Minneapolis: Fortress Press, 2016.

Betz, Hans Dieter. *The Sermon on the Mount: A Commentary on the Sermon on the Mount*. Minneapolis: Augsburg Fortress, 1995. https://muse-jhu-edu.eu1.proxy.openathens.net/book/45975.

Berlant, Lauren. *Cruel Optimism*. Durham, NC: Duke University Press, 2011.

Brock, Rita Nakashima. *Journeys by Heart: A Christology of Erotic Power*. Eugene, OR: Wipf & Stock, 1988.

Brown, Austin Channing. *I'm Still Here: Black Dignity in a World Made for Whiteness*. New York: Convergent, 2018.

"Calumet Connect Databook." Chicago: Alliance for the Great Lakes, 2021. https://greatlakes.org/wp-content/uploads/2021/02/Final_Calumet_Connect_Databook_2.0_January_2021.pdf.

Carter, Gregory T. "Race and Citizenship." In *The Oxford Handbook of American Immigration and Ethnicity*, edited by Ronald H. Bayor, 166–82. New York: Oxford University Press, 2013. https://doi.org/10.1093/oxfordhb/9780199766031.001.0001.

Choi Hee An. *A Postcolonial Relationship*. Albany: SUNY Press, 2022.

Choi, Ki Joo. *Disciplined by Race: Theological Ethics and the Problem of Asian American Identity*. Eugene, OR: Cascade Books, 2019.

Cone, James H. *Black Theology and Black Power*. 1989 ed. 1969. Reprint, Maryknoll, NY: Orbis Books, 1997.

———. *A Black Theology of Liberation*. 20th anniversary ed. Maryknoll, NY: Orbis Books, 1990.

———. *The Cross and the Lynching Tree*. Maryknoll, NY: Orbis Books, 2011.

———. *For My People: Black Theology and the Black Church*. Maryknoll, NY: Orbis Books, 1984.

———. *God of the Oppressed*. Rev. ed. 1975. Reprint, Maryknoll, NY: Orbis Books, 1997.

———. *Martin & Malcolm & America: A Dream or a Nightmare*. Maryknoll, NY: Orbis Books, 1991.

———. *My Soul Looks Back*. 1982. Reprint, Maryknoll, NY: Orbis Books, 1986.

———. *Said I Wasn't Gonna Tell Nobody*. Maryknoll, NY: Orbis Books, 2018.

Crawley, Ashon T. *Blackpentecostal Breath: The Aesthetics of Possibility*. New York: Fordham University Press, 2017.

Curry, Michael, and Sara Grace. *Love Is the Way: Holding On to Hope in Troubling Times*. New York: Avery, 2020.

Day, Keri. *Religious Resistance to Neoliberalism: Womanist and Black Feminist Perspectives*. New York: Palgrave Macmillan, 2016.

DiAngelo, Robin. "White Fragility." *International Journal of Critical Pedagogy* 3, no. 3 (2011): 54–70.

———. *White Fragility: Why It's So Hard for White People to Talk about Racism*. Boston: Beacon Press, 2018.

Douglas, Kelly Brown. *Resurrection Hope: A Future Where Black Lives Matter*. Maryknoll, NY: Orbis Books, 2021.

Emerson, Michael O., and Glenn E. Bracey II. *The Religion of Whiteness: How Racism Distorts Christian Faith*. Oxford: Oxford University Press, 2024. https://doi.org/10.1093/oso/9780197746288.001.0001.

Equal Justice Initiative. "Black Children Are Six Times More Likely to Be Shot to Death by Police." December 2, 2020. https://eji.org/news/black-children-are-six-times-more-likely-to-be-shot-to-death-by-police/.

Florer-Bixler, Melissa. *How to Have an Enemy: Righteous Anger and the Work of Peace.* Harrisonburg, VA: Herald Press, 2021.

Gaspar, David. "What the Rest of America Can Learn from Illinois on Criminal Justice Reform." *Time*, September 19, 2023. https://time.com/6315615/illinois-ends-cash-bail-essay/.

Gaulke, Thomas R. *An Unpromising Hope: Finding Hope Outside of Promise for an Agnostic Church and for Those of Us Who Find It Hard to Believe.* Eugene, OR: Pickwick Publications, 2021.

Gebara, Ivone. *Longing for Running Water: Ecofeminism and Liberation.* Minneapolis: Fortress Press, 1999.

Glancy, Jennifer A. *Slavery in Early Christianity.* Minneapolis: Fortress Press, 2002.

Hardt, Michael, and Antonio Negri. *Empire.* Cambridge, MA: Harvard University Press, 2000.

Harvey, Jennifer. *Dear White Christians: For Those Still Longing for Reconciliation.* 2nd ed. Grand Rapids, MI: Eerdmans, 2020. https://ebookcentral.proquest.com/lib/jkmlibrary/detail.action?docID=6260724.

Hengel, Martin. *Crucifixion in the Ancient World and the Folly of the Cross.* Translated by John Bowden. Philadelphia: Fortress Press, 1977.

Henricks, Kasey, Amanda E. Lewis, Iván Arenas, and Deana G. Lewis. "A Tale of Three Cities: The State of Racial Justice in Chicago Report." Chicago: Institute for Research on Race and Public Policy, University of Illinois Chicago, 2017. https://stateofracialjusticechicago.com/a-tale-of-three-cities/.

Jennings, Willie James. *Acts.* Louisville, KY: Westminster John Knox Press, 2017.

———. "Can White People Be Saved?" In *Can "White" People Be Saved?: Triangulating Race, Theology, and Mission*, edited by Love L. Sechrest, Johnny Ramírez-Johnson, and Amos Yong, 27–43. Downers Grove, IL: IVP Academic, 2018.

———. *The Christian Imagination: Theology and the Origins of Race.* New Haven, CT: Yale University Press, 2010.

Kahl, Brigitte. *Galatians Re-Imagined: Reading with the Eyes of the Vanquished.* Minneapolis: Fortress Press, 2010.

King, Martin Luther Jr. "An Address before the National Press Club." In *A Testament of Hope: The Essential Writings and Speeches of Martin Luther King, Jr.*, edited by James M. Washington, 99–105. 1962. Reprint, San Francisco: HarperSanFrancisco, 1986.

———. "The Answer to a Perplexing Question." In *Strength to Love*, 133–143. Minneapolis: Fortress Press, 2010.

———. "Black Power Defined." In *A Testament of Hope: The Essential Writings and Speeches of Martin Luther King, Jr.*, edited by James M. Washington, 303–312. 1967. Reprint, San Francisco: HarperSanFrancisco, 1986.

———. "An Experiment in Love." In *A Testament of Hope: The Essential Writings and Speeches of Martin Luther King, Jr.*, edited by James M. Washington, 16–20. 1958. Reprint, San Francisco: HarperSanFrancisco, 1986.

———. "Loving Your Enemies." In *Strength to Love*, 43–52. Minneapolis: Fortress Press, 2010.

———. "Loving Your Enemies." Sermon presented at the Dexter Avenue Baptist Church, Montgomery, AL, November 17, 1957. https://kinginstitute.stanford.edu/king-papers/documents/loving-your-enemies-sermon-delivered-dexter-avenue-baptist-church.

———. "Nonviolence and Racial Justice." In *A Testament of Hope: The Essential Writings and Speeches of Martin Luther King, Jr.*, edited by James M. Washington, 5–9. 1957. Reprint, San Francisco: HarperSanFrancisco, 1986.

———. "Paul's Letter to American Christians." In *Strength to Love*, 145–153. Minneapolis: Fortress Press, 2010.

———. "Pilgrimage to Nonviolence." In *A Testament of Hope: The Essential Writings and Speeches of Martin Luther King, Jr.*, edited by James M. Washington, 35–40. 1958. Reprint, San Francisco: HarperSanFrancisco, 1986.

———. "Showdown for Nonviolence." In *A Testament of Hope: The Essential Writings and Speeches of Martin Luther King, Jr.*, edited by James M. Washington, 64–72. 1968. Reprint, San Francisco: HarperSanFrancisco, 1986.

Lartey, Jamiles, and Wilbert L. Cooper. "Tyre Nichols' Death: How Black Officers Alone Can't Stop Brutal Policing." *The Marshall Project*, January 28, 2023. https://www.themarshallproject.org/2023/01/28/tyre-nichols-memphis-black-police-brutality.

Lester, Neal A. "The Disturbing 'Monkey Business' of U.S. Black-White Race Relations." Learning for Justice, February 24, 2017. https://www.learningforjustice.org/magazine/the-disturbing-monkey-business-of-us-blackwhite-race-relations.

Lipsitz, George. *The Possessive Investment in Whiteness: How White People Profit from Identity Politics*. 20th anniversary ed. Philadelphia: Temple University Press, 2018.

Lopez, Davina C. *Apostle to the Conquered: Reimagining Paul's Mission*. Minneapolis: Fortress Press, 2010.

Lorde, Audre. *Sister Outsider*. 1984. Reprint, Berkeley: Crossing Press, 2007.

McFague, Sallie. *Blessed Are the Consumers: Climate Change and the Practice of Restraint*. Minneapolis: Fortress Press, 2013.

———. *The Body of God: An Ecological Theology*. Minneapolis: Fortress Press, 1993.

Mikulich, Alex. *Unlearning White Supremacy: A Spirituality of Racial Liberation*. Maryknoll, NY: Orbis Books, 2022.

Moe-Lobeda, Cynthia. *Resisting Structural Evil: Love as Ecological-Economic Vocation*. Minneapolis: Fortress Press, 2013.

Morley, Neville. *The Roman Empire: Roots of Imperialism*. London: Pluto Press, 2010. https://doi.org/10.2307/j.ctt183pb5x.

Moten, Fred. "Black Op." *PMLA* 123, no. 5 (October 2008): 1743–47.

———. "Blackness and Nothingness (Mysticism in the Flesh)." *South Atlantic Quarterly* 112, no. 4 (Fall 2013): 737–80.

———. "The Case of Blackness." *Criticism* 50, no. 2 (Spring 2008): 177–218.

Pavlić, Ed. *Who Can Afford to Improvise? James Baldwin and Black Music, the Lyric and the Listeners*. New York: Fordham University Press, 2016.

Povinelli, Elizabeth A. *Economies of Abandonment: Social Belonging and Endurance in Late Liberalism*. Durham, NC: Duke University Press, 2011.

Roberts, J. Deotis. *Liberation and Reconciliation: A Black Theology*. 2nd ed. 1971. Reprint, Louisville, KY: Westminster John Knox Press, 2005.

Sanburn, Josh. "All the Ways Darren Wilson Described Being Afraid of Michael Brown." *Time*, November 25, 2014. https://time.com/3605346/darren-wilson-michael-brown-demon/.

Scarborough, William, Faith R. Kares, Iván Arenas, and Amanda E. Lewis. "Adversity and Resiliency for Chicago's First: The State of Racial Justice for American Indian Chicagoans Report." Chicago: Institute for Research on Race and Public Policy,

University of Illinois Chicago, 2019. https://stateofracialjusticechicago.com/adversity-and-resiliency-for-chicagos-first-the-state-of-racial-justice-for-american-indian-chicagoans/.

Scarborough, William, Amanda E. Lewis, and Iván Arenas. "A Tale of Diversity, Disparity, and Discrimination: The State of Racial Justice for Asian American Chicagoans." Chicago: Institute for Research on Race and Public Policy, University of Illinois Chicago, 2018. https://stateofracialjusticechicago.com/a-tale-of-diversity-disparity-and-discrimination-the-state-of-racial-justice-for-asian-american-chicagoans/.

Susskind, Lawrence E., and Jeffrey L. Cruikshank. *Breaking Robert's Rules: The New Way to Run Your Meeting, Build Consensus, and Get Results*. New York: Oxford University Press, 2006.

Walker-Barnes, Chanequa. *I Bring the Voices of My People: A Womanist Vision for Racial Reconciliation*. Grand Rapids, MI: Eerdmans, 2019.

Warrior, Robert Allen. "Canaanites, Cowboys, and Indians: Deliverance, Conquest, and Liberation Theology Today." In *Native and Christian: Indigenous Voices on Religious Identity in the United States and Canada*, edited by James Treat, 93–104. 1989. Reprint, New York: Routledge, 1996.

Wilderson, Frank B., III. *Afropessimism*. New York: Liveright, 2020.

———. *Red, White, and Black: Cinema and the Structure of U.S. Antagonisms*. Durham, NC: Duke University Press, 2010.

———. "Wallowing in the Contradictions." Interview by Percy Howard, July 9, 2010. https://percy3.wordpress.com/2010/07/09/frank-b-wilderson-%E2%80%9Cwallowing-in-the-contradictions%E2%80%9D-part-1/.

Wilkerson, Isabel. *Caste: The Origins of Our Discontents*. New York: Random House, 2020.

Williams, Delores S. *Sisters in the Wilderness: The Challenge of Womanist God-Talk*. Maryknoll, NY: Orbis Books, 1993.

Winters, Joseph R. *Hope Draped in Black: Race, Melancholy, and the Agony of Progress*. Durham, NC: Duke University Press, 2016.

Wootson, Cleve R., Jr., and Derek Hawkins. "The Charlotte Police Shooting That Hasn't Gone Away." *Washington Post*, September 21, 2016. https://www.washingtonpost.com/news/post-nation/wp/2016/09/21/the-charlotte-police-shooting-that-hasnt-gone-away/.

Index